D1417418

The Color of Privilege

Three Blasphemies on Race
and Feminism

Aída Hurtado

Ann Arbor

THE UNIVERSITY OF MICHIGAN PRESS

Copyright © by the University of Michigan 1996
All rights reserved
Published in the United States of America by
The University of Michigan Press
Manufactured in the United States of America
⊗ Printed on acid-free paper

1999   1998   1997   1996   4   3   2   1

HQ
1421
.H87
1996

No part of this publication may be reproduced, stored in a
retrieval system, or transmitted in any form or by any means,
electronic, mechanical, or otherwise without the written per-
mission of the publisher.

*A CIP catalog record for this book is available
from the British Library.*

Library of Congress Cataloging-in-Publication Data

Hurtado, Aída.
     The color of privilege : three blasphemies on race and feminism /
Aída Hurtado.
        p.   cm.   —   (Critical perspectives on women and gender)
     Includes bibliographical references and index.
        ISBN 0–472–09531–5 (alk. paper).   —   ISBN 0–472–06531–9 (pbk. :
alk. paper)
        1. Minority women—United States.   2. Feminism—United States.
     3. Marginality, Social—United States.   4. United States—Ethnic
     relations.   5. United States—Race relations.   I. Title.
     II. Series.
     HQ1421.H87   1996
     305.42'0973—dc20

                                                            96-21187
                                                            CIP

9/98

*To all women of Color
who struggle every day
to overcome humiliation,
pain, and oppression
through resistance and strength
but, above all,
through humor and joy*

Preface

This book contains what I consider my three blasphemies found in the first three chapters: "Relating to Privilege and Political Mobilization: Toward a Multicultural Feminism," "The Poetics of Resistance: Sexual Dynamics in the Gender Subordination of Chicanas," and "Invitation to Power: The Restructuring of Gender in the Political Movements of the 60s." In the fourth chapter, "On a Reflexive Feminist Theory of Gender Subordination," I integrate the dynamics explored in the first three chapters to propose the beginning of a feminist framework for studying gender that integrates race and class privilege in the process of theorizing about subordination.

Each of these blasphemies began with a concrete and perhaps overly simple question. In "Relating to Privilege" my question was: Why don't women of Color[1] unite with the white feminist movement when many of the political and economic goals promoted by this movement would obviously benefit them? In this chapter I attempt to provide a structural answer about why many women of Color feel alienated from most of the organized segments of the white Women's movement. I argue that the practices within these segments are at odds with the way most women of Color have been treated by the power structure and therefore feel alien to them. In essence, women of Color, as a group, have been used primarily as laborers as well as exploited for their sexuality. Women of Color are not needed by white men to reproduce biologically pure offspring and therefore have been subordinated through *rejection,* whereas white women have been *seduced* into compliance because they are needed to reproduce biologically the next generation for the power structure. Rejection as potential biological childbearers (not necessarily as child caretakers) creates distance for women of Color from the *intimate* and familial centers of structural power. For white women, who are essential for survival of the status quo, have to be seduced through material and psychological rewards to accept the role of biological bearers. White women as biological carriers are squarely placed in the intimate circles of power and therefore are familially connected (through biological ties) to those who subordinate them—white men. Their allegiance to white men through familial ties means that they cannot be subordinated in the same way as women of Color. The difference in access to structural power between white men and white women has to be made palatable, attractive, and rewarding; otherwise, rebellion would ensue. In fact, white families are organized and united around the notion of the male breadwinner's access to socioeconomic power and success; his success is the entire family's success. Therefore, gender subordination, as imposed by white men, is experienced *differently* by white women and by women of Color. It is in this experiential difference that many of the conflicts around political mobilization occur. It is this difference that has produced much of the disunity in the women's movement from its inception in the nineteenth century to the present.

I focus in chapter 1 on the relationships of white women and women of Color to white men and how these relationships have affected political coalitions between feminists from both groups. "Relating to Privilege" allowed me to struggle with how to write about subordination processes that are not static; that do not apply to all members of a category equally; and that, by being *relational* in nature, are difficult to pinpoint. I conclude, however, that theorizing can take place for groups of people without essentializing them and that the only way to fully dismantle oppressive practices is through the dissection of social structure. Although I'm a psychologist and a feminist, I have difficulty with individual experience that is not connected to a broader social framework, although individual experiences can add up to powerful insights about patterns that ultimately help us dismantle entire social structures.

The concept of gender subordination as relational paved the way for deciphering other relationships between different groups of women and men that would allow me to further document the specificity of the dynamics of gender subordination. This was especially helpful in writing my second blasphemy, "The Poetics of Resistance: Sexual Dynamics in the Gender Subordination of Chicanas." In this chapter the simple question I was trying to answer was: Why do Chicanas refuse to leave their communities when they experience so much gender subordination, especially when they have acquired skills that insure their survival outside their group? Despite very strong critiques by Chicana feminists of Chicano communities, there has never been a formal proposal to form a separate feminist community nor a group addendum to the existing agenda of white radical feminists who have proposed separatism from *all* men for group survival. Chicana feminists of all persuasions have a deep commitment to their communities of origin—whether it is in the heart of Texas, the inner city of Chicago, or the vast Arizona desert. Our feminism is a commitment to our mothers as well as our fathers and to all community members. Women of Color in the United States have always theorized about their gender subordination, although not always in traditionally academic forms. To garner the full complexity of Chicanas' experiences it becomes necessary to tap sources of knowledge not used by scholars steeped in mainstream positivist ideology. Therefore, in the "Poetics of Resistance" I had to experiment with other kinds of data from which to theorize. Instead of conventional materials, I use oral histories collected by Yolanda Broyles from the actors in El Teatro Campesino and poetry written by Chicanas and Chicanos to specify how sexuality is used in Chicano communities to restrict and subordinate Chicanas.

My analysis includes the dynamics of resistance as well as oppression. I conclude by reviewing the latest developments in Chicana feminist research in which Chicana feminists, within and outside of El Teatro, have wrested from men the right to invent themselves, and they have done so through many avenues, including creative and academic production. Undoubtedly, oppression always results in casualties, but a by-product is the ability of some of its survivors to further the group's collective consciousness. The ability of some Chicanas to move between many worlds— for example, having experienced farm labor while being a university professor and raising her children in a Chicano neighborhood—has resulted in the creation of a new consciousness about gender relations that is class and race specific—the result of the cultural and historical evolution of Chicanos. Chicanas' and other women of Color's ability to cross *fronteras* (borders) holds potential for formulating theories of liberation.

In my third blasphemy I examine the Black Civil Rights movement and the Chicano movement to scrutinize their articulation of gender relations. These movements forced their participants to articulate the necessity of presenting a unified political front to dominant forces and to avoid bringing gender issues to the forefront for fear of fragmenting the fragile solidarity these movements had accomplished. Thus, I attempt to answer the question: What explains the unshakable (in political terms) solidarity between men of Color and women of Color? The answer to this question lies partially in how the political upheavals of the 1960s provided a radical departure from previous forms of leadership at the national level. Men of Color, by being leaders of their own communities, becoming visible at the national level, and negotiating with the highest levels of government, were validated as men and, by default, as human beings. An essential part of this definition as men was that women of Color enact their womanhood as defined by hegemonic standards, which at the time were predominantly white. To question the sexism of men of Color in public would have been to tear down not only their manhood but, even more important, their chance to be fully human, perhaps for the first time in the history of this country.

The possibility of being human was seductive also for women of Color because hegemonic definitions of gender roles entailed that men take care of women and children, at least financially. This would have relieved an enormous burden from women of Color, who not only worked a second shift but also, historically, have been perceived as beasts of burden— exploited for their labor as well as for their sexuality. Men of Color and women of Color share very similar material conditions, especially in comparison to the white population, which provides the overarching political goal of economic and social justice. Therefore, to be considered a woman was a step closer to being a human being, with the privileges and considerations that humanness entails. It was the first time that men of Color could offer the women in their group the potential rewards of seduction.

Despite the intense political solidarity between men and women of Color during this time, many women of Color still questioned the gendered arrangements within their own communities, either through political action or in the form of artistic production. These forums maximized the possibility of their critique remaining inside their groups and reduced the likelihood of them being picked up by the mainstream media. In this way the solidarity between women of Color and men of Color, though not without tension, could be based on a common fight for the recognition of their humanity, not only by the dominant group but also by each other.

The tension between men of Color and women of Color has resurfaced recently as white feminists and feminists of Color have formed alliances, as women of Color's intellectual production has been recognized and celebrated, and as women of Color scholars have broadened the topics of their inquiry to include gender subordination within their own communities. At times this intellectual work has been perceived by both men and women of Color as treason because it may lead to the political demise of our communities or, worse yet, to the erosion of the slight advancement we have made in convincing others, and perhaps ourselves, that indeed we are human.

By now the reader must be asking why I consider these particular questions blasphemous; blasphemy in the sense of questioning what in many ways we have been required not to question—our loyalty and silence to those who may oppress us because they have also been our *compañeras/compañeros* in struggle. As feminists of Color, many of us have allied ourselves with white feminists to push forward a political agenda that places gender issues at the forefront. As feminists of Color, many of us have also allied ourselves with activists of Color that place race/ethnicity at the forefront of their political mobilization. To question these allegiances is to potentially serve the role of saboteur when the progress we have made in remedying racism and sexism is yet in its infancy.

More specifically, the answers to these questions can undermine the nationalist arguments that most ethnic/racial movements in the United States have used as their political templates and moral essences. Nationalist arguments have struggled to build a sense of peoplehood and unity based on the ethnic/race backgrounds of different communities in the United States. Whether these communities are Chicano, Asian American, African American, or Native American, nationalist political mobilization has been based on trying to rebuild previously derogated identities by the reacquisition of the groups' languages, ethnic identities, and cultures—all of which are political acts because they have been in defiance of the dominant hegemony of cultural and political assimilation. Nationalist arguments pull at the heartstrings of all of us who grew up in a barrio or ghetto, who had parents who were farmworkers or unskilled workers, and who have "made it" in the Anglo world—precisely, those of us who are likely to pose a challenge to their logic. Nationalist rhetoric is full of passion, love, and idealism in a modern framework, in which the "hard" facts of life such as putting food on the table and having a roof over one's head are the primary basis for political solidarity. The requirement that internal criticism of our group remains within the confines of the group is not imagined paranoia but, in fact, necessary for group survival. The answers to these questions are not "betrayal" because betrayal implies the rejection of the group or knowledge that the articulation of the answers will result in expulsion from the group. We have had many traitors in our groups—those who have joined with the dominant forces to oppress and dismantle the slight progress ethnic/racial groups have made in this country during the last two hundred years. Traitors, although painful, are easy to deal with. Blasphemy is much more profound, because it is based not on rejection of the group but on love of the group. To be blasphemous is not to want to leave the group but, rather, to want to make it better for those who belong to the group as well as for future generations. Blasphemy involves confrontating unpleasant, unvoiced, often ignored, social relations, which have been suspended for the sake of political survival. If oppression and domination are relational, they are therefore not the property of individuals but, rather, the outcome of context-specific relationships. And yet these social contexts are not independent of a ruthless, relentless, and pervasive social structure that still uses gender, race/ethnicity, class, and sexual orientation to enforce privilege and subordination. The answers to the simple questions I pose are blasphemous because, by definition, they implicate all of us—within certain contexts we can be victims of subordination, and within others we can be the oppressors. Yet, wherever we go, certain group memberships still make it easier for us to be victims and more difficult to be oppressors. If there are no inherent good guys or bad guys, inevitably what I speak of will be blasphemy to one group or another depending on where the relational lens is focused. My struggle to articulate this "border" consciousness, to quote Anzaldúa, is the topic of the last chapter "On a Reflexive Feminist Theory of Gender Subordination." There I struggle to provide a framework for dismantling our inability to integrate our own privilege based on group memberships into our theorizing about subordination. Central to my argument is my belief that only a feminist paradigm is capable of theoretically incorporating privilege as an essential part of producing knowledge that will lead to dismantling existing economic and social inequality. Feminists' epistemologies are the only frameworks that have within them the seeds of their own destruction so that other frameworks can emerge to challenge their assertions: they have in them the breeding ground for blasphemy, which ultimately is what will be needed to blast us out of the continuing construction of structures of oppression.

Acknowledgments

In many ways this book has been in the making since my arrival in Santa Cruz, California, in August 1983. Since then I have encountered many people who generously gave of their time and energy to educate me beyond my narrow conception of categorical memberships. I arrived in Santa Cruz a Chicana nationalist who perceived feminism as nothing more than a middle-class preoccupation available to those who did not have to struggle for their daily bread. I hope I have through this book, in some small way, been educated into a feminist who struggles with understanding power as part of a structural arrangement in which we all play a part.

Of the individuals who helped me understand this are all of the students I have encountered in my classes at the University of California, Santa Cruz as well as at the University of Michigan. Especially close to my education have been all the research assistants whom I have had the pleasure to work with: José Sahagún, Melinda Nabor, Francie Cordova, Virginia Espino, Pattye Crespo, Alejandra Díaz, Sobeida Vizcarra, Letty Recio, Reynold Gonzalez, Raúl Rodriguez, Verónica Rodriguez, José Cuellar, Rebeca Burciaga, Manuel Fonseca, Manuel Arteaga, Sandra Márquez, and Hector Torres.

Among the colleagues who took special care not to write me off when I often refused education are: Candace West, Beatríz López-Flores, Annie Valva, Gini Matute-Bianchi, Gloria Cuadraz, Sophia García-Robles, Liz Martín-García, Abby Stewart, Pat Mora, Elba Sánchez, Norma Cantú, Patricia Zavella, Clara Lomas, and Hale Bolak.

Most of all, because they have the most consistent, intimate, and contentious contact with me, to my ever-expanding family—Craig, Chelita, Bonnie, Lynne, Erin, Pepe, Chanel, Matt, Alyson, Gerry, Pat, Jennifer, Bryan, Chloe, and Rebbekah. And to my dad, wherever he may be.

Of course, whatever miseducation remains is for me to acknowledge and remedy.

Contents

CHAPTER 1

Relating to Privilege and Political Mobilization: Toward a Multicultural Feminism

I see that as an artist, with my Latino artist friends, to be able to have that charge, that sense of creating a space, to create fifteen or twenty years of paintings, music, film or video. Twenty years of writing grant after grant, having your children going through their changes, and been left by men, and families, and women, all the things that we go through, and still have a moment of joy. We can appreciate life. We look at the world and it is palatable to us, all the beauty, to me just can't be stopped. It gives me so much joy and so much hope to know that.

—Ana Castillo

It was the fall of 1983. I'd just been hired as an assistant professor of psychology at the University of California, Santa Cruz. Santa Cruz, the pseudoresort town on the edge of the Pacific, with its radical political roots, had just been declared by *Ms.* magazine as one of the country's foremost feminist havens. I was sitting at a dinner party with four other women colleagues from various departments. We were discussing sexism in our respective areas when one of them burst into tears over her salad and began, between sobs, to describe how inferior she felt and how she often thought she was crazy because nobody in her department saw the flaws in the discipline as she did. I was startled but bent over and put my arm around her. The other women stared at their plates and sat quietly, trying to give our distressed colleague time to compose herself. She eventually did, and the first thing she said when she stopped crying was, "I just want somebody in my field to say that most of what gets published in main-

A shorter version of this chapter appeared under the title "Relating to Privilege: Seduction and Rejection in the Subordination of White Women and Women of Color" in *Signs 41* (1989), 833–55.

The epigraph is taken from an interview with Ana Castillo, poet and artist (quoted in Barrera 1991, 131–32).

stream journals is bullshit." And I replied without hesitation, "Everything that gets published in mainstream journals is bullshit." And she burst out laughing. The rest of the women also joined in with uncomfortable laughter, and we continued our discussion and our dinner.

I went away that evening deeply perplexed. Here were these extremely attractive, highly educated women (all of them trained in the top five Ph.D. programs in the country in their respective fields), mostly in their late twenties early thirties, with the top academic jobs in the country, middle class (some would say upper middle class), white, living in the *Ms.*-anointed feminist haven in the country, with deep sadness that at times resulted in crippling depression. In fact, two were already on antidepressant medication. Here I was with the same current socioeconomic characteristics, except I was brown, the daughter of farmworkers, and nowhere near as talented as they were in academic skills. I wasn't particularly happy to be living in Santa Cruz (feminist or not), mostly because I missed my Chicano community and there was nowhere to get a decent Mexican breakfast on the weekend, but I thought I had died and won the lottery to be able to teach what I wanted and to write as I pleased. Why were they so sad when, whichever way it was analyzed, structurally, they had more power and control than 99.99 percent of all women in the world? I did not know, and yet I did not doubt, what they felt. My job, I thought that night, was to figure out why they were so sad and I was not (at least not all the time) and what we could do, as women, to help one another.

It seemed to me that the answer to why these women were so much like me and yet so different did not lie in personality characteristics or individual temperaments. Instead, I struggled to understand how structural factors may be impinging on us differently that would result in such different reactions to our newly acquired status as assistant professors. This is how this chapter was born.

Each oppressed group in the United States is positioned in a particular and distinct relationship to white men, and each form of subordination is shaped by this relational position. Men of Color and white men maintain power over women, particularly within their respective groups. Gender[1] alone, however, does not determine either a superordinate or subordinate position. In a highly industrialized society run by a complex hierarchical bureaucracy and based on individualistic competition, many socially constructed markers of group membership are used to allocate power (Apfelbaum 1979). Class, ethnicity, race, and sexuality are but a few. As we develop a discourse for discussing our group memberships, as our consciousness about the mechanisms of subordination evolves, and as previously silenced groups speak, we can begin to form a picture of contemporary forms of subordination and their psychological effects (Connell 1985, 264).

I focus on the relationships of white women and women of Color to white men and how these relationships have affected feminists from both groups.[2] The conflicts and tensions between white feminists and feminists of Color are viewed too frequently as lying solely in woman-to-woman relationships. These relationships, however, are affected in both obvious and subtle ways by how each of these two groups of women relate to white men through linkages that Nancy Henley calls "the everyday social relationships that glue together the social superstructure" (1986, 21).[3]

The Structural Position of Women in the United States

In the United States Blacks, Native Americans, and Latinos are predominantly working class, as are some Asian groups.[4] On every measure of standard of living (income, years of education, household makeup) most groups of Color are positioned structurally below the white population. This is especially the case for women in these racial and ethnic groups. The socioeconomic position of women of Color, as a group, affects their relational position to the highest income holders in the United States—white men. Women of Color's structural position has not historically been an integral part of white feminist analyses, primarily because most white feminists have overemphasized gender oppression as overriding other socioeconomic characteristics as the basis for subordination. Although in the last five years the infusion of race and class into feminist analyses has been one of the most heated and prolific debates in feminist writings, it is still very much the practice to collapse differences among women, especially when comparing them to men (specifically, when the comparison involves white men).

The recent awareness about the differences among women from different ethnic/racial groups has not erased the persistent practice in statistical reporting in the media to aggregate the socioeconomic status of all groups of women, thus hiding their substantial differences (*San Jose Mercury News* 1988; *Los Angeles Times* 1992; James 1994). The reports usually begin by stating the aggregate differences in pay for women and men, which state, for example, that women have reached 70 percent of pay parity with men (*San Jose Mercury News* 1988). A closer examination of the statistics quoted usually shows that not only do the headlines collapse differences among women; they usually also exaggerate women's gains and so reduce the differences between women and men. In fact, most of the stories that follow show that white women reach, on average, 68 percent of pay parity with white men, but Black women reach only 61 percent, and Hispanic women reached barely 55 percent.[5]

White women tend to earn more money than women of Color because, as a group, they tend to be able to stay in school longer than many women of Color (Ortíz 1995). White women are more likely to finish high school (86 percent, in contrast to 77 percent of Black women and 63 percent of Hispanic women) and receive more of the bachelor's degrees awarded to women (83.5 percent, in contrast to 7 percent of Black women, 0.4 percent of Native Americans, 3.5 percent of Hispanic women, and 3.6 percent of Asian Americans, based on the total number of bachelor's degrees awarded to women nationwide in 1991) (Carter and Wilson 1993, 47–49, 55). White women therefore earn substantially higher incomes, even though certain groups of women of Color (e.g., Black women) are more likely than white women to stay in the labor force without interruption. Recent figures show that the median annual income for women of Mexican descent is $4,556; for Puerto Rican women, $4,473; for Vietnamese women, $4,694; for Japanese women, $7,410; for Filipina women, $8,253; and for Black women, $14,036. On the other hand, the median income for white women is $15,575 (Taeuber 1991; Bennett 1995; Ortíz 1995). All women experience job segregation, but white women's current educational attainment gives them a brighter future than that of women of Color (Woo 1985).[6] In the past few years in the United States the college enrollment of all women fourteen to thirty-four years old has been nearing that of men. Close to half (49 percent) of all graduate students in 1980 were women, compared to less than a third (29 percent) in 1970 (Taeuber and Baldisera 1986, 13–15). In fact, between 1982 and 1992 the number of Ph.D. degrees received by women rose 28.8 percent while falling 7.5 percent for all men and 8.9 percent for white men specifically. Although these school figures do not include a separate category for women of Color, it is safe to conclude that, given the high school and college graduation rates quoted earlier, the doctoral degrees increasingly going to women are predominantly going to white women (Kelley 1994).[7] Moreover, the 1991 figures for first-time professional degrees verifies this assumption: of the 39 percent professional degrees granted to women that year, 3.7 percent went to Hispanics, 6.8 percent went to African Americans, 5.6 percent to Asians, 0.4 percent to Native Americans, but 82.3 percent went to white women (Carter and Wilson 1993, 57). Of most relevance to my argument that white women have an economic cushion because of their relationship to male family members are the figures that show that, on average, about 89 percent of Hispanic and African American college students come from families with annual incomes less than $40,000 (Wyche and Graves 1992) and from families that, on average, have two more family members than white families (Hurtado et al. 1993).

Increasingly, women are becoming the sole supporters of their families. The number of single-parent families has almost doubled since 1970; one in five families with children is now maintained by a woman. Women of Color are more likely than white women, however, to maintain families (44 percent of Black women, 39 percent of Puerto Rican women, 23 percent of Native American women, 20 percent of Mexican American women, and 20 percent of Cuban women, compared to 13 percent of white women) (Ortíz 1995).[8] Furthermore, women of Color are more likely to be heads of households living in poverty (52 percent of Black households and 53 percent of Hispanic households, compared to 27 percent of white households), more likely to be divorced (35 percent of Black women, compared to 14 percent of white women), and more likely to have larger families (40 percent of Black women, 60 percent of Hispanic women, but only 20 percent of white women had four or more people to support). In addition, teenage mothers are more likely to be Black women than white women (58 percent of teenage mothers are Black, compared to 13 percent white) (Taeuber and Baldisera 1986, 9–10). These figures remained virtually unchanged in 1991 (*Poverty in the United States: 1991,* Ser. P-60, no. 181 1993).

These measures reveal that women of Color stay fewer years in school, have fewer dollars to spend, and bear more economic burdens than any other group in this country. White women also suffer economically, but their economic situation is not as dire as that of women of Color. More specifically, white women's relationship to white men (the highest earners in society) as daughters, wives, or sisters gives them an "economic cushion" (Palmer 1983). Given these data, when I discuss feminists of Color I will treat them as members of the working class, unless I specifically mention otherwise. When I discuss white feminists, I will treat them as middle class. Labels are not easy to assign because of the complexity of human experience and because of the insidious and changing nature of subordination. My purpose is not to provide neat categories to be used regardless of social context but, rather, to provide a framework for discussion by defining the different positions of these groups of women in relation to white men. I believe this will help us to understand the differences between women of Color and white women in general and feminists in particular.

The Exclusion of Women of Color in Feminist Theory

The economic cushion that many white women, as a group, enjoy because of their relationship to white men has influenced the development of feminist writing. Academic production requires time and financial resources. Poverty hampers the ability of all working-class people, especially racial and ethnic groups, to participate in higher education: without financial assistance few low-income and racial/ethnic students can attend universities; without higher education few working-class and ethnic/racial intellectuals can become researchers, scholars, and professors.[9] Not surprisingly, therefore, most contemporary published feminist theory in the United States has been written by white, educated women (hooks 1981). The experiences of other women (including white working-class women) are absent in much of white academic feminist theory (Joseph and Lewis 1981).

Much of white feminist theory focuses on the condition of women qua women.[10] There are many examples of this tendency. There are also numerous examples of impressive and comprehensive reviews of contemporary white feminist theory (e.g., Jaggar 1983). Many of these works readily acknowledge that most white feminist theory fails to integrate race into its analysis of women's subordination. While many authors lament this failure, it is not uncommon for them to proclaim that women of Color have not developed a distinctive and comprehensive theory of women's liberation and that the existing writings are "mainly at the level of description" (ibid., 11). Most white feminist theorists do not dismiss them altogether, however; they either fit writings by feminist of Color theorists within the existing white feminists' frameworks or claim that writings by feminists of Color, while descriptive, are not theoretical. Or, as Caraway points out, if Black women's writings do not "replicate in style and tone the official feminist discourse, it is [they are] often ignored, exoticized as a 'funky' or 'gutsy' backdrop to the 'real' project of theorizing" (1991, 39).[11] In doing so, many white feminists gloss over important differences between feminists of Color and white feminists, differences that may elucidate the race/class nexus so lacking in white feminist theory (Zavella 1994). For example,

Alison Jaggar notes that "a very few [Black feminists] are radical feminists, though almost none seem to be lesbian separatists" (1983, 11), but she does not discuss why this is so, beyond locating it within choices that white women have made. Jaggar continues by saying that "radical feminism . . . was sparked by the special experiences of a relatively small group of predominantly white, middle-class, college-educated, American women in the later 1960s. . . . Today, those who are attracted to radical feminism still tend to be primarily white and college-educated" (83–84). Jaggar also fails even to speculate about why Black feminists might be reluctant to separate from Black men while simultaneously recognizing their gender subordination.

Recently, white feminist theorists have begun to recognize the theoretical implications of embracing diversity among women (e.g., Caraway 1991). White feminist theory is moving beyond biological determinism and social categoricalism to a conception of gender and sex as an outcome of power and subordination (Connell 1987, 140, 264).[12] Rejecting the binary categorization of "man" and "woman," this new conceptualization opens up the possibility of diversity among women and men and the possibility of many feminisms (Rabine 1988, 19). Despite these advances, however, white feminist theory has yet to integrate the facts that, for women of Color, race, class, and gender subordination are experienced simultaneously and that their oppression is carried out not only by members of their own group but also by whites of both genders (Hurtado 1988; Zavella 1994; Cuadraz and Pierce 1995). White feminist theorists have failed to grasp fully what this means, how it is experienced, and, ultimately, how it is fought (Collins 1986). Many white feminists have an intellectual commitment to addressing race and class, but the class origins of the participants in the movement as well as their relationship to white men have prevented them, as a group, from understanding the simultaneity of oppressions for women of Color (Palmer 1983, 154; Collins 1986; Crenshaw 1989, 64). To understand why white feminist theory has not fully addressed race and class in its analysis of gender subordination, it becomes necessary to examine the historical origins of the white feminist movement.

The Historical Context

Before the Civil War nearly all white women advocates of equal rights for women were committed abolitionists. Yet, as bell hooks indicates, this did not mean they were all antiracist (1981, 124). White abolitionists did not all want to destroy the racial hierarchy or provide broad citizenship rights to

freed slaves. Instead, they were motivated by religious and moral senti-
ments to take a stand against slavery as an institution (Stimpson 1971).
Because many white abolitionists were not antiracist, working relationships between Black and white activists were sometimes strained. When it
was expedient, white women in the abolitionist movement would compare
their plight to that of the slaves. Elizabeth Cady Stanton, speaking before
the New York State Legislature in 1860, stated:

> The prejudice against Color, of which we hear so much, is no stronger
> than that against sex. It is produced by the same cause, and manifested
> very much in the same way. The Negro's skin and the woman's sex
> are both prima facie evidence that they were intended to be in subjec-
> tion to the white Saxon man. The few social privileges which the man
> gives the woman, he makes up to the (free) Negro in civil rights.
> (Stanton, Anthony, and Gage 1889, 456–57)

Stanton, unfortunately, cast her argument in terms that pitted white
women against Black men in a competition for privileges that erased Black
women altogether.

The strained bonds between Black and white women involved in the
fight for equal political rights finally ruptured after the Civil War. When
only Black men received the vote, Black and white activists together
decried the exclusion of women's rights, but their protests took different
forms. Black suffragists did not abandon Black men; white suffragists
quickly abandoned Black women (A. Y. Davis 1981, 76–77; hooks 1981,
127). White women's rights advocates such as Elizabeth Cady Stanton, who
had never before argued woman suffrage on a racially imperialistic platform, in 1869 stated her outrage at the enfranchisement of Black men:

> If Saxon men have legislated thus for their own mothers, wives and
> daughters, what can we hope for at the hands of Chinese, Indians, and
> Africans? . . . I protest against the enfranchisement of another man of
> any race or clime until the daughters of Jefferson, Hancock, and
> Adams are crowned with their rights. (Stanton, Anthony, and Gage
> 1887, 222)

Aptheker rightly points out that Stanton and Anthony were probably
no more, and probably less, racist than their contemporaries (1982, 51–52).
Black suffragists, however, could not afford such disengagement from

their group. Instead, many Black women leaders of the time fought for the just treatment of all people, with the recognition that women of Color experienced multiple oppressions because of their gender, race, and class. Black women suffragists struggled with white suffragists to obtain women's right to vote as they fought against lynchings, poverty, and segregation (Wells 1970; Sterling 1979; Hutchinson 1982). In 1893 Anna Cooper addressed the Women's Congress in Chicago and eloquently outlined the position many other Black activists were advocating at that time:

> We take our stand on the solidarity of humanity, the oneness of life, and the unnaturalness and injustice of all special favoritisms, whether of sex, race, country, or condition. . . . Least of all can women's cause afford to decry the weak. . . . Not till the universal title of humanity of life, liberty, and the pursuit of happiness is conceded to be inalienable to all; not till then is woman's lesson taught and woman's cause won—not the white woman's, not the black woman's, not the red woman's, but the cause of every man and of every woman who has writhed silently under a mighty wrong. (quoted in Hutchinson 1982, 87–88)

Racial conflict emerged in the suffrage movement for many reasons, the most important of which was the white women's privileged relationship to white men. Elizabeth Cady Stanton, Susan B. Anthony, and Lucy Stone were all *familially related* to prominent white men who supported them during their involvement in political work, while Black activists such as Sojourner Truth, Ida B. Wells, and Ellen Craft were at birth *owned* by white men (Sterling 1979). In an ironic twist, because of Stanton, Anthony, and Stone's familial ties, they too owned, or could potentially co-own, the relatives of Truth, Wells, and Craft.

Despite the abolition of slavery, the difference between the relationship of white women to white men and of women of Color to white men has persisted to the present. The conflict that this difference causes between contemporary white feminists and feminists of Color is but a replay of old divisions that are perpetuated with amazing consistency. Like their political ancestors, contemporary feminists of Color do not attribute their oppression solely to their gender and are reluctant to abandon the struggle on behalf of their racial/ethnic group. For example, the largest organization of Chicana academics, Mujeres Activas en Letras y Cambio Social, explicitly states its class and ethnic solidarity:

We are the daughters of Chicano working class families involved in higher education. We were raised in labor camps and urban barrios, where sharing our resources was the basis of survival. . . . Our history is the story of working people—their struggles, commitments, strengths, and the problems they faced. . . . We are particularly concerned with the conditions women face at work, in and out of the home. We continue our mothers' struggle for social and economic justice. (Sosa-Ridell 1983, 2)[13]

Rejection versus Seduction

Sojourner Truth, speaking at the Women's Rights Convention in 1851, highlighted the crucial difference between women of Color and white women in their relationships to white men. Frances Dana Gage, the presiding officer of the convention, describes Sojourner Truth marching down the aisle to the pulpit steps, where she addressed her audience:

At her first word there was a profound hush. . . . "That man over there say that women needs to be helped into carriages, and lifted over ditches, and to have the best place everywhere. Nobody ever helps me into carriages, or over mud-puddles, or gives me any best place!" And raising herself to her full height, asked, "And ain't I a woman? Look at me! Look at my arm!" (and she bared her right arm to the shoulder, showing her tremendous muscular power). "I have ploughed, and planted, and gathered into barns, and no man could head me! And ain't I a woman? I could work as much and eat as much as a man— when I could get it—and bear the lash as well! And ain't I a woman? I have borne thirteen children and seen them most all sold off to slavery, and when I cried out with my mother's grief, none but Jesus heard me! And ain't I a woman?" (Stanton, Anthony, and Gage 1887, 115–17)

Now, as then, white middle-class women are groomed from birth to be the lovers, mothers, and partners (however unequal) of white men because of the economic and social benefits attached to these roles (de Beauvoir 1952, xxiv; Lorde 1984, 118–19). Upper- and middle-class white women are supposed to be the biological bearers of those members of the next generation who will inherit positions of power in society. Women of Color, in contrast, are groomed from birth to be primarily the lovers, mothers, and partners (however unequal) of men of Color, who are also oppressed by white men.[14] The avenues of advancement through marriage that are open to white women who conform to prescribed standards of middle-class femininity are not even a theoretical possibility for most women of Color (Ostrander 1984).[15] Ramón Gutiérrez (1991, xviii) rightly indicates that marriage provides a "window into the social, political, and economic arrangements of a society," and that it is through marriage that people "create social alliances, establish a new social unit, change residence, exchange property, and gain rights to sexual service." It is the most intimate linkage, besides biological ties, that two individuals may engage in—therefore, it is not surprising that like tend to marry like because it is through the ritual of marriage that defines the local contours of class and status (xviii). Equally important is the gendered nature of the institution of marriage—it requires a male and a female and "how this marital relationship between two gendered individuals is culturally defined often becomes a gender representation of relations of domination and subordination in other realms" (xviii). Therefore, it is not surprising that in 1993, only 2.2 percent of U.S. marriages were interracial. More to the point, even a smaller number, .4 percent, were Black-white unions. In actual numbers, there were 246,000 Black-white marriages out of a total of 1,200,000 interracial married couples and a total of 54,000,000 married couples in the United States (Graham 1995, 33). Moreover, 71 percent of all Black-white couples in the U.S. involve a Black man and the Census Bureau figures in 1992 indicate that Black women are "half as likely to marry outside the race than black men" (ibid., 40, 58). This is not to say that women of Color are more oppressed than white women but, rather, that white men use different forms of enforcing oppression on white women and on women of Color.[16] As a consequence, these groups of women have different political responses and skills, and at times these differences cause the two groups to clash.[17]

Women of Color came to the United States either through slavery (e.g., Blacks), conquest of their homeland (e.g., Chicanas, Puerto Ricans, American Indians, Filipinas), or through forced and semiforced labor migration (e.g., Japanese, Chinese). Unlike European immigrants who become culturally and linguistically assimilated within two generations (Neidert and Farley 1985), these groups of women constitute racially/ethnically distinct groups. Thus, even if a Black career woman were to marry a white professional man, her offspring would *not* inherit the power positions accorded to white sons and daughters of the same class.[18] If, however, a working-class white woman were to marry a white professional man, her offspring would automatically acquire the privileged position of the father. In certain circles a white woman's humble beginnings are a source of pride because they reaffirm the dominant hegemonic belief in the availability of equal opportunity (Pettigrew and Martin 1987; Haney and Hurtado 1994). In contrast, race privilege is not assured even to offspring of a white father and Black mother. Indeed, some argue that being half-Black is a greater stigma than having remained within the subordinate group's boundaries, because these individuals are ostracized by both whites and Blacks (Du Bois 1973; Malcolm X 1973; Root 1992, 5).

A similar type of stigma is attached to offspring of white men and non-Black women of Color. Often the offspring of these unions are referred to as "half-breeds" and not fully accepted socially, especially if phenotypically they resemble their nonwhite mothers (Pérez 1991, 184). For Latinos, this "pigmentocracy"—that is, privilege based solely on skin color—has its historical precedence in colonial Spanish rule because "honor, status, and prestige were judged by skin color and phenotype" (Gutiérrez 1991, 198–99). Granted, legally, offspring of mixed unions may inherit the white father's race privilege because the one-drop rule only applies to Blacks; however, structurally, biological assimilation into the dominant group is very much dependent on complete obliteration of any visual vestige that may identify the individual as part of the nonwhite group. For all practical purposes, then, nonstigmatized intermarriage is only possible when it does not appear to be an intermarriage at all and when the offspring of such unions do not identify with nor look like the nonwhite group. Under such conditions the effect of intermarriage on dismantling white privilege is very limited, and to a large extent, structurally, it almost has no effect at all. What will become relevant for feminist theory in the near future will be when the growing numbers of offspring of intermarriage who can potentially pass as white *refuse* their inherited white privilege and join subordinate groups to sabotage existing power arrangements (ibid., 184; also see chap. 4 for a more extensive discussion of these issues).

White men need white women in a way that they do not need women of Color because women of Color cannot fulfill white men's need for racially pure offspring. This fact creates differences in the relational position of the groups—distance from and access to the source of privilege, white men. Thus, white women, as a group, are subordinated through seduction, women of Color, as a group, through rejection. Class position, of course, affects the probability of obtaining the rewards of seduction and the sanctions of rejection. Working-class white women are socialized to believe in the advantages of marrying somebody economically successful, but the probability of obtaining that goal is lower for them than for middle- or upper-class white women (Ostrander 1984). Class position affects women of Color as well. Although rejected by most white men as candidates to reproduce offspring, middle-class women of Color may be accepted into some white middle-class social circles in the well-documented role of token (Apfelbaum 1979, 199; Pettigrew and Martin 1987). Class privilege functions to one degree or another regardless of race, and white privilege functions to one degree or another regardless of class (Higginbotham 1985).

The Dual Construction of Womanhood

> This was one of the supreme ironies of slavery: in order to approach its strategic goal—to extract the greatest possible surplus from the labor of slaves—the black woman had to be released from the chains of the myth of femininity. . . . In order to function as slaves, the black woman had to be annulled as woman.
>
> —A. Y. Davis 1971, 7

For the most part, white feminist theory has difficulty elucidating the condition of women of Color because much of this theorizing takes the categories of "women" and "men" as "in no need of further examination or finer distinction" (Connell 1985, 264). There is an implicit biological determinism even in the works of those theorists who have rejected it.[19] When Sojourner Truth, baring her muscular arm, asked "ain't I a woman?" the reply might not have been obvious, even though she had borne thirteen children. The answer to her question involves defining *woman*. The white women in the room did not have to plough the fields, side by side with Black men, and see their offspring sold into slavery, yet they were clearly women. Sojourner Truth had worked the fields, and she had borne children, but she was not a woman in the sense of having the same experiences as the white women at the meeting. The questioning of Sojourner Truth's gender was further underscored by the white ministers' insistence that she bare her breasts to prove that she was not an impostor and, "indeed, that she was a woman at all" (Caraway 1991, 76). Truth militantly obliged and appropriated the moment by indicating that her black breasts had suckled many a white man (White 1985, 162).[20]

The definition of *woman* is constructed differently for white women and for women of Color, though sexuality is the marking mechanism through which the subordination of each is maintained.[21] The construction of white womanhood also eroticizes potency (as male) and victimization/frailty (as female). As Catherine MacKinnon surmises:

> Women who resist or fail, including those who never did fit—(for example, black and lower-class women who cannot survive if they are soft and weak and incompetent, assertively self-respecting women, women with ambitions of male dimensions—are considered less female, lesser women. Women who comply or succeed are elevated as models, tokenized by success on male terms or portrayed as consenting to their natural place and dismissed as having participated if they complain. (1982, 530)

White women are persuaded to become the partners of white men and are seduced into accepting a subservient role that meets the material needs of white men. As Audre Lorde describes it:

> White women face the pitfall of being seduced into joining the oppressor under the pretense of sharing power. This possibility does not exist in the same way for women of color. The tokenism that is sometimes extended to us is not an invitation to join power: our racial "otherness" is a visible reality that makes it quite clear. For white women there is a wider range of pretended choices and rewards for identifying with patriarchal power and its tools. (1984, 118–19)

The patriarchal invitation to power is only a pretended choice for white women because, as in all cases of tokens, their inclusion is dependent on complete and constant submission. As John Stuart Mill observed: "It was not sufficient for [white] women to be slaves. They must be willing slaves, for the maintenance of patriarchal order depends upon the consensus of women. It depends upon women playing their part . . . voluntarily suppressing the evidence that exposes the false and arbitrary nature of man-made categories and the reality which is built on those categories" (quoted in Spender 1980, 101–2).

The genesis of the construction of "woman" for Black women in the United States is in slavery.[22] During slavery Black women were required to be as masculine as men in the performance of work and were as harshly punished as men, but they were also raped (A. Y. Davis 1981, 5). Many Black women were broken and destroyed, but the majority who survived "acquired qualities considered taboo by the nineteenth-century ideology of womanhood." As Angela Davis puts it: "[Black women's] awareness of their endless capacity for hard work may have imparted to them a confidence in their ability to struggle for themselves, their families, and their people" (1981, 11).[23]

Many white men perceive women of Color primarily as workers (Castillo 1991, 27) and as objects of sexual power and aggression.[24] Their sexual objectification of women of Color allows white men to express power and aggression sexually, without the emotional entanglements of, and the rituals that are required in, relationships with women of their own group (Rich 1979, 291–95; hooks 1981, 58; Palmer 1983, 156). In many ways the dual conception of woman based on race—"white goddess / black she-devil, chaste virgin / nigger whore, the blond blue-eyed doll / the exotic 'mulatto' object of sexual craving"—has freed many women of Color from the distraction of the rewards of seduction (Rich 1979, 291). Women of Color "do not receive the respect and treatment—mollycoddling and condescending as it sometimes is—afforded to white women" (Joseph 1981, 27).

Identity Invention versus Reaffirmation of Cultural Roots

A prominent theme in the activities of the white feminist movement has been the deconstruction of patriarchal definitions of gender in order to develop women's own definitions of what it means to be a woman (Chodorow 1978; Friday 1982). This is similar to the process of decolonization that minority groups underwent in the 1960s (Apfelbaum 1979, 203). In both instances socially stigmatized groups have reclaimed their history by taking previously denigrated characteristics and turning them into positive affirmations of self (ibid.; Tajfel 1974). For example, radical feminism glorifies the menstrual cycle as a symbol of women's capacity to give birth, while Black liberation uses skin color in the slogan "Black Is Beautiful" (Tajfel 1974, 83; Jaggar 1983, 94–95).

White women are at a greater disadvantage than women of Color in reclaiming their identity—or perhaps it is more accurate to say, in inventing their identity. For white women "the struggle for consciousness is a struggle for world: for a sexuality, a history, a culture, a community, a form of power, an experience of the sacred" (MacKinnon 1983, 637). Unlike people of Color, who can refer to a specific event in history (e.g., slavery, military conquest) as the beginning of their subordination, white women in the

United States have always been subordinated to white men, and hence their dependency is not the result of a specific historical event or social change (de Beauvoir 1952, xxi). People of Color in the United States retain the memory of the days before slavery or conquest: they share that past, a tradition, and sometimes a religion or culture (ibid.).

White feminists have had to uncover a history and simultaneously define what they want to become in the future. With patriarchal ideology so deeply ingrained, it is difficult for white feminists to reconstruct womanhood in adulthood (hooks 1984, 47–49). Existing academic paradigms, emanating from male culture and distorting women's experience, are virtually useless for this task (Smith 1978, 293). With few academic, historical, and cultural paths to follow, white feminists have nevertheless undertaken the task of redefining gender. It is to their credit that white feminists have succeeded in building feminist theory and in obtaining concrete political results when they started with little more than an intuitive dissatisfaction with their subordination (Friedan 1963, 11).

As part of their subordination, most white women have been denied equal participation in public discourse with white men (Smith 1978, 281; Candace West, forthcoming).[25] Shirley Ardener (1975) argues that (white) women are socialized in the "art of conversation," while (white) men are trained in the more formal "art of rhetoric," or the "art of persuasion." Socialization to a feminine mode of discourse deprives white women of a political medium through which to voice and define their oppression (Spender 1980, 78–79). In 1963 Betty Friedan called this the "problem that has no name" because white middle-class women's discontent did not fit into the categories of the problems already named (by men) (1963, 15). In the late 1960s consciousness-raising groups were formed not only to delineate women's discontent but also to develop a discourse for discussing it (Spender 1980, 92–94).[26] Feminist inquiry, then, began with a "broad unmasking of the attitudes that legitimize and hide women's status, the ideational envelope that contains women's body" (MacKinnon 1982, 529).

Despite their exclusion from participation in the "manufacturing of culture," white women have not been segregated from the "makers of culture," white men (Smith 1978, 282). White middle-class women's relational position to white men has given them at the very least a spectator's seat. For example, Dorothy E. Smith relates how women who become mathematicians generally discover mathematics by accident, in "sharing a brother's lessons, the interest of a family friend, the paper covered with calculus used to paper a child's room—some special incident or relation which introduced them to the territory of their art" (1978, 284). Elizabeth Cady Stanton was exposed to the white man's culture by her father, a prominent, conservative judge, who taught her law and supported her obtaining a high school diploma at the age of sixteen (A. Y. Davis 1981, 48–49).

Most women of Color are not groomed to be the parlor conversationalists that white women are expected to be. Working-class women of Color come from cultures whose languages have been barred from public discourse, as well as from the written discourse, of society at large. Many people of Color speak varieties of English (e.g., Black English) not understood by most white people. Nonetheless, people of Color often excel in verbal performance among their own peers. They embrace speech as one medium for expression. Older women are especially valued as storytellers with the responsibility of preserving the history of the group from generation to generation (Brant 1984; Ybarra-Fraustro 1986). Patricia Hill Collins argues that a rich tradition of Black feminist thought exists, much of it produced orally by ordinary Black women in their roles as mothers, teachers, musicians, and preachers (1986, 80). This oral tradition celebrates the open and spontaneous exchange of ideas. The conversation of women of Color can be bawdy, rowdy, and irreverent, and, in expressing opinions freely, women of Color exercise a form of power.

What this means is that, for white women, the first step in the search for identity is to confront the ways in which their personal, individual silence endorses the power of white men that has robbed them of their history. For women of Color the challenge is to use their oral traditions for specific political goals.

The Public-Private Distinction

The public-private distinction that exists among the white middle class devalues "women's work" done in the home and arbitrarily upgrades (men's) work performed in the public sphere (Joseph and Lewis 1981, 33–35). Throughout the history of the white feminist movement in the United States, white women have gained political consciousness about gender oppression by examining their personal lives. They have realized that what happens in the intimacy of their own homes is not exempt from the political forces that affect the rest of society (Friedan 1963, 32). The contemporary notion that "the personal is political" identifies and rejects the public-private distinction as a tool by which women are excluded from public participation while the daily tyrannies of men are protected from public scrutiny.

Yet the distinction is relevant only for the white middle and upper classes, since, historically, the state in the United States has intervened constantly in the private lives and domestic arrangements of the working class. Women of Color have not had the benefit of the economic conditions that underlie the public-private distinction. Instead, the political consciousness of women of Color stems from an awareness that the public is *personally* political.[27] Welfare programs and policies have discouraged family life, sterilization programs have restricted reproduction rights, government has drafted and armed disproportionate numbers of people of Color to fight its wars overseas, and, locally, police forces and the criminal justice system arrest and incarcerate disproportionate numbers of people of Color (Joseph 1981, 20; Haney 1985). There is no such thing as a private sphere for people of Color except that which they manage to create and protect in an otherwise hostile environment.

The differences between the concerns of white feminists and those of feminists of Color are indicative of these distinct political groundings. White feminists' concerns about the unhealthy consequences of standards for feminine beauty, their focus on the unequal division of household labor, and their attention to childhood identity formation stem from a political consciousness that seeks to project private sphere issues into the public arena (Chodorow 1978; Orbach 1978; Spender 1980; Hartmann 1981, 18). Feminists of Color focus instead on public issues such as affirmative action, racism, school desegregation, prison reform, and voter registration—issues that cultivate an awareness of the distinction between public policy and private choice.

Because white feminists focus on politicizing the personal, their political consciousness about gender oppression emerges primarily from examining everyday interactions with men. As Nancy Henley observes, as wives, secretaries, or assistants to white men, white women are physically integrated around centers of power, which makes it necessary for powerful white men to have "frequent interaction—verbal and nonverbal—with women" (1986, 15). These frequent interactions promote and reinforce white women's socialization to docility, passivity, and allegiance to white men, so that white women experience an individualized and internalized form of social control. As a result, the white feminist movement is the only political movement to develop its own clinical approach—feminist therapy—to overcoming oppression at the interpersonal level (Henley 1979).

In contrast, other oppressed groups in U.S. society "are often physically separated, by geography, ghettos, and labor hierarchies, from power centers" (Henley 1986, 15). People of Color, as a group, do not have constant familial interactions with white men, and social control is exerted in a direct and impersonal manner. Instead of developing a culturally specific therapy exclusively, ethnic and racial political movements in the United States fight vehemently against the use of therapeutic treatments that depoliticize and individualize their concerns by addressing social problems as if they emerged from the psychology of the oppressed (Ryan 1971; hooks 1993, 4).

These differences in political approaches reflect differences in women's relational position to white men. When white middle-class women rebel, they are accused of mental illness and placed in mental institutions (Gilman 1973). When people of Color rebel, they are accused of violence and placed in prisons (Blumstein 1983). This difference in treatment is related to the distance of each group from the centers of power.

Political Socialization and Survival Skills

Women of Color are marginalized in U.S. society from the time they are born. Marginalization is not a status conferred on them as they step outside the confines of ascribed roles; rather, as Audre Lorde poignantly describes, it is a condition of their lives that is communicated to them by the hatred of strangers. A consciousness of this hatred and the political reasons behind it begins in childhood:

> I don't like to talk about hate. I don't like to remember the cancellation and hatred, heavy as my wished-for death, seen in the eyes of so many white people from the time I could see. It was echoed in newspapers and movies and holy pictures and comic books and Amos 'n' Andy radio programs. I had no tools to dissect it, no language to name it.
>
> The AA subway train to Harlem. I clutch my mother's sleeve. . . . On one side of me a man reading a paper. On the other, a woman in a fur hat staring at me. Her mouth twitches as she stares and then her gaze drops down, pulling mine with it. Her leather-gloved hand plucks at the line where my new blue snowpants and her sleek fur coat meet. She jerks her coat closer to her. I look. I do not see whatever terrible thing she is seeing on the seat between us—probably a roach. But she has communicated her horror to me. It must be something

very bad from the way she is looking, so I pull my snowsuit closer to me away from it, too. When I look up the woman is still staring at me, her nose holes and eyes huge. And suddenly I realize there is nothing crawling up the seat between us: it is me she doesn't want her coat to touch. . . . No word has been spoken. I'm afraid to say anything to my mother because I don't know what I've done. I look at the sides of my snowpants, secretly. Is there something on them? Something's going on here I do not understand, but I will never forget it. Her eyes. The flared nostrils. The hate. (Lorde 1984, 147–48)

Experiences such as these force women of Color to acquire survival skills as early as five years of age (A. Y. Davis 1974; Joseph 1981, 32–33, 40; Moraga and Anzaldúa 1981). Many children of Color serve as the official translators for their monolingual relatives in disputes with companies and agencies unresponsive to poor, working-class people. Early interaction with the public sphere helps many women of Color to develop a public identity and the political skills to fend off state intervention. Women of Color do not have the rewards of seduction offered to them. Relatively few get a high school diploma, even fewer finish college, and only an infinitesimal number obtain graduate degrees (Segura 1986; Cuadraz 1992). Most women of Color have to contribute to the economic survival of their families, and therefore their commitment to obtaining an education, acquiring economic independence, and practicing a profession is part of economic survival (Pesquera 1985). In addition, the low-income status of most women of Color means that they must acquire such survival skills as sustaining informal networks of support, practicing alternative forms of health care, and organizing for political and social change (Trotter and Chavira 1981; Brant 1984; Hurtado 1987–88; Castillo 1995).

By comparison, the childhoods of many white middle-class feminists were protected by classism and racism. As a consequence, many do not acquire their political consciousness of gender oppression until they become adults (Friedan 1963, 73–94). Lacking experience in challenging authorities, and white men in particular, white feminists often seem surprised at the harshness with which the power structure responds to threat, and they do not have well-developed defenses to fend off the attacks. They often turn their anger inward rather than seeing it as a valid response (Tavris 1982, 25–45). In planning political actions, some adopt white men's approaches, others reject them totally. White liberal feminists, for instance, have had a significant impact at the macro level because they have adopted the bureaucratic language and sociopolitical rules that are congenial to the power structure (Jaggar 1983, 197, 286–87). White radical feminists reject men's approaches and are successful at the micro level of interaction in developing modes of political organizing that are consensual and nonhierarchical (Trebilcot 1979).

In contrast, the political skills of feminists of Color are neither the conventional political skills of white liberal feminists nor the free-spirited approaches of white radical feminists. Instead, feminists of Color train to be urban guerrillas by doing battle every day with the apparatus of the state (Moraga and Anzaldúa 1981; Sandoval 1991). Their tactics are not recorded or published for others to study and are often misunderstood by white middle-class feminists. One basic tactic is using anger effectively (Moraga and Anzaldúa 1981; hooks 1984; Lorde 1984, 129; Anzaldúa 1987, 15–23).

> Women of color in America have grown up within a symphony of anger, at being silenced, at being unchosen, at knowing that when we survive, it is in spite of a world that takes for granted our lack of humanness, and which hates our very existence outside of its service. And I say symphony rather than cacophony because we have had to learn to orchestrate those furies so that they do not tear us apart. We have had to learn to move through them and use them for strength and force and insight within our daily lives. Those of us who did not learn this difficult lesson did not survive. And part of my anger is always libation for my fallen sisters. (Lorde 1984, 119)

The loss of children is one of the main reasons for the anger felt by many women of Color. There is a contemporary ring to Sojourner Truth's words, "I have borne thirteen children and seen them most all sold off to slavery" (Stanton, Anthony, and Gage 1889, 117). Drugs, prison, discrimination, poverty, and racism continue to deprive women of Color of their children at alarming rates in contemporary U.S. society.[28] For example, in 1990 the homicide rate for nonwhite males ages fifteen to nineteen was 92 per 100,000, in comparison to white males in that age group, for whom the rate was 13 per 100,000. The 1990 rate among nonwhite teenage males was twice that of 1985. In 1990 Blacks of all ages made up half of the nation's homicide victims, although they constitute about 12 percent of the nation's population (*San Francisco Chronicle*, 3 February 1995). These losses and their meaning for the survival of future generations often distinguish the concerns of feminists of Color from those of white women. "Some problems we share as women, some we do not. You fear your children will grow up to join the patriarchy and testify against you, we fear our children will be dragged from a car and shot down in the street and you will turn your backs upon the reasons they are dying"(Lorde 1984, 131–32).

These differences in childhood experiences with racism and classism, the necessity of developing survival skills, and using anger create conflict between white feminists and feminists of Color.

> When women of Color speak out of the anger that laces so many of our contacts with white women, we are often told that we are "creating a mood of hopelessness," "preventing white women from getting past guilt," or "standing in the way of trusting communication and action." . . . One woman wrote, "Because you are Black and Lesbian, you seem to speak with the moral authority of suffering." Yes I am Black and Lesbian, and what you hear in my voice is fury, not suffering; anger, not moral authority. There is a difference. (ibid., 130)

Lesbianism as Resistance to Seduction

> Sex, on heterosexual terms, is then mere manifestation of our unconscious assertion that the world is arranged in a hierarchical order by nature.
>
> —Hernández 1991, 39

One way that white women have resisted the rewards of seduction is through homosexuality.[29] Lesbianism may or may not be a conscious or political choice, but the consequences are *always* political.[30] Lesbianism is subversive because it undermines the unconquerable biological divide of patriarchal inheritance laws through biological ties. How can race (and to a certain extent class) privilege be maintained if there are no "pure" biological offspring? Furthermore, the seat of patriarchal subordination is in the intimacy of the domestic sphere—how can lesbians be kept in check if the patriarch is only present in the public sphere? MacKinnon asserts that women's subordination, moreover, is not a result of patriarchy (which is an outcome) but, rather, of sexuality (1982, 529). Women are inferior because they are nothing more than their sex. Their value, if any, is measured by who they can please sexually. Therefore, if lesbians are sex objects only for other women, they are of no value whatsoever for men. In MacKinnon's

words, "Lesbians so violate the sexuality implicit in female gender stereotypes as not be considered women at all" (530).

White feminists have struggled with these profound questions, and
some have advocated complete abstention from men, restricting them to
only the social sphere or living with them outside the legal sanctions of
marriage. Lesbians, however, in having distance from white patriarchy,
are more likely to have the psychological, social, and physical space to
invent themselves outside the confines of gender seduction. This is
extremely threatening to the institution of patriarchy because it gives
women the potential to be indifferent to men and "allowed sexual and
emotional—therefore economic—access to women *only* on women's
terms" (Rich 1986, 43).

For lesbians of Color their rejection of men as sexual partners alienates
them from their communities of origin (Barrera 1991, 118; Hernández 1991,
139). As Carla Trujillo indicates:

> Our culture seeks to diminish us by placing us in a context of an Anglo
> construction, a supposed *vendida* to the race. More realistically, it is
> probably due to the fact that we do not align ourselves with the con-
> trolling forces of compulsory heterosexuality. Further, as Chicanas,
> we grow up defined, and subsequently confined, in a male context:
> daddy's girl, some guy's sister, girlfriend, wife, or mother. By being
> lesbians, we refuse to need a man to form our own identities as
> women. This constitutes a "rebellion" many Chicanas/os cannot han-
> dle. (1991, ix)

Many lesbians of Color are not only thought of as traitors to their
ethnic/racial communities but also are often accused of catching "white
women's disease" (Sternbach 1989) and are openly ostracized by many
members of their ethnic/racial communities (Frye 1992, 128). Many times
the only peaceful coexistence between lesbians of Color and their communities of origin comes from their remaining closeted and not living their
choices openly. The stress of either having to move away from family and
community or to remain closeted adds an enormous burden in these
women's lives (Barrera 1991).

The distance white lesbians have from white men and the distance
from their ethnic/racial communities that many lesbians of Color are
forced into creates a bond across ethnic/racial lines. Many lesbian communities, especially in academic environments, tend to be much more

ethnically/racially mixed than society at large. Furthermore, lesbian communities are more likely to transgress the usual rules of coupling, with a greater number of cross-ethnic/racial relationships, more cross-generational relationships, and more cross-class relationships than in society generally. Part of this transgression also includes challenging the hegemonic standards of beauty for a more diverse and inclusive view of desirable aesthetics (Castillo 1991, 39). This intimate contact among lesbians of different ethnic/racial groups, although not unproblematic, lends itself to developing common political goals that go beyond issues of sexuality because of the intimate knowledge that daily interaction brings about class and ethnic/race differences.

Implications for Theorizing Women's Subordination and Its Relationship to Political Mobilization

> The problem here is not to explain why women acquiesce in their condition but why they ever do anything but.
>
> —MacKinnon 1982, 539

Clearly, whether women are subordinated by white men through seduction or rejection, the results are detrimental to women's humanity. Advantages gained by women of Color because of their distance from white men amount to nothing more than the "deformed equality of equal oppression [to that of men of Color]" (A. Y. Davis 1971, 8). The privileges that white women acquire because of their closeness to white men give them only empty choices. As a seventy-three-year-old Black woman observes: "My mother used to say that the black woman is the white man's mule and the white woman is his dog. Now, she said that to say this: we do the heavy work and get beat whether we do it well or not. But the white woman is closer to the master and he pats them on the head and lets them sleep in the house, but he ain't gonna' treat neither one like he was dealing with a person" (quoted in Collins 1986, 17). Seen as obstinate mules or as obedient dogs, both groups are objectified. Neither is seen as fully human; both are eligible for race-, class-, and gender-specific modes of domination (18). In a patriarchal society all women are oppressed, and ultimately that is what unites them.

Neither a valid analysis of women's subordination nor an ethnically and racially diverse feminist movement is likely to emerge if white middle-class feminists do not integrate their own privilege from association with white men into their analysis of gender subordination (Frye 1992, 9). This requires an awareness that their subordination, based on seduction, has separated them from other women who are subordinated by rejection. This separation can be bridged, but first white women must develop a new kind of consciousness and renounce the privilege that comes from their relationship to white men.

If women of Color are to embrace a feminist movement, then they, too, must expand their consciousness of gender oppression. They, too, must understand differences in the dynamics of seduction and rejection and, in particular, that seduction is no less oppressive than rejection. Gloria Anzaldúa, a Chicana scholar, advocates a consciousness that simultaneously rejects and embraces, so as not to exclude, what it critically assesses. It is a mestiza consciousness that can perceive multiple realities at once:

> It is not enough to stand on the opposite river bank, shouting questions, challenging patriarchal, white conventions. A counterstance locks one into a duel of oppressor and oppressed; locked in mortal combat, like the cop and the criminal, both are reduced to a common denominator of violence. The counterstance refutes the dominant culture's views and beliefs, and, for this, it is proudly defiant. . . . But it is not a way of life. At some point, on our way to a new consciousness, we will have to leave the opposite bank, the split between the two mortal combatants somehow healed so that we are on both shores at once, and, at once, see through serpent and eagle eyes. . . . The possibilities are numerous once we decide to act and not react. (Anzaldúa 1987, 78–79)

The experiences of women of Color in the United States expose other aspects of patriarchal society that are only beginning to emerge in feminist theory and feminist political action. It is only through feminist theory's integration of a critique of the different forms of oppression experienced by women that a progressive political women's movement can grow, thrive, and last. But what are some of the principles that this "cross-over feminism" must put forth (Caraway 1991, chap. 6)? Moreover, feminist paradigms do not separate political mobilization from theorizing, so it necessarily follows that the way we think about women's subordination will also be influenced by the advocacy of political praxis.

Although white feminists have done a brilliant analysis of the victim-ization inherent in the "rewards" of seduction, feminists of Color empha-size the *strength* acquired as result of rejection.

> There is joy in struggle. Those of us who are old enough to remember segregated schools, the kind of political effort and sacrifice folks were making to ensure we would have full access to educational opportu-nities, surely remember the sense of fulfillment when goals that we struggled for were achieved. When we sang together "We shall over-come," there was a sense of victory, a sense of power that comes when we strive to be self-determining. When Malcolm X spoke about his journey to Mecca, the awareness he achieved, he gives expression to that joy that comes from struggling to grow. When Martin Luther King talked about having been to the mountain top, he was sharing with us that he arrived at a peak of critical awareness, and it gave him great joy. In our liberatory pedagogy, we must teach young Black folks to understand that struggle is process, that one moves from cir-cumstances of difficulty and pain to awareness, joy, fulfillment. That the struggle to be critically conscious can be that movement which takes you to another level, that lifts you up, that makes you feel better. You feel good, you feel your life has meaning and purpose. (hooks and West 1991, 16–17)

Feminists of Color steadfastly hold onto, as a core of their political mobi-lization, the politics of hope and joy in victory for their communities as a whole (Cuadraz and Pierce 1994, 9–10). White feminists, on the other hand, have had strategic victories by highlighting victimhood. It is not to say that one strategy is better than another but, rather, that they have to be recog-nized in order to build substantive political alliances. The emphasis on the strengths that result from oppression or the weaknesses that result from victimhood are the outcome of *structural relationships*, not essentialist racial characteristics. If these differences are not perceived as structural in nature, it leads to an overemphasis on women of Color's strengths, which essen-tially converts them into the exotic "other," placing them in a realm in which all spirituality, strength, and joy reside upon which whites can "feast" for their political and spiritual nurturance (duCille 1994, 591–92).[31]

Historically, among communities of Color there has been a strong commitment to advancing the group through acts of self-help because there were very few other avenues for group advancement (hooks and

West, 1991, 15). Solidarity with one's group is socialized in the home and supported by institutions in racial/ethnic communities such as Black churches among African Americans (hooks 1994, 167–68) and Catholic churches among Chicanos or by service and political organizations such as the National Association for the Advancement of Colored People (NAACP), the League of United Latin American Citizens (LULAC), and Sociedades Mutualistas. There is a linkage between obtained privilege of individual ethnic/racial group members and the political struggles of the group. Therefore, group responsibility is assumed, and its absence has to be justified (hooks and West 1991), whereas in the white women's movement individual advancement is assumed, and collectivity has to be socialized.

White feminists by definition have a more circumscribed community than feminists of Color because to include their community *as a whole* would entail including the white patriarchal order. Feminists of Color can, in fact, include their entire communities because their communities have also been subordinated by white patriarchy.

The effects of domination by rejection have dramatically affected the life chances of communities of Color in this country. Whereas for white feminists seduction still implies certain restricted areas of comfort and success. The very livelihood of communities of Color is at stake if they do not mobilize politically. Therefore, feminists of Color have a sense of urgency once they become politically active. The sense of urgency leaves less time for discussing or evaluating endlessly what the proper courses of action are and even about which tactics are the most desirable. There is a deep pragmatism that at times may appear Machiavellian and politically contradictory. Yet, as Lorraine Hansberry stated in 1962:

> Negroes must concern themselves with every single means of struggle: legal, illegal, passive, active, violent and nonviolent. They must harass, debate, petition, give money to court struggles, sit-in, lie down, strike, boycott, sing hymns, pray on steps—and shoot from their windows when the racists come cruising through their communities. (quoted in Caraway 1991, 34)

This statement captures not only the eclectic resources Blacks have needed to survive but also the sense of urgency Black feminist theory brings to its politics (Caraway 1991, 34). I am not saying that the white feminist movement does not have a sense of urgency but, rather, that their sense of urgency has different origins. For feminists of Color the direct attack on members of their ethnic/racial group makes them feel that, if something is not *done* immediately, they will disappear as a group. It is the sense of urgency that the early suffragists felt, what white feminists felt in fighting for abortion rights and what they will also feel if abortion rights are revoked—a sense that one's very existence is at stake.

White feminists have been much more concerned with theorizing from an academic framework rather than from political praxis. They have, in the last twenty years, made impressive inroads into academia; perhaps in no other time in history has a nontraditional academic discipline, in this case women's studies, gotten such a foothold in the most prestigious universities in this country. There is also no doubt that the development of the discipline has been unconventional in its emphasis on a multidisciplinary perspective, its political commitment to ignoring traditional academic hierarchies, such as allowing full participation by students and its emphasis on political activism. Women's studies has also stressed its production of *knowledge*, whereas feminist theory written by women of Color has often been skeptical of knowledge without *wisdom*. Caraway points to Collins's (1986) work in making the distinction: "'This distinction between knowledge without wisdom is adequate for the powerful, but wisdom is essential to the survival of the subordinate.' For ordinary African-American women who have to navigate the terrain of gender, race, and economic subordination, experiential wisdom is more credible than that provided by reading or thinking about a social situation" (1991, 49–50). Certainly, the discipline of women's studies has emphasized experiential knowledge in its formation, yet in terms of academic production it is not surprising that much of its yield has followed theory as developed in traditional disciplines, because many of its practitioners have been trained, and mostly work, in the most prestigious universities of this country (hooks 1989).[32]

Collins suggests an example of the distinction between knowledge with and without wisdom:

> In Collins' discussion of the final criteria for an Afrocentric feminist epistemology, the ethic of personal accountability, she presents the most rigorous test of adequacy for feminist theory. Not only must individuals develop knowledge claims in a democratic, accessible, dialogic manner and present them with a core of empathy—"urging one another on"—but also the theorist must, as Collins says, be accountable. (Caraway 1991, 49–50)

Accountability is related to the expectation of personal responsibility to the ethnic/racial community by each individual member as they become successful. That is, individuals of Color are considered an integral part of a well-defined community that holds them accountable for their political choices.[33] In Kurt Lewin's (1948) terms, accountability is the outcome of a common fate as the basis for group formation. Each individual member's behavior reflects on the community as a whole, and therefore community members have a right to scrutinize that behavior. More to the point, however, is that most feminists of Color internalize accountability, and it is an integral part of their theorizing.

Accountability is the political aspect of reflexivity now being advocated in cultural studies discourse. As Caraway points out, "Reflexivity is the keyword here, inscribing our feminist theories with the constant imperative to keep looking back over our shoulders to see what and whom we have left out of the identities we present to the world" (1991, 193). While reflexivity implies an individual self-assessment of one's perspective in the course of theorizing, accountability is a collective process of a similarly defined group with politically agreed-upon goals to make an individual aware of their perspective. Accountability implies that we are incapable of assessing our own blind spots and that a group is essential in helping us "see" the political implications of our perspective for our group. Oddly enough, there has been a tremendous confusion in both accountability and reflexivity about individual freedom.

In fact, it was the implementation of both of these processes among progressive communities that led to the often misunderstood movement of political correctness—an almost constant reflexivity that makes social interaction extremely cumbersome.[34] The goal of political correctness is actually the opposite of curtailing individual freedom (MacKinnon 1993; Matsuda, Lawrence, Delgado, and Crenshaw 1993; Williams 1995, 24–25). The goal is to increase the potential for freedom for individuals who are normally excluded from our collective conception of freedom—the physically challenged, the overweight, the unattractive, the racially/ethnically different. The resulting cumbersomeness is a result of how our man-made language is based on hierarchy and domination (Spender 1980). In fact, the worst application of reflexivity is when all social interaction is nothing more than reflexive analysis without being able to communicate fully political intent. The political correctness movement has been distorted not only by conservative forces but also by many of its own practitioners. The constant surveillance of language, which was supposed to free speakers from their biases, ends up being experienced as repression—the exact thing it is supposed to be fighting. The circularity of this social process is the result of change in language without an accompanying discussion of the underlying political issues involved in the advocacy for change. In fact, the political correctness movement at its core is supposed to be an educational move-ment in which there is collective enlightenment about our unconscious biases—in other words, accountability. Instead, it becomes a battle of words that defeats the purpose of the war. Accountability, on the other hand, is a political assessment in reference to the group memberships the individual identifies with, to whose members, therefore, she or he has implicitly agreed to listen. In many ways accountability has nothing to do with personal lifestyle but only with those actions that are political in nature and that affect the group directly (Graham 1995, 66–67).[35]

There are some feminists of Color (and politically progressive men of Color) who have refused the process of accountability and have disen-gaged from the group. Examples are scholars such as Shelby Steele (1990) and Richard Rodriguez (1982). They ignore how their public stands nega-tively affect their respective ethnic/racial groups politically. Unlike other scholars of Color who belong to academic communities of Color and who use their colleagues as sounding boards for the political implications of their work, Rodriguez and Steele refuse such networks and perceive them as curtailing their individual freedom. I might point out that their personal lifestyles, which we know very little about, are not the basis for scholars of Color's critique of their work. Rather, it is their lack of accountability to the communities they are harming, by their negative assertions about the com-munities they are identified with. These individuals may or may not act politically on behalf of their ethnic/racial and gender group, but, clearly, they no longer participate in the feedback loop many feminists of Color advocate in their writings, a feedback loop provided by same-status mem-bers as well as by the general ethnic/racial community outside the confines of the academic environment (Boynton 1995). That is, many of these schol-ars of Color who speak against their communities in such forums as con-gressional hearings (for example, Richard Rodriguez speaking against bilingual education) do not participate in any ethnic organizations, work in ethnic communities, or associate with ethnic studies activities. Their ideo-logical positions are not influenced by everyday interactions or by close scholarly contact with individuals whose work is to defend and promote the advancement of ethnic/racial groups.

Boynton reviews the emergence of a new group of public intellectuals,

African American writers and thinkers who explore in the public arena the consequences of race in the United States for themselves and for their communities of origin, most of which are working-class, segregated communities. Caraway quotes Patricia Hill Collins about this process:

> First black feminist thought must be validated by ordinary African-American women who grow to womanhood "in a world where the saner you are, the madder you are made to appear." To be credible in the eyes of the group, scholars must be personal advocates for their material, be accountable for the consequences of their work, have lived or experienced their material in some fashion, and be willing to engage in dialogues about their findings with ordinary, everyday people. (1991, 51)

Caraway argues that accountability is the cornerstone of collectivism and an essential part of a crossover (or multicultural) feminism. Yet she recognizes astutely that, "in a culture of white privilege, this condition imposes a greater burden on white feminists to take the first step toward making things right" (179).

Accountability, for the most part, works well within ethnic/racial struggles and could offer mainstream white feminism a new level of development in interethnic/interracial coalition building. Marxist literary critic Terry Eagleton has written that oppressed peoples are "natural hermeneuticists, skilled by hard schooling in the necessity of interpreting their oppressors' language. They are spontaneous semioticians, forced for sheer survival to decipher the sign systems of the enemy and adept at deploying their own opaque idioms against them" (1984, 45). The real question, however, is how to implement accountability without reversing hierarchies and reproducing systems of power, because, as Caraway points out, in commenting on Eagleton's quote: "This understanding speaks to those truths and is vital to a progressive politics. But it is not in itself theoretically adequate to prevent the erection of equally repressive 'other' hierarchies" (1991, 181). That is, I believe, the uncharted terrain that a multicultural feminism should address. While some white feminists argue that the only road to a multicultural feminism is to reverse the existing racial/ethnic and class hierarchies and position women of Color on top (Spelman 1988), others argue that reversal is nothing more than substituting one oppression by another (Caraway 1991, 181).[36]

This dichotomous approach to power reversals is based on two fallacies. First, that having power will result in its abuse and that those who have been dominated will learn nothing by being in power. This position inadvertently assumes the fundamental "sameness" based on gender. Women in subordinate or dominant structural positions will not act the same as other women if their structural positions are temporarily reversed (Castillo 1991, 32). Privilege as well as subordination takes a lifetime to socialize and are such ingrained patterns that it takes conscious action to change them. I contend that having experienced oppression does result in making an individual much more sensitive to its effects. This is one of the arguments for promoting women into positions of authority—that they will act differently than men, who have traditionally held these positions. Furthermore, power reversals among white feminist and feminists of Color can only happen in very restricted arenas because, obviously, a feminist politics is not likely to be implemented in society at large. These reversals are likely to happen in classrooms, conferences, and feminist organizing. All of these arenas build in accountability and restrictions. Power reversals do not mean that one group punishes another in any form but, rather, that authority is shifted so that previously silenced groups become the centerpiece of the social interaction.

The second fallacy is that the reversals are only for the benefit of the previously dominant; that only they will learn from being decentered. I would argue that both the positive and negative aspects of being in the center will be learned by temporary, constrained reversals.[37] I take an existential approach to power. Power entails both privilege and responsibility; it entails both freedom and restriction. That is why reversals are an essential part of redefining power; both dominant and subordinate have to learn the other side of the mirror in order to build consciously a new social arrangement that is more democratic in nature than what we have experienced so far. Not only will white feminists learn from experiencing what it is like to be even further down the social hierarchy, but women of Color may learn the seductive aspects of power at the same time that they are conscious of them—a reversal that does not at all have the same social psychological dynamics as when power is "naturally" conferred and therefore not conscious. I believe that reversal is a necessary prerequisite to healthy and authentic coalitions, however uncomfortable it may be for all parties involved.

Why are reversals so necessary for coalition politics? What is being accomplished through temporary, context-restrained reversals is the knowledge of what it is to be treated according to group membership either for privilege or for oppression. Many white feminists handle gender accountability well, and some embrace it as an essential part of a radical feminist politics. This is not the case with race accountability. That is, many white feminists find it difficult even to see their white privilege and how the history of such privilege creates a divide between themselves and feminists of Color (Caraway 1991). Caraway provides a magnificent analysis of how first-wave feminism was torn apart by white feminists' and abolitionists' inability to fully integrate their white privilege into account in their political mobilization efforts with African American feminists.[38] Also, most white feminists carry their communities in their heads, living as they do dispersed among white men and nonfeminists. Most communities of Color are still extremely geographically isolated, which makes "checking out" accountability pragmatically much easier; there are well-defined constituencies that can voice their political goals as a group that feminists of Color can listen to. In fact, white feminist theory is still struggling with fully developing a paradigm that sees gender subordination primarily as a structural mechanism in which individual, or personal, characteristics are for the most part irrelevant. One of the reasons for this is that a feminist paradigm tries to avert the masculinist pitfall that is so mechanistic in nature that it does not leave room for individual experience or for feelings. In averting such a danger, at times a feminist paradigm can fall into personalism[39]—the exaltation of personal experience over any other kind of evidence, or into a relativism of oppression that can only be understood through context-specific interaction, which leaves us without a comprehensive theory for understanding the very real structural oppression that exists based on the simultaneity of gender, race, and class *group membership.*

Many white feminists' discussions of differences between feminists of Color and themselves fall into personalism; they dredge up personally damaging things that feminists of Color say and write about white women in general and white feminists in particular. Take, for example, Caraway's account, which she readily admits is a selection of quotes that is entirely arbitrary and out of context, of the negative things that have been written by women of Color about white women:

> [White women] were like clear, dead water . . . they were frivolous, helpless creatures, lazy and without ingenuity. Occasionally one would rise to the level of bitchery. (Walker 1976, 103–4)

I couldn't stand the idea of a white person touching me. Eventually I realized that it wasn't the white skin I hated, but it was their culture of deceit, greed, racism, and violence. . . . Their manner of living appeared devoid of life and bordered on hostility even for one another. . . . The white people always seemed so loud, obnoxious, and vulgar. . . . After spending a day around white people, I was always happy to go back to the reservation where people followed a relaxed yet respectful code of relating with each other . . . a welcome relief after a day with the plastic faces. (Cameron 1981, 46)

Caraway cites these and several other quotes by Black women that denigrate white women (1991, 189); although she admits that she may have taken things out of context, I do not think the question is whether these negative perceptions exist or how widespread they are. The fact of the matter is that they do exist, and even a cursory review of women of Color's writings will show that they are not the exception. The real question, and one whose answer will yield more possibilities of alliance, is, why do they exist, and what do they tell us about the intergroup relations between women of Color and white women?

Personalism leads us to evaluate these quotes as being unkind, and Caraway goes so far as seeing them on the verge of representing reverse racism. I think the answer lies in the notion that Caraway explores in linking postmodernist thought and Black feminist theory[40]—"that all knowledge can be *located*, as a point of view, as perspectival. . . . It mandates that our theories be self-critical and self-referential about where (and on whom) we stand in communities and cultures" (53). I would add that not only is this done at the individual level for people of Color, but, equally important, it is done at the group level as well. Like many white feminists, Caraway is making an *individually* based reflexive judgment about the quotes; she concludes that there is not much "goodness" in them, which is a personality characteristic, and equates this quality with women of Color's capacity also to oppress white women *politically*, which is a structural characteristic. Significantly, it does not matter how good you are, as a person, if the political structures provide privilege to you individually based on the group oppression of others; in fact, individuals belonging to dominant groups can be infinitely good because they never are required to be personally bad. That is the irony of structural privilege: the more you have, the less you have to fight for it. Conversely, it does not matter how "good" you are as a subordinate; your actions are almost entirely independent of your individual character, and social judgments about you are based on your group membership (Haney and Hurtado 1994).[41] That is what many white feminists do not understand. Their structural privilege is independent of their individual actions, and therefore accountability feels like a burden to them, because there is not a one-to-one correspondence between behavior, attitudes, values, and merit. Regardless of a white individual's actions, many times she will still be judged as a racist because, as a white person, she benefits from a system of privilege that functions beyond people as individuals (Harris 1990).[42] Peggy McIntosh is one of the few white feminist writers who openly acknowledges that "In my class and place, I did not see myself as racist because I was taught to recognize racism only in individual acts of meanness by members of my group, never in invisible systems conferring racial dominance on my group from birth" (1992, 81). That is what dominance and liberation are about; they are not about individuals. In a structural system of oppression, there is hardly any room for individual will— that is why liberatory politics are necessary.

Some day we will be able to judge one another as individuals, and we will either like one another or detest one another on the basis of individual merit not based on the group memberships that confer privilege or domination on us. Until then clashes are inevitable, and also unfair, because the structures we are fighting are arbitrary, man-made, and have little if anything to do with individuals' character, personality, or behavior—that is the tragedy of racism, classicism, heterosexism, and sexism. Yet with more power comes more responsibility. The truth of the matter is that judgments about the individual character of women of Color, such as that they are "nasty" or "backstabbing," are difficult to make because so much of their character, their personalities, in this country are made in relation to oppression. The quotes Caraway (1991) provides may indeed accurately reflect feminists of Color's intergroup perceptions but not necessarily be true in individual interactions. Sandoval (1991) calls the ability of many women of Color to shift between group versus individual perceptions a *differential consciousness*. The ability to shift is what allows many women of Color to have intimate friends, colleagues, and even husbands who are white without blunting their perceptions of the group's damage to people of Color as a group. Similarly, for white women it is hard to say, for example, how "nice" or how "strong" they are when they have been shaped in relation to white patriarchy. MacKinnon (1982) takes the radical position that in fact we do not know what or who woman is because the concept has not existed outside of what men desire women to be. If woman is constructed as men's projection of their desires and we are trained to make ourselves that desire, what are we independent of that projection? That is the project of a radical, multicultural feminist theory and politics.

The categories used for subordination—class, race, and gender/ sexuality—are not equal; they have different historical bases and consequences, which are an integral part of how they are used to dominate. The challenge to feminist theory is to document those differences rather than mesh them into an existing hierarchical system of oppression or into a "whole" system that supersedes these histories (Zavella 1988, 126, 130). Worse yet is a domination framework that is relativist in nature and can only be played out through "social interaction"—that is, the notion that we can only understand group memberships such as race, class, and gender within the specific social context in which they are enacted. Donna Haraway astutely observes that:

> Relativism is a way of being nowhere while claiming to be everywhere equally. The "equality" of positioning is a denial of responsibility and critical inquiry. Relativism is the perfect mirror twin of totalization in the ideologies of objectivity; both deny the stakes in location, embodiment, and partial perspective; both make it impossible to see well. Relativism and totalization are both "god tricks" promising vision from everywhere and nowhere equally and fully, common myths in rhetorics surrounding Science. (1988, 584)

From contextually based relativism, any attempt to document social structure falls into "essentialist" thinking and is therefore invalid. If race, class, and gender do not exist outside of social interaction because these categories do not exist outside of specific social contexts, it leaves us in a quandary as to how to explain the mechanisms by which social structure uses these categories of individuals to oppress at a group level. There is no doubt that there are individual variations in how they express these group memberships, but there is also no doubt that regardless of individual variations, oppression is enforced at a group level. That is, regardless of how individuals express their ethnicity/race, there is no doubt that being of Color has definite structural consequences as reflected in differences in income, education, health, and other quality-of-life outcomes. The attempts of social interactionists to explain the simultaneity of oppression from various derogated categories only subverts the political project of dismantling power for the purpose of a more equitable distribution. It privileges social science "understanding" for the radical feminist praxis of political activism. It also feeds into a liberal paradigm that at its core is elitist and "standard" driven rather than committed to a radical restructuring of existing power arrangements.

If it is only in the *doing* of social interaction that we can understand inequality, then, obviously, we only need to *not do* social inequality and it will not exist. The fact of the matter is that it is only through the redistribution of material wealth that social inequality will cease. More than likely, social interaction will follow, and, if it does not, what does it matter if white people do not like people of Color so long as everybody has equal access to health care, education, and decent employment? The challenge to feminism, to reiterate Anna Cooper's point, is not to stop the struggle, not till all of humanity is granted life, liberty, and the pursuit of happiness. Not till then will woman's cause be won—"not the white woman's, not the black woman's, not the red woman's, but the causes of every man and every woman who has writhed silently under a mighty wrong" (Hutchinson 1982, 87–88).

Theorizing by Feminists of Color

I come from a long line of eloquent illiterates
whose history reveals what words don't say.
Our anger is our way of speaking,
the gesture is an utterance more pure than word.
　　　　　　　　　　　　　　　　—Cervantes 1981, 45

Regardless of the exclusion of feminists of Color by practices within women's studies (Zinn, Cannon, Higginbotham, and Dill 1986) and academic publishing outlets, women of Color have always theorized about their gender subordination, although not always in traditionally academic forms (Collins 1991). The history of women of Color's feminism has gone largely undocumented because, in order to garner the true complexity of women of Color's experiences, it becomes necessary to tap into sources of knowledge not used by scholars steeped in mainstream positivist ideology. Yet, as Lorna D. Cervantes's poem above indicates, this lack of documentation does not mean a lack of action by feminists of Color on behalf of women's issues.

Feminists of Color's theorizing, as mentioned earlier, has been constrained by their access to academic resources, but within these constraints they have produced impressive frameworks that contribute to our understanding of gender subordination (Cotera 1977; Zavella 1988; Fernández 1994). They have theorized not only about structures of oppression but have simultaneously tried to devise methods of deconstructing the very structures they are discovering and all within the framework of intergroup ethnic/racial solidarity—no easy task indeed.

Women of Color in the United States have been forced to resist gender subordination within their own communities as well as gender, class, and race/ethnic discrimination in society at large (Zavella 1987, 1988). Women of Color's "triple" oppression has resulted in earning less, receiving less education, and having more children to support than whites or than men within their own groups. The core issues of women of Color feminists are material conditions such as employment, poverty, education, health, child care, and reproductive rights (Zavella 1988, 125). Their political mobilization historically has not only revolved around these material conditions, issues that affect them disproportionately, but also has involved matters of political empowerment for themselves and their communities. A model of this type of leadership is exhibited by Antonia Pantoja, founder of the Puerto Rican Association for Community Affairs who echoes the Black feminists organizers of the antislavery movement in emphasizing collective decisionmaking, the development of new leaders, especially among the youth, and the good of the group over the personal gain of the individual. The concerns of feminists of Color have always been intimately tied to those of their communities (Zavella 1988; Fernández 1994).

Because U.S. women of Color are composed of native-born individuals as well as immigrants, their feminism has been influenced by the history of other lands as well as experiences in the United States. A case in point are Latinas.[43] Some Latinas are recent immigrants, and others are descendants of the original Mexicans who resided in the Southwest since 1848, when the Treaty of Guadalupe Hidalgo ended the Mexican American War and Mexico lost over 50 percent of its territory to the United States. Most Latinas reside in the five southwestern states (California, Texas, Arizona, New Mexico, and Colorado). There are, however, a sizable number of Latinas of Puerto Rican descent in New York, of Cuban descent in Miami, and of Mexican and Puerto Rican descent in Chicago. The complexity of Latinas' feminism in the United States is represented in their history of struggle (Zavella 1988). For example, many Latinas have fought side by side in revolutionary struggles in Cuba, Nicaragua, or El Salvador and have worked to unionize miners and farmworkers in the Southwest as well as garment workers in the Northeast. From Dolores Huerta in California, one of the foremost leaders of the United Farmworkers Union, to Esperanza Martell, cofounder of the Latin Women's Collective in New York City, their political efforts on behalf of women's issues have been embedded in their political activities on behalf of their entire communities.

Historically, all communities of Color in the United States have had strong women leaders. For example, in the Latino community there are such leaders as Emma Tenayuca, a famous labor leader in Texas, and María Mercedes Barbudo, who was jailed in 1824 in Puerto Rico for conspiring against the Spanish colonizers, to *las soldaderas*, who fought in the Mexican Revolution of 1910. *Soldadera* literally means "female soldier." *Soldaderas* helped democratize Mexico from a feudal country to one in which land was distributed among peasants.

Currently, there is a flurry of academic and artistic production from feminists of Color who are making connections with activists in the United States and in the rest of the Americas. Some of the most exciting work is being created by feminists of Color who are questioning the sexism (Zavella 1988, 126–27) and heterosexism in their communities and documenting the lives of lesbians of Color (Trujillo 1991). These scholars are also working to form domestic and international alliances around women's issues. In the domestic arena organizations such as the Women of Color Resource Center in Oakland, California, are committed to creating inclusive political agendas that span ethnic and cultural differences. International alliances have been built between women of Color in the United States and those in other countries such as in Latin America through scholarly conferences and political mobilization along the U.S.- Mexico border. Feminists of Color residing on the mainland, for example, have been cultivating cultural and political alliances with feminists residing in Puerto Rico.

In summary the impetus for much of the theorizing by women of Color has been political mobilization, largely around labor issues (Zavella 1987). Their theorizing and political praxis are not separate, however, and feminists of Color have made impressive inroads in the number of organizations they have built (Fernández 1994, 29), their artistic production, as well as their scholarly output. Regardless of their diversity, there are some overarching principles that characterize their theorizing about gender subordination. First, almost all feminists of Color resist arranging their derogated group memberships into a hierarchy of oppressions; instead, they insist on deciphering the complexity of their gender, class, and ethnic/racial status simultaneously (Zavella 1988, 126). Second, almost all feminists of Color claim their individual group's history as part of their activist legacy. They see the connections between their current political activism as being part of their group's historical trajectory of resistance. For groups that have a history of forced and semiforced migration, it includes struggles in their native lands. Third, almost all feminists of Color do not make a distinction between theorizing that emerges in the academy and theorizing that emerges from political organizing, everyday interaction, and artistic production. Feminist theorizing by women of Color is trying to build a paradigm that is inclusive in nature, nonelitist, and does not reside exclusively within the academy. Fourth, currently there is an emphasis on attacking head-on the previously taboo subject of heterosexism in their communities. These emphases, which are not exhaustive, provide a valuable road map for the work of a multicultural feminism. Among the principles that can be gleaned from the extensive and diverse writings of feminists of Color are: strength and pragmatism, predisposition to political coalitions, and an inclusive paradigm.

Interracial/Interethnic Coalition Politics: What Feminists of Color Can Offer

> . . . Eventually, if we speak the truth to each other, it will become unavoidable to ourselves.
>
> —Lorde 1984, 175

Strength and Pragmatism

Feminists of Color have theorized from a position of strength rather than victimhood (Harris 1990, 254; Sandoval 1991). First-wave Black feminism, ignited by the abolitionist movement, is an impressive platform from which to launch the current women's movement. Even then Black feminist abolitionists were urging white feminists to recognize their power to stop the violence and domination by white men. Their power was not only present within the political arena, but, because of their intimate links with white men, they could also modify the socialization of children and therefore affect future power relations. As Caraway advocates, "we [white feminists] also must be able to see ourselves as justice-seeking changers (not just victims) of those grids of history and power" (1991, 64).

Because of the construction of white womanhood as fragile and in need of protection, educated white women have never fully seen their power to take an active role in the suppression of violence against people of Color (ibid., 162).[44] Mary Church Terrell's 1904 essay "Lynching from a Negro's Point of View" saw the liberatory potential in white women's refusal to support lynching: "But what a mighty foe to mob violence Southern white women might be, if they arise . . . to implore their fathers, husbands and sons no longer to stain their hands with the black man's blood!" Terrell's words remain relevant today.

The recognition of one's power brings with it a deep pragmatism and the knowledge that fighting back is a dirty business. There is no doubt that, in seeking justice, individuals must join the political debates—no one who is actively opposing oppression remains uncontaminated by the existing power structures. Activists become enforcers of existing hierarchies at the same time that they fight to dismantle them; many people of Color have understood this intuitively, if not consciously. Survival is dependent on maintaining a separate consciousness, to quote W. E. B. Du Bois (1973), at the same time that the individual becomes *like the other* in temporary contexts (Sandoval 1991, 2).[45] Many feminists of Color participate in community activism, electoral politics, the academy, at the same time that they are part of working class ethnic/racial communities. It requires that in certain contexts they speak standard English, and in others, Spanish, Vietnamese, Black English. It requires that in certain contexts they act assertively and outspoken and that in others, they be part of the background and curtail their participation. For successful feminists of Color, these transitions are part and parcel of their social and political survival (Hurtado 1996). The knowledge that joining the fray is a necessary tool to redistribute justice has made feminists of Color open to political coalition building.

Predisposition to Political Coalitions

> At times, I must separate from you, from your invasion. . . . I think of myself as one who must separate to my space and language of women to revitalize, to nurture and be nurtured. Then, I can resurface to build the coalitions that we must build. . . . All of us together . . . without a hierarchy of oppression. Anglo men and women, heterosexuals, white feminists, men of color, women of color, gay men, lesbians, lesbians of color, etc.
>
> —Pérez 1991, 178

From the beginning of Black feminist theory its practitioners were committed to "an egalitarian and inclusive political theory which demonstrates a public voice of advocacy for all women and all oppressed persons. They consistently called for a transformed women's movement, one project which could align with other human rights, religious, labor, and racial coalitions for social justice" (Caraway 1991, 164). But, before coalitions can exist on an equal level, much of what women of Color have produced theoretically has to be addressed in the *spirit* in which it was produced. There are not many examples of white feminists embracing women of Color's writings without cannibalizing them. Michelle Cliff (1990, 20) deplores not the cannibalization of writing by women of Color as much as the instrumental distortions "which deny its spirit" and, in doing so, also deny the historical and material conditions that created the spirit of the theory. Writing by women of Color is used by many white feminists not to understand the sufferings and travails of women of Color and to see how white women contribute to this oppression but, rather, to "understand and rise above not necessarily the pain of black women but their own" (duCille 1994, 62). Instead, feminists of Color propose a collaborative relationship that engages individuals with strong core identities whose aim is a wider freedom, not a need to subsume others (Caraway 1991, 51). Collins sees this collaboration as a web of reciprocity (1989, 771).

Historically, feminists of Color have been receptive to coalitions (Fernández 1994, 37) but not at the expense of excluding other causes. What is clear, however, is that the coalition has to be on their own terms. And the terms are also clear: all forms of oppression afflicting their groups have to be taken into account simultaneously; otherwise, they will continue to struggle independently from white feminists, which ultimately will weaken everybody's cause. As Patricia Zavella rightly indicates, feminists of Color pose a profound challenge to white feminists who conceptualize gender subordination as grounded in the commonalties of women's experiences. Instead, feminists of Color propose that social structure should be the analytical focus, which allows for profound differences among women. More specifically, Zavella proposes that

> feminists discourse should borrow from and "reconstruct" the discourse on race, the "new ethnicity," and the social construct of "other." This literature is not just about people of color but about dynamics and meanings of white/other, and inextricably, male/female. Chicanas, on the other hand, should formulate a variety of feminist expressions, for I believe our solidarity with other femi-

nists is primarily ideological, with common interests based on shared feminist principles that place women at the center. As we struggle towards many feminisms—perhaps the ambivalence of Chicana "womanists" will become less pronounced. (1988, 130)

An Inclusive Paradigm

Feminists of Color offer an inclusive paradigm but one that does not deny differences and does not deny anyone's history. Incorporating history into a multicultural feminism, however, entails confronting both "emancipation and shame" (Caraway 1991, 166–67). History has to be taken into account, both for its transformative potential as well as for its recognition of shame—acknowledging the structural and social apartheid that still exists between different groups of women.

It is in examining, truthfully, differences between *groups* of women that an authentic multicultural feminism can be built (ibid., 61). The examination of women's differences can serve as the standpoint from which to build a creative critique of what an inclusive feminism should look like. Truthful examination of women's differences could serve the purpose Iris Young attributes to any alternative community in building progressive politics:

> Black Americans find in their traditional communities, which refer to their members as "brother" and "sister," a sense of solidarity absent from the calculating individualism of white professional capitalist society. Feminists find in the traditional female values of nurturing a challenge to a militarist world view, and lesbians find in their relationships a confrontation with the assumption of complementary gender roles in sexual relationships. From their experience of a culture tied to the land, Native Americans formulate a critique of the instrumental rationality of European culture that results in pollution and ecological destruction. (1990, 301)

Just as Ida B. Wells was able to make the connections between lynching and the dehumanization of Black men, the debasement of Black women, and the construction of white women as property, contemporary feminists of Color struggle with building the same connections among the problems affecting their communities. The purpose of making these connections is to create a framework from which to *fight back*. Wells represents the first wave of Black feminists—their hallmark being the practice of talking back under all circumstances, regardless of the consequences. Talking back and acting back, through whatever means necessary, are what feminists of Color have to offer to an inclusive multicultural feminism.

The Poetics of Resistance: Sexual Dynamics in the Gender Subordination of Chicanas

But I loved my father. A broad-shouldered man with black, curly hair, he adored my mother's beauty. He raged jealously when she paraded into town with her sisters. . . . She feared my father's jealousy like abuse, and often stayed home to appease. I misunderstood her compliance. In time, I recognized her strength, his weakness.

—Emma Pérez

The sense of submission and docility that we see is . . . about survival . . . a powerful mechanism. It's like when you're in the ocean and a shark is coming; if you stay still, it'll go right by you. If you can stay still enough, and you survive it, then you can go on, and do what you have to do. But the nuances and the dynamics are intricate. It's like a dance in a person's life, and it's a continuous conflict about which it is tremendously difficult to make conclusive remarks.

—Ana Castillo

One of the challenges for feminist theory is to begin to document the culturally specific ways that gender subordination is imposed. If subordination is relational, then so is power. This is not to be confused, however, with structural power that is institutionalized and independent of the actors that are cast as its inheritors. But, in order to understand the specific nature of the subordination of women and before a multicultural feminism can be built, it is necessary to examine different ethnic/racial groups in the

A shorter version of this chapter, entitled "The Politics of Sexuality in the Gender Subordination of Chicanas," appears in the forthcoming book edited by Carla Trujillo, *Xicana Theory: Consciousness and Practice*. Berkeley, Calif.: Third Woman Press.

The first epigraph is from Emma Pérez's novel *Gulf Dreams*, 1996, 19.

The second epigraph is taken from an interview with Ana Castillo, poet and artist (quoted in Navarro 1991, 132).

United States. The opportunity for this shift in the research lens comes from the development of many feminisms (Cotera 1977; Marks and de Courtivron 1981; Brant 1984; hooks 1984, 1990; Anzaldúa 1990; Collins 1991; Sandoval 1991; de la Torre and Pesquera 1993; Fernández 1994; Pesquera 1994; Segura 1994; Zavella 1994; Castillo 1995). Gender is now conceptualized by many feminist theorists as the result of power relations between the sexes rather than as a binary biological category. This theoretical shift away from biological determinism provides an aperture through which to theorize about how race and class affect gender relations in our society because it allows for diversity in the expression of the "essential" natures of women and men. That is, every society has "normative conceptions of attitudes and activities appropriate for one's sex category" that help to "bolster claims to membership in a sex category" (West and Zimmerman 1987, 127).

Not all groups in U.S. society ascribe to the same definitions of *womanhood* and *manhood* (Brod 1987; Stoltenberg 1993; Zavella 1994, 206; Connell 1995). There is systematic variation according to race and class (hooks 1981, 1989; Hurtado 1989). White feminist theorists have made impressive contributions to the understanding of gender as manifested among white middle-class people (Jaggar 1983). The incisiveness of their analysis has also advanced our understanding of the lives of all women regardless of race and class. Only recently, however, have feminist theorists begun to explore the socioculturally specific ways in which gender is accomplished and ultimately used to allocate privilege and to impose subordination (West and Fenstermaker 1993, 151–74). Some feminist theoreticians propose that women of Color are triply oppressed by their race, class, and gender (hooks 1984; Segura 1984; Pesquera 1985; Zavella 1987), and we need to extend this concept to elucidate the intragroup *relations* that restrict women's spheres of action.

Women of Color's "No-name Feminism"

> Even as I keep before me the memory of Esperanza's laughter breaking the evening stillness whenever I would get too serious about trying to analyze what she was telling me. My aim is to work the dialectic between Esperanza's no-name feminism and my feminism of too many names, to go beyond the search for heroines on either side of the border.
> —Behar 1993, 276

There is a growing body of feminist theory produced by women of Color, although, as a group, they have not had as much access as white feminists to traditional forms of theorizing (see chap. 1). Feminist thought has also been generated by women of Color, however, through everyday verbal interaction and through creative production such as poetry and song. Consequently, the broadening of the paradigm of how gender is conceptualized also requires that other materials besides conventional academic production be used to theorize about women of Color. Patricia Hill Collins (1986) proposes the use of oral histories to uncover feminist thought in African American communities, and Alvina Quintana advocates the use of literary texts to see Chicanas as "their own ethnographers" (1989, 189). I propose to use a combination of both. In this chapter I use the analysis of the oral histories collected by Yolanda Broyles (1986; 1989; 1994) that chronicle the role of women in the theatrical group El Teatro Campesino and poetry written by Chicanas and Chicanos to elucidate how intragroup sexism is imposed within structurally subordinated Chicano communities. I intertwine the oral histories of Chicanas in El Teatro Campesino and the conflicts generated by gender issues among the actors with the use of poetry to further elucidate how gender subordination is imposed on Chicanas by members of their own group. I do not analyze the actual portrayals of Chicanas in El Teatro Campesino. Although the plays performed by the group were primarily created through collective improvisation by both male and female actors in El Teatro (Broyles 1994, xii–xiii), Luis Valdez, as director, had an inordinate influence on how the improvisations got sifted and constructed as final productions (Broyles 1989, 213). I am interested in how the women in El Teatro Campesino dealt with Valdez's constructions and how they struggled with the male actors in trying to broaden El Teatro Campesino's portrayal of women. When I turn to the use of literary texts, I use poetry written by men to contrast how they see women and then how women see themselves. Unfortunately, there was no simultaneous production of plays by women in El Teatro Campesino, so I am unable to use this device to further elucidate the gender dynamics in this arena.

Just like the white Women's movement spoke loud and clear primarily to middle-class, educated women, many of the cornerstones of white middle-class feminism, however, also spoke equally loud and clear to large groups of white women who had many internal variations: by region, by profession, by ethnic background, by family size, and by family socialization. Even though there were many white communities represented in the white Women's movement, there were also overarching similarities in their experience of sexism. So too with Chicanas; they come from many different communities, from the southern borders of Texas to immigrant communities in the midwestern United States (Zavella 1993; 1994b). The cornerstone of sexism experienced in these communities, however, has certain dynamics that are overarching regardless of the internal diversity of Chicano communities. The overarching similarities stem largely from the Catholic undergriding of Chicano culture (Espín 1984, 151) and because of the common history of conquest and immigration of Chicanos to the United States (Almaguer 1994). It is from this historical materialist perspective that produce many similarities in U.S. Chicano culture, especially around gender ideology and practice.

Furthermore, in the better part of this chapter I deal with the constraints that many Chicana women have to negotiate. More recently, however, many Chicana feminists have focused on these women's resistance to these barriers (Peña 1987; Lamphere, Zavella, Gonzalez, with Evans 1993).[1] It is important, however, to give ethnic specificity to these gender ideologies to better understand within what boundaries these variations occur. Yet, to fully understand Chicanas' resistance, it is necessary to view their strategies within the context of their oppression—resistance under this frame gains its full significance and non-resistance also becomes much more understandable.

The Creation of El Teatro Campesino

El Teatro Campesino was formed in 1965 by Luis Valdez in Delano, California. Its initial purpose was to support César Chávez and the farmworkers' unionization struggle by performing improvised political skits urging farmworkers to join the union for United Farmworkers (UFW) (Sánchez 1985). Although it severed its ties with the UFW in 1967, El Teatro Campesino currently operates as an independent theatrical company producing plays written by Luis Valdez and exploring new avenues of artistic expression (Diamond 1977). Its most recent accomplishments include the play (and eventual film) *Zoot Suit* and the film *La Bamba.*

From the beginning El Teatro Campesino's goal was to represent the collective social vision of Chicanos and to reflect all that is valued in these communities: family ties, preservation of the Spanish language, Chicano culture, and political mobilization.[2] The main dramatic devise developed by El Teatro was *el acto*—short, one-act skits with rapid dialogue, sharp wit, incorporating a critique of the day's events. The purpose of *el acto*, in Luis Valdez's words, was to: "Inspire the audience to social action. Illuminate specific points about social problems. Satirize the opposition. Show or hint at a solution. Express what people are feeling" (Valdez 1971, 6). The emphasis of *el acto*, unlike other dramatic forms, was to express not the individual vision of Luis Valdez as a dramatist and an artist but, rather, the collective social vision of Chicano communities. As such, the characters in *el acto* are archetypes that are supposed to be representative of *la raza*[3] and therefore particularly helpful in uncovering the collective representations of gender in Chicano communities. It is not surprising that El Teatro Campesino's treatment of intimacy, cultural nationalism, and political goals reproduces the intragroup gender dynamics found in Chicano communities.

The Stage as Metaphor

Of the many analyses of El Teatro Campesino only a few focus on the position of Chicanas within the troop (Morton 1974; Ramirez 1974; Frischmann 1982; Huerta 1982; Xavier 1983; Yabro-Bejarano 1985, 1986; Broyles 1986, 1989; 1994; Flores 1986; Bruce-Novoa 1988). Broyles's analysis, in particular, shows that "the stereotyped roles found in the work of El Teatro Campesino are in many ways related to the stereotyped views of Chicanas found within society at large" (1986, 164). More succinctly, art imitates life.[4] Using El Teatro Campesino as metaphor, and in particular the stage on which the plays get acted out, I explore how Chicanas experience gender subordination.

The Definition of Chicana Sexuality

The construction of Chicanas' sexuality is at the core of the gender dynamics that results in sexism in Chicano families and communities (Pérez 1993, 51–71; Zavella 1994, 206). By and large, the women characters in El Teatro Campesino are cast into one of two roles: whores or virgins (*putas* or *virgenes*). In the interstices of the bipolar conception of Chicanas' sexuality is the neuter woman, one who does not fit either sexual pole. In El Teatro this neuter role takes the form of allegorical characters that are neither men or women such as la Muerte (Death) or el Diablo (the Devil).[5] In Chicano communities the neuter woman is represented by what Abelardo Delgado (1978) calls the "femme-macho," a woman who is attractive to men because she is strong and powerful but not like a whore or meek like a wife. In fact, her psychological characteristics are grotesquely exaggerated, so much so that none of them are human. The femme-macho's sexuality, in particular, is so accentuated and objectified that she is in effect neutered. The construction of Chicanas' womanhood around the virgin, whore, and femme-macho are not meant to be *types* but social locations that are given cultural space to exist. As Joan Scott states: "Subjects have agency. They are not unified autonomous individuals exercising free will, but rather subjects whose agency is created through situations and statuses conferred on them" (1991, 793). Certainly there is a certain amount of flexibility of movement between these different social locations, especially through normatively sanctioned cultural rituals—for example, from virgin to wife to grandmother. The shifting from "deviant" (and therefore defiant) locations, however, to culturally sanctioned locations is much more difficult. For example, from whore to wife or from lesbian to (hetero) wife is much more problematic and much less likely.

In El Teatro Compesino, as in Chicano communities, the assignment into the social locations of "virgins" or "whores" is based largely on physical characteristics and a woman's assertiveness and strength. The virgin is a woman who is small, fragile, fair-skinned, and has a pretty face.[6] In El Teatro, she is referred to as "soft." The potential whore is an Indian-looking woman who speaks up and is "difficult." Broyles (1986) says that this rigid dichotomy reflects the *offstage* judgment of the female actors. Socorro Valdez (Luis Valdez's sister), a longtime actor in El Teatro Campesino, describes the "rigidification process" as follows:

> As it were, the actresses that were "soft" offstage and just *muy buenas, muy buenas* [very nice, very nice] got the "soft roles." And the ladies that were *medias cabronas* [tough] and had a beer and a cigarette hanging out of their mouth, well you know what role they got. . . . I always ended up with that other stuff. I know those choices. And I know there were moments in the group when there was to be a "girlfriend." Well, can Socorro be the girlfriend? No, Socorro can't be the girlfriend. Socorro is either the old lady or she's the jokester. But I was never in this company as a "soft" woman, because they confuse softness and hardness and they attach those two things to strength or weakness. But there is no such thing in my mind. You can't put those two things together like that. They fluctuate. (quoted in Broyles 1986, 171)

The femme-macho, unlike the virgin or the whore, can either be attractive or unattractive. A strong personality is what characterizes her. The strength of the femme-macho does not lie in her racial/physical appearance but, rather, on remaining emotionally uninvolved though sexually active. The man's challenge is to deflower the femme-macho emotionally; the power of the femme-macho is to remain an emotional virgin. The Achilles' heel of the femme-macho is her emotions. Yet she will only be punished for showing particular emotions. The femme-macho can be sarcastic, funny, outrageous, aggressive, mean, or belligerent, but she cannot be tender, loving (except in a political or abstract sense), frightened, or insecure. In fact, femme-machos are always in mortal combat with men to emasculate them and overpower them. Although femme-machos are able to express a wider range of emotions than other kinds of women and therefore obtain some sense of freedom, they are still emotionally trapped because they are never allowed to show weakness.

Many Chicanas, struggling to escape the narrow confines of the whore-virgin dichotomy embrace the femme-macho characteristics as a form of liberation. A prototype of this adaptation is the persona cultivated by the popular Mexican movie star María Félix. Whereas María Félix came from a working-class background, had no education, was not very talented, but was decidedly beautiful, she was able to forge a career in Mexican cinema and reached international acclaim and wealth. There were many beautiful actors in the 1940s and 1950s when María Félix was at the height of her popularity but few who were femme-machos. In fact, most of María Félix's movies rested on a formula in which she was an arrogant, indomitable, and belligerent woman who eventually was tamed by a strong man, like Katherine in Shakespeare's comedy *The Taming of the Shrew*. Yet, although most of her movies ended with her submission, in public life she never submitted and, instead, flaunted her freedom, including her economic independence and her shrewd sense for business (Taibo 1985).[7] The femme-macho also plays with the notion of bisexuality—her taunting is attractive to men because of the morbid curiosity it stirs up by the potential of watching women make love to each other. Félix, as a femme-macho, is reported to have had an affair with Frida Kahlo, which further enhanced her power by demonstrating her defiance of established sexual conventions (Herrera 1983).[8] She even committed the ultimate sin of keeping emotional distance from her only son and did not exalt her motherhood (Fuentes 1967). Carlos Fuentes dramatized this relationship in his novel *Zona Sagrada* (Sacred Zone) [1967]. In his novel, loosely based on Félix's life and her relationship with her son, he details the characteristics of the femme-macho. In the novel the mother goes so far as to emasculate her son by denying him her approval (usually the relationship depicted between a powerful father and his son). The main character of *Zona Sagrada* also teases about her potential bisexuality further threatening men in the novel.[9]

Sandra Cisneros in her poem "Loose Woman" also exalts the characteristics of the femme-macho as a form liberation:

LOOSE WOMAN

They say I'm a beast.
And feast on it. When all along
I thought that's what a woman was.

They say I'm a bitch.
Or witch. I've claimed
the same and never winced.

They say I'm a *macha,* hell on wheels,
viva-la-vulva, fire and brimstone,
man-hating, devastating,
boogey-woman lesbian.
Not necessarily,
but I like the compliment.

The mob arrives with stones and sticks
to maim and lame and do me in.
All the same, when I open my mouth, they wobble like gin.

Diamonds and pearls
tumble from my tongue.
Or toads and serpents.
Depending on the mood I'm in.

I like the itch I provoke.
The rustle of rumor
like crinoline.

I am the woman of myth and bullshit.
(True, I authored some of it.)
I built my little house of ill repute.
Brick by brick. Labored,
loved and masoned it.

I live like so,
Heart as sail, ballast, rudder, bow.
Rowdy. Indulgent to excess.
My sin and success—
I think of me to gluttony.

By all accounts I am
a danger to society.
I'm Pancha Villa.

I break laws,
upset the natural order,
anguish the Pope and make fathers cry.
I am beyond the jaw of law.
I'm *la desperada*, most-wanted public enemy.
My happy picture grinning from the wall.

I strike terror among the men.
I can't be bothered what they think.
¡Que se vayan a la ching chang chong![10]
For this, the cross, the Calvary.
In other words, I'm anarchy.

I'm an aim-well,
shoot-sharp,
sharp-tongued,
sharp-thinking,
fast-speaking,
foot-loose,
loose-tongued,
let-loose,
woman-on-the-loose
loose woman.
Beware, honey.

I'm Bitch. Beast. *Macha.*
¡Wachale!
Ping! Ping! Ping!
I break things.

(1994, 112)

The poet uses hyperbole to exalt the appropriation of the femme-macho gender adaptation. Every single characteristic of the femme-macho is covered in this poem. If women are thought of as less human than men, the poet outright claims her bestiality ("I'm a beast"; "I'm a bitch"). If women are thought of as dangerous because they cannot control their passions (as animals often cannot) and they devour men, the poet "feasts" on the notion and claims herself "a danger to society," a "*desperada*," who "breaks laws," all the while her "happy picture grinning from the wall." She defies patriarchal power and usurps a male identity for herself by becoming "Pancha Villa"—after the only Mexican hero to openly defy the U.S. army at the turn of the century—furthering her transgression by feminizing the name Pancho. She rebels against all authority and violates all sacred boundaries, including that of heterosexuality (*viva-la-vulva*) and defies the Holy Father by "anguishing the Pope" as well as "mak[ing] fathers cry." She has fashioned herself into a crime of nature and rejoices in her transgression ("man-hating, devastating / boogey-woman lesbian"). She does not regret, apologize, or otherwise feel anything but passion and power ("I like the itch I provoke"). Her emotion is not tempered by sympathetic response to anybody, but, instead she thinks of no one but herself "to gluttony." She relishes her selfishness and laughs out loud at how she is the creator of her own image (not real but made out of bullshit through the appropriation and mockery of hegemonic masculinity). She laughs deep, and she laughs hard, and at the end only she is left standing because all her accusers have run away in fear ("The mob arrives with stones and sticks"; "All the same, when I open my mouth, they wobble like gin"). And all the while she claims, sarcastically, with an implied wicked smile, that this is what she thought "a woman was."

Whereas the femme-macho has her will, her source of strength, whores have no volition. As Emma Pérez indicates, "For Paz, *la india* personifies the passive whore, who acquiesced to the Spaniard, the conqueror, his symbolic father—the father he despises for choosing an inferior woman who begot an inferior race and the father he fears for his powerful phallus" (1993, 61). In El Teatro Campesino's portrayals whores are not women who give themselves willingly in exchange for a predetermined amount of goods. Instead, they are fallen women and by definition, damaged merchandise. Most important, Chicana *putas* are traitors—traitors to the essence of *la cultura*. As *putas*, Chicanas betray all that is sacred to Chicano/Mexicano culture. At the root of the image of the *puta* is Chicanos' dread of the symbolic meaning of sexual penetration, especially the equation of penetration and the Spanish conquest of Mexico (Del Castillo 1974; Alarcón 1981; Paz 1985; Pérez 1991, 67) .

Historically, la Malinche, a woman, is the ultimate traitor of Mexico. La Malinche supposedly facilitated Hernán Córtes's conquest of the Aztec empire by acting as translator between the Spanish and the different Mixteca tribes. From this betrayal modern Mexico was born both figuratively and literally, since la Malinche converted to Catholicism *and* bore the children of Hernán Córtes's soldier Jaramaillo.[11] Thus began Mexican *mestisaje*.[12] La Malinche's betrayal was both cultural and sexual. El Teatro Campesino's version of la Malinche has emphasized cultural betrayal. In *Los Vendidos* (The Sell-outs) the antagonist is an assimilated Chicana, Miss Jimenez (pronounced *Jim*enez onstage), who acts as la Malinche by being a tool of the Reagan Administration, the symbolic conqueror Hernán Córtes of California. In *No Saco Nada de la Escuela* (I Don't Get Anything Out of School), la Malinche is Esperanza, who denies her Mexican heritage and wants to "pass" as Hawaiian (Brown 1980). More to the point of cultural betrayal is the la Malinche in *La Conquista de Mexico* (The Conquest of Mexico), who is described for didactic purposes by Piedra, the main narrator of the play:[13]

> This woman was to become infamous in the history of Mexico. Not only did she turn her back on her own people, she joined the white men and became assimilated serving as their guide and interpreter and generally assisting in the conquest. She was the first Mexican-American. (Valdez 1978, 58)

La Malinche in this play further underscores her cultural betrayal also by wanting to "pass," as she distances herself from the other Indians about to be branded by Hernán Córtes "so I can tell you [them] apart." La Malinche chimes in: "son Indios estupidos" (they are stupid Indians). When one of the Indians questions her distancing herself from other Indians by calling her a *prieta* (darkie), she replies, "Yo no soy India, I'm Spanish" (I'm not Indian, I'm Spanish) (58).

"Chicana Primero" or "My Culture, Hell"

El Teatro's portrayal of la Malinche as both a sexual and cultural traitor paralleled the debates in the Chicano Movement around gender issues. According to Alma Garcia, during the 1970s as Chicana feminism emerged within the Chicano movement, there was a strong ideological debate between two groups of women. First there were the cultural loyalists who viewed any kind of organizing around gender issues as divisive and as "a threat to the Chicano movement as a whole" (García 1989, 225). Chicana loyalists "believed that the Chicano movement did not have to deal with sexual inequities since Chicano men as well as Chicano women experienced racial oppression" (ibid., 225). Cultural loyalists saw racism as the central issue for the Chicano movement and they feared any feminist organizing as potentially divisive, and even Anglo-inspired. These women rallied around the slogan "Chicana primero" (Chicana first) claiming their loyalty to their ethnic identity first and everything else second.

On the other hand, there was a group of Chicana feminists who disagreed with the Chicano movement's nationalist rhetoric that made it necessary for women to suppress any criticism of the movement for the purpose of "cultural survival" (ibid., 222). Chicana feminists who held this perspective "criticized the notion of the 'ideal Chicana' that glorified Chicanas as strong, long-suffering women who had endured and kept Chicano culture and the family intact. To Chicana feminists, this concept represented an obstacle to the redefinition of gender roles" (ibid.). Furthermore, Chicana feminists wanted to modify the cultural nationalist position that viewed "machismo as a source of cultural pride" (ibid., 223) rather than as an excuse to oppress women. Chicana feminists from this ideological camp in response to the accusation by cultural loyalists that they were betraying Chicano culture responded with the slogan "Our culture, hell" (Flores 1971, quoted in García 1989, 228).

The split between cultural loyalists and Chicana feminists had its counterpart in the politics of sexuality. As García notes, "Lesbianism was identified as an extreme derivation of feminism. A direct connection was frequently made that viewed feminism and lesbianism as synonymous" (ibid., 226). Thus, cultural betrayal became sexual betrayal, which left intact the existing gender disparities between women and men in a politically progressive movement devoted to the struggle of equality as it remained also in El Teatro Campesino, an organization dedicated to the struggle for human dignity.

Reclaiming Malinchismo

Although the ideological struggles between Chicana feminists and cultural loyalists persisted throughout the 1970s (García 1989, 226), most recently

Chicana feminists have reinterpreted la Malinche's role in the conquest of Mexico from traitor to that of a brilliant woman whose ability to learn different languages was unsurpassed by any of her contemporaries. There is historical evidence that demonstrates that la Malinche believed the Spanish would deliver many of her people from the cruelty of the Aztec religion, which required human sacrifice. In contrast, Catholicism offered love and compassion as a philosophy of life. She was just as shocked as the rest of her people when the Spanish massacred thousands as they approached the conquest of Mexico City.[14]

Yet this recent reinterpretation has not yet displaced the old analysis. For example, Octavio Paz (1985) proposes that the conquest of Mexico is a violation and that la Malinche represents the violated mother country because she is the mistress to the leader of the conquest. Mestizos are *hijos de la Chingada*,[15] or "the offspring of violation." La Malinche is *la Chingada* because she consented to be opened and conquered by Córtes:

> The *Chingada* is the Mother forcibly opened, violated or deceived. The *hijo de la Chingada* is the offspring of violation, abduction or deceit. If we compare this expression with the Spanish *hijo de puta* [son of a whore]. . . . To the Spaniard, dishonor consists in being the son of a woman who voluntarily surrenders herself: a prostitute. To the Mexican it consists in being the fruit of violation. . . . *The Chingada* is the mother who has suffered—metaphorically or actually—the corrosive and defaming action implicit in the verb that gives her name. (Paz 1985, 79–80, 75).

Although the word *chingar* has many meanings in the Spanish-speaking world, according to Paz:

> The verb denotes violence, an emergence from oneself to penetrate another by force. . . . *Chingar* . . . is to do violence to another. The verb is masculine, active, cruel: it stings, wounds, gashes, stains. And it provokes a bitter, resentful satisfaction. . . . The *chingón*[16] is the *macho*, the male; he rips open the *chingada*, the female, who is pure passivity, defenseless against the exterior world. The relationship between them is violent, and it is determined by the cynical power of the first and the impotence of the second. The idea of violence rules darkly over all the meanings of the word, and the dialectic of the "closed" and the "open" thus fulfills itself with an almost ferocious precision. (76–77)

Luis Valdez also appropriates the metaphor of conquest as sexual penetration as the "basic human experience" and "by implication, sexual experience is likened to the historical process of raw conquest" (Broyles 1989, 229). Luis Valdez's views, elaborated below, certainly have influenced how he has portrayed relations between women and men in his theater productions as well as in his films:

> We who are of the Third World and are victims of colonization have been subjected with the rest of the world to the phenomenon of Europe for the last five hundred years. These people left that section of the world and they went out and conquered other vast sections of the world. Now conquest and that warriorlike stance is not peculiar to this period of history, it has been all throughout the history of the human race and also in the Americas. Perhaps what is upsetting us is that we are still in this period, that we are still stuck. The modern Genghis Khan is still with us and he came from Europe in all of his forms. He came in a particularly masculine form. In the case of the Spanish he came in iron armor. The male erection made flesh, if you will, *"Chingate, Cabron!"* [Fuck you, you bastard."] If I may refer to basic mythical experience of the male in the sex act—that is what it takes. In order to do your stuff as a man, you have to have armor and a spear and you have to penetrate and the more you penetrate the better it is. *Dime que no* [Tell me that's not true]. On the other hand, there is the other part which is just as natural which is the female experience which is *"Vente Cabron"* [Fuck me, you bastard"]. Those two fit together. I am not trying to embarrass you. I am talking basic human experience. (quoted in Broyles 1989, 229–31)

When all "basic human experience" is conceptualized from this phallocentric perspective, then the victim of the violence, *la Chingada*, is not deserving of pity or compassion but is, instead, worthless. *La Chingada* is the vanquished one; the conquered one who succumbed to male power and therefore, she is, by definition, not his equal, and perhaps even subhuman. Women, although condemned from birth to eventually be vanquished because of their sexual opening, are valuable only before they are penetrated and therefore "unconquered." When virginity, the only gift women have to offer men, is gone, women join the ranks of *las Chingadas*. According to Paz, even if a woman willingly partakes in the act of lovemaking, the fact that she is "penetrated" constitutes a violation. Because woman is conceptualized as not fully human but, rather, as property (Trujillo 1991, 188) that can be damaged by sexual violation, nothing she does is perceived as a choice (Alarcón 1981, 184). Only femme-machos, who are hybrids of man/woman and not really women, can, to a certain extent, have a will. But theirs is not a *human* (therefore male) will; rather, it is an animalistic will that needs to be tamed. Femme-machos are also the only women who are allowed sexual pleasure. Virgins and wives are not supposed to feel sexual desire; it is seen as a necessary evil for accomplishing the higher goal of becoming a mother. As Oliva Espín states: "To shun sexual pleasure and to regard sexual pleasure as an unwelcome obligation toward her husband and a necessary evil in order to have children may be seen as a manifestation of virtue. In fact, some [Latina] women even express pride at their own lack of sexual pleasure and desire" (1984, 156). The enjoyment of sexual pleasure is particularly threatening in lesbians because they are asserting their sexuality by explicitly choosing the sexual object, other women (Trujillo 1991, 191). Any wife or girlfriend who seems to "enjoy sex" too much is suspected of having the potential to betray her possessor (Castillo 1991, 28).

Thus, in Chicano culture, as in many other cultures, women are the possessions of men (ibid.; Navarro 1991, 115; Behar 1993, 282); her virginity determines her property value (Alarcón 1981, 184; Espín 1984, 151).[17] Courtship and marriage include very specific rules for measuring the degree to which a woman is damaged merchandise. The least damaged is the virgin, followed by the once-married woman with children, then the divorced woman with no children (no evidence of having been opened), then the woman who lives with a man. Among the most damaged is the woman who sleeps with different men, regardless of her motivations for doing so.[18] Women who sleep with different men cease to be *mujeres de respeto* (respectable women) and instead become *mujeres del gusto*, women who "like pleasure, that is, sex" (Behar 1993, 281). Behar elaborates further from ethnographic data gathered in the course of studying Esperanza, a Mexican street peddler:

> The accusation is one of the best put-downs in a society where church teachings and the dominant gender ideology make women feel that they are not supposed to admit they get any pleasure from sex. In fact, many women do have relationships with more than one man. . . . It seems clear that many women are not content to leave sexuality safely confined to the house. But those women who become publicly known

as mujeres del gusto pay a price: they lose status and respectability and become associated with the lower working class in the local social hierarchy. Such women are viewed as *locas;* they are 'crazy women' because they flaunt their bodies and their desire openly. (ibid.)

Even though these observations are made about women in rural Mexico, many of these norms continue to thrive in U.S. Chicano communities as many Mexican residents migrate north to the United States.

Yet the ultimate violation is committed by lesbian women, who are opened by other women. Once a woman opens herself to another woman, she can never again redeem herself, not even through motherhood. Trujillo indicates that Chicana lesbians who choose to become mothers are perceived as aberrations of the traditional concept of motherhood (1991, 190).[19] Within Chicanos' cult of virginity Chicanas have to maneuver to be less rather than more *chingada.*[20] As Alma Villanueva laments:

(mamacita)
when a man opens a woman, she
is like a rose, she
will never close
again.
ever.

(quoted in Sánchez 1985, 335)

Their redemption, as women, is possible only through celibacy and, to a lesser extent, marriage, because women's potential for betrayal is present from birth. It is in the very fact of being a woman that she is suspect and therefore in need of redemption. As Anzaldúa indicates, "'*Tu no sirves pa' nada*— / you're good for nothing. / *Eres pura vieja.*'/ 'you're nothing but a woman' means you are defective" (1990, 382). Redemption through celibacy is obvious because a woman has never been opened; redemption through marriage at least insures that she is open only to spew forth children in the image of *el Chingón.*[21] Femme-machos can to some degree escape this categorization but only through a constant battle of wills and wits. They must be prepared to lose strength, to then recover and keep fighting. A femme-macho who does not fight back also joins the ranks of *Chingadas.*

Not surprisingly, these different sexual categories for the most part do not get applied in Chicano communities to white women,[22] who are not the descendants of la Malinche and therefore do not have the potential for subverting the mestizo race (Pérez 1991, 169). Although lesbians of all races are derogated, the rules about virginity are suspended when white women are evaluated (Anzaldúa 1990, 380). If anything, white women, as a group, are thought of as sexually immodest because of "their culture" (Espín 1995, 227).

Emma Pérez (1993, 62) combines the politics of conquest with a psychoanalytical framework to explain the complexity of Chicanos' views on white-Chicano intermarriage. According to Pérez:

> The Oedipal-conquest triangle dictates the sexual politics of miscegenation in the twentieth century. Although Chicanos are usually incensed when Chicanas marry the "enemy," white men, they exercise male prerogative by marrying white women to both defy and collaborate with the white father. In having half-white children, they move their sons a step closer to the nexus of power—the white colonizer-father. The Chicana who marries a white male, by contrast, embraces the white Oedipal-colonizer ambivalently, because—although theoretically she gains access to power—realistically she is still perceived as *la india* by a white dominant culture that disapproves of miscegenation. (ibid.)

Pérez continues by examining how skin color is an essential part of these dynamics:

> Skin color, however, plays an important role for half-breeds. The lighter the skin, the more possible it is to pass through doors of power and privilege. Of course, skin color does not just apply to half-breeds. But when one has the white skin and the white name of a white father and a *mestiza* for a mother, one is likely to have access to more power in a racist society. What one does with that power politically is a different issue altogether. Of course, class status is also a prominent factor to consider in these matchings. (ibid., 70)

Granted that the dynamics of white-Chicano intermarriage are extremely complex, the point is, however, that white women are still not held accountable as Chicanas to the same standards of proper sexual conduct. Take, for example, the poem by Mario Garza:

TUS JEFITOS	YOUR PARENTS
Pobre Chicano	Poor Chicano
tus jefitos have	your parents have
been victimized by	been victimized by
the gabacho racism.	white racism.
When you went out	When you went out
with a gabacha feminist,	with a white feminist,
she neglected you for	she neglected you for
her anglo friends.	her anglo friends.
She tried to castrate	She tried to castrate
your manhood.	your manhood.
Tus jefitos would say,	Your parents would say,
"Es gringuita	"She's a little white one,
es muy linda."	so beautiful."
When you went out	When you went out
with your second gabacha,	with your second white woman,
she fucked around with	she fucked around with
your best friends.	your best friends.
Tus jefitos would say,	Your parents would say,
"Es gringuita	"She's a little white one,
es muy buena."	she's very nice."
Now you have a chicana	Now you have a chicana
Chicana like yourself	Chicana like yourself
she loves you	she loves you
she cares for you	she cares for you
she cleans for you	she cleans for you
she cooks for you	she cooks for you
she worries for you	she worries for you
Chicana like yourself	Chicana like yourself
But sometimes	But sometimes
she drinks and dances.	she drinks and dances.
Tus jefitos say,	Your parents say,
"Es chicana	"She's chicana
es muy puta!"	she's a whore!"

(1976, 98)

The male narrator in this poem is aware of the different, and unfair, standards that his parents apply to Chicanas in comparison to white women. Yet the narrator is a mere observer, with no apparent role in responding to the accusations, although he benefits from the relationships with these women. Also, the object of the analysis are the women, not his conduct, so there is no way for the reader to judge what the white woman who is "fucking" around with his best friends is responding to, nor do we know whether the Chicana's domestic behavior represents a fair exchange in their relationship. Instead, the reader can only assess the behavior of both white and Chicana women as disembodied stereotypes who exist in relationship to an omnipotent and neutral Chicano male. More to the point of the discussion here, however, is the rigid perception of Chicana women: she is the *girlfriend* (who can potentially enter the other rigid role of wife if she behaves appropriately—cleans, cooks, and worries for the implicitly perfect male) who transgresses, acting like a whore by drinking and dancing. All her previous "girlfriend" behavior is defaulted by crossing the rigid line through drinking and dancing. Chicanas are effectively fenced in by the threat of accusation of being whores—by having sexual intercourse outside the protected boundaries of a monogamous heterosexual relationship. The transgression is not the drinking or dancing but, rather, the potential for unsanctioned sex.

The feminist critique of this double standard for sexual conduct is voiced strongly by Chicana poets. Marcela Christine Lucero Trujillo unknowingly responds to "Tus Jefitos" in her poem "Machismo is Part of Our Culture":

> Hey Chicano bossman
> don't tell me that machismo is part of our culture
> if you sleep
> and marry W.A.S.P.
>> You constantly remind me,
>> me, your Chicana employee
> that machi-machi-machismo
> is part of our culture.
>> I'm conditioned, you say,
> to bearing machismo
> which you only learned day before yesterday.
>> At home you're no patrón
>> your liberated gabacha
>> has gotcha where
>> she wants ya,

> y a mi me ves cara
> de steppin' stone.
> Your culture emanates
> > from Raza posters on your walls
> > from bulletin boards in the halls
> > and from the batos who hang out at the barrio bar.
> Chicanismo through osmosis
> acquired in good doses
> remind you
> to remind me
> that machi-machi-machismo
> is part of our culture.
>
> > > (quoted in Gutiérrez 1993, 48)

Here the poet does not take the "jefitos" [parents] to task, nor some abstract concept of "Chicano culture," but rather she directly puts the perpetrator's feet to the fire by pointing out the contradiction between his behavior at home with his white wife who is his "liberated gabacha / has gotcha where she wants ya" and his behavior at work where he treats his Chicana employee as a "steppin' stone." The perpetrator is willing to accept "liberated" behavior from his white wife but if the Chicana employee protests his sexist behavior, he claims "that machi-machi-machismo / is part of our culture" effectively fencing-in the Chicana employee through a cultural defense of his behavior. But the employee is unwilling to accept that explanation because she does not see oppression as an authentic expression of Chicano culture. Instead she feels that the perpetrator has gleaned a superficial understanding of Chicano culture to justify his behavior: "Your culture emanates from Raza posters on your walls / from bulletin boards in the halls / and from the batos who hang out at the barrio bar." This assertion by the employee effectively sabotages the perpetrator's cultural defense and simultaneously rescues Chicano culture from distortion and creates a pocket of resistance.

Interestingly, Andrea Dworkin (1987), a white feminist, also conceptualizes sexual intercourse as violation. In her analysis, however, the Chicano meaning of sexual intercourse is turned on its head. Whereas for Chicanos abstention from sexual intercourse is a mechanism used to control and subordinate Chicanas, in Dworkin's paradigm abstention from sexual intercourse is, for white women, a revolutionary step toward liberation.

The outcome of sexual penetration outside of marriage for the value of Chicana womanhood is the same whether it happens by force or consent. Symbolically, women are always the potential enemy, even when they are most adored. A pampered, valued daughter can easily be disowned by her parents if she consents to be penetrated without the sanction of marriage (Behar 1993, 282). Overnight the parent's devotion can turn to strong hatred that will not subside until the ever elusive family honor is repaired through marriage or revenge (Ibid., 283). If *la hija despojada* (the damaged daughter) remains within the family and has offspring, they too are judged as dishonorable and not legitimate.

The reward for women who save their virginity until marriage is entering the revered status of wife and eventually mother and grand-mother. Mothers and grandmothers have legitimate realms of authority within Mexicano/Chicano culture, as they do in many other cultures; how-ever, the family centeredness that characterizes Mexicano/Chicano culture *idealizes* motherhood.[23] Also, the respect that is supposed to be accorded to older people in general also facilitates the potential authority of mothers as they become grandmothers and great-grandmothers. Mothers are sup-posed to be superhuman beings who can perform miraculous deeds on behalf of their families (Behar 1993, 271). Their comforts and rewards are to see their children grow up and to support their husbands. Mothers and grandmothers are the nurturant warriors who heal the wounds inflicted by an oppressive, racist society (Zinn 1975a). As such, they have been mythol-ogized in much of the Chicano literature produced in the 1960s. Consider José Montoya's poem "La Jefita" (The Little Boss):[24]

When I remember the campos	When I remember the fields
Y las noches and the sounds	And the nights and the sounds
of those nights en carpas o	of those nights in tents or
Bagones I remember my jefita's	train cars I remember my mother's
Palote	Rolling pin
Clik-clok; clik-clak-clok	Clik-clok; clik-clack-clok
Y su tocesita.	And her little cough.
(I swear, she never slept!)	(I swear, she never slept!)
Reluctant awakenings a la media	Reluctant awakenings in
	the middle of the
Noche y la luz prendida,	Night and the light on,
PRRRRRRINNNNGGGGGGG!	PRRRRRRINNNNGGGGGGG!

A noisy chorro missing the
	Basin.

Que horas son, ama?
Es tarde mi hijito. Cover up
Your little brothers.
Y yo con pena but too sleepy,

	Go to bed little mother!

A maternal reply mingled with
The hissing of the hot planchas
Y los frijoles de la hoya
Boiling musically dando segunda
A los ruidos nocturnos and
The snores of the old man

	Lulling sounds y los perros

Ladrando—then the familiar
Hallucinations just before sleep.

	And my jefita no more.

But then it was time to get up!
My old man had a chiflidito
That irritated the world to
Wakefulness.

	Wheeeeeeeeeet! Wheeeeeeet!

Arriba, cabrones chavalos
Huevones!

	Y todavia la pinche
	Noche oscura

Y la jefita slapping tortillas.

	Prieta! Help with the lonches!

	Calientale agua a tu 'apa!

A noisy drip missing the
	Basin.

What time is it, mom?
It's late my little son. Cover up
Your little brothers.
And I with embarrassment but
	too sleepy,

	Go to bed little mother!

A maternal reply mingled with
The hissing of the hot iron
And the homemade beans
Boiling musically singing backup
To the night noises and
The snores of the old man

	Lulling sounds and the dogs

Barking—then the familiar
Hallucinations just before sleep.

	And my little boss no more.

But then it was time to get up!
My old man had a little whistle
That irritated the world to
Wakefulness.

	Wheeeeeeeeeet! Wheeeeeeet!

Get up, goddam kids,
Lazy!

	And still the goddam
	Night was pitch black

And my little boss slapping
	tortillas.

	Dark one! Help with the
		lunches!
	Heat up the water for your dad!

(Me la rayo ese! My jefita never slept!)	(I'll be damned! My little boss never slept!)
Y en el fil, pulling her cien Libras de algoda se conreis Mi jefita y decia, That woman—she only complains in her sleep.[25]	And in the field, pulling her one hundred pounds of cotton My little boss That woman—she only complains in her sleep.

The mother in this poem is rendered central to the family by her ability to nurture, care, be the voice of reason, and keep the family functioning. She performs household chores while the rest of the family sleeps and then works side by side with them picking cotton in the fields. According to the son, the narrator, she does not express needs, pains, or frustrations. Her silence is a direct measure of her sainthood. Her capacity to give is infinite; she expects no reward other than seeing her family survive. In fact, the father in this poem is portrayed as insensitive to the children and the mother. The family survives because the mother's saintly behavior is the glue that keeps all the family members together. This portrayal is not uncommon. In the film *La Bamba* the mother is dedicated to her children and especially to her son Ritchie's success.[26] Also in El Teatro Campesino's *Soldado Razo* the father is a hard-drinking, authoritarian individual, while his wife is the "traditional long-suffering Latin mother figure" (Brown 1980). In this idealization of motherhood the Indo-Hispanic notion of devotion is equated with obedience (Alarcón 1981, 186). *La Madrecita* (The Little Mother) enacts and inculcates the cultural ideals of respect, devotion, and the legitimacy of gender hierarchies (regardless of how little she believes or follows them). As Abelardo Delgado proclaims, "as long as women obey we make saints of them" (1978, 34), and Carla Trujillo reaffirms this: "Martyrdom, the cloth of denial, transposes itself into a gown of cultural beauty" (1991, 188).

This poem strikes a cord of truth for many working-class Chicanas and Chicanos because the survival of the group has been possible precisely because of women's constant work, at home and in the fields (ibid., 189). However, *la jefita* is converted into the other, and in her objectification she is dehumanized.[27] By contrast, the project of Chicana feminists, especially Chicana poets, is to allow the other to speak. Contrast "La Jefita" with these stanzas from Alma Villanueva's poem "Mother May I":

18

and then began the years
of silence, the years
my mouth would open
and no words would speak,
my mouth locked tight.
and a loneliness grew

that I couldn't name.

19

I looked for it
in my husband's eyes.
I looked for it
in my children's eyes.
I looked for it
in supermarkets.
I looked for it
in the oven.
I looked for it
in the dustpan.
I looked for it
in the sink.
in the tv.
in the washing machine.
in the car.
in the streets.
in the cracks
on my linoleum.
I polished
and cleaned and cared for everything silently. I put on my
masks, my costumes and posed for each occasion. I conducted myself
well, I think, but an emptiness grew
that nothing could fill. I think

I hungered for myself.

(quoted in Sánchez 1985, 323–24)

This poem almost seems to be a mother's reply to the son in "La
Jefita." The droning work has a cost for *la jefita*—the loss of a voice with

which to speak of her pain. The loss of her voice results in a loss of herself because nobody, no matter how noble their intentions, can live entirely for others. More important, the son in "La Jefita" expects her to live for others. I argue that it is this *expectation* that subordinates and controls Chicanas.[28] If *la jefita* were to stop the rolling of tortillas and look up and say to the son, "I think / I hungered for myself," the arrangement between Chicanos and Chicanas would collapse. Silence is imperative to maintain the image of mothers as self-sacrificing saints.

As Chicanas acquire political consciousness about gender subordination, they become aware of the restricted social constructions of Chicana womanhood. Socorro Valdez expresses her consciousness of the restricted definition of women within El Teatro Campesino:

> It was like walking the same path over and over. There was the mother, the sister, or the grandmother or the girlfriend. Only four. You were either the *novia, la mamá, la abuela, o la hermana*. And most of the time these characters were passive. The way those females are laid out are for the most part very passive and laid back, *y aguantaban todo*. I think that is what really chewed me up at the time. (quoted in Broyles 1986, 166)

The comment that the female characters *aguantaban todo* (withstood everything) is pivotal in understanding the gender subordination of Chicanas. The structural position of Chicanos, as a group, has not permitted many of its women to be passive, because physical survival is at stake. Historically, there have always been strong women leaders within the Chicano/Mexicano community, from *las soldaderas*[29] who fought in the Mexican Revolution of 1910 to Emma Tenayuca, a famous labor leader in Texas. As a community, the fact that there is a type of adaptation, femme-macho, that allows for the expression of *will* leaves an aperture through which Chicanas can enforce their power. Even though the "gender blending" (Behar 1993, 293) of the femme-macho often amounts to taking on both male and female burdens, there is also attraction to the freedom that is often only reserved for men in Mexicano/Chicano communities. Behar eloquently describes this dialectical relationship between restriction and freedom in her ethnography of Esperanza, a Mexican street peddler:

> Esperanza has a keen sense of her gender blending, of how she has had to be father and mother, economic provider and nurturer,

upholder of the social-religious order, and a mirror in which her daughters can read a past that threatens to become their future. . . . One sees both Esperanza's pride in pulling off each role and her ambivalence about being a women who has taken on male roles. I read in Esperanza's narrative a desire to be a macha—a women who won't be beaten, won't forgive, won't give up her rage. A macha, too, in the sense of wanting to harness a certain male fearlessness to meet evil and danger head on. (ibid.)

For women in El Teatro Campesino their freedom of expression took the form of allegorical characters and even the appropriation of male characters by performing "in drag." In Socorro Valdez's words:

At the time there were no men in the group who could be made to play pachucos, or old men, etc. And it was important to play the men's roles well; because the truth is that Luis writes for men. He always has. His point of view is male and it will always be so. But it was kind of strange that he had no men to play the men. So I figured, "Hell, what's holding me back? Just let me put on a pair of pants and jump into it and see." And in fact I ended up playing men better than the men! . . . It wasn't that I was trying to get the role; I was trying to *establish* the role within the group. Those characters of men needed to be played. But unfortunately the men in the group at the time were not able or capable or free or whatever the problem was. (quoted in Broyles 1989, 224)

Broyles rightly concludes that

For Socorro, playing a male role provided a new adventure in role-playing: as a male she was now in an *active* position. In the Teatro Campesino repertoire, action was typically centered around male protagonists, with women characters generally functioning as auxiliary figures. The women figures were those *affected* by men; they were peripheral: the one *to whom* things happened. Not that the reverse would be desirable. The overpowering centrality of one character (usually male) creates limitations of dialogue, space, and action in the development of other characters. In Teatro Campesino plays in which the main character (male) has been balanced by other characters, those other characters are invariably also male (such as in *Fin del*

mundo, 1980; or *La Gran Carpa Cantinflesca*) or they are sexless characters like La Muerte (Death) or El Diablo (the Devil) (such as in *La
Carpa de los Rasquachis*). Women characters fill the spaces in between.
(ibid.)

Oddly enough, women actors could only fulfill their creative potential not
by being women but by being men! Therefore, "assuming a male role represented a major step in the explorations of new possibilities as a per-
former. And that step was an outgrowth of the living, creative impulse that
had become frustrated within the narrow confines of stereotyped women's
roles" (ibid.). Similarly, for some Chicanas outside of El Teatro, fulfilling
their potential took the form of taking positions of leadership in the political struggles on behalf of their group. Thus, Chicanas' apparent "passivity"
is much more complex than it appears and may, in fact, disguise a tremendous amount of strength and will. Many Chicanas are passive yet strong
enough to withstand their oppression (Castillo 1991, 35). Their subordination lies in the contradiction between having strength and refusing to use it
all of the time on those who obviously oppress them.

Chicana poets have embraced the hybrid image of human/animal to
exalt their liberation. This appropriation sabotages the negative image of
the femme-macho and turns it into a celebration of the breaking with gender boundaries. Consider the poem "Lagartija" ("Lizard") by Elba
Sánchez:

aqui me ves	here I am
lagartija contenta	contented lizard
paso los días	I spend my days
panza al sol	belly to the sun
cuerpo extendido	stretching out
sin miedo	without fearing
al filo	the dagger
de mis imperfecciones	of my imperfections
soy quien soy	I am who I am
desperté	I awoke
de un largo sueño	from a long dream
me comí las telarañas	ate the spiderwebs
que antes me enredaban	that entangled
las pestañas	my eyelashes
vendàndome los ojos	blindfolding me

ahora ya no como	I do not eat
moscas	flies any more
ni soy de sangre fría	nor am I cold blooded
yo misma	I am
mi propia partera	my own midwife
luciendo escamas	showing off scales
de cobre terrenal	of earthen copper
de cabeza a cola	from head to tail
me doy a luz	give birth to myself

(1992, 14)

Here the poet takes the image of a *lagartija,* not only an animal but a cold-blooded reptile and a hermaphrodite, to represent herself. In fact, the indigenous beliefs about the lizard are that "it is a sexual animal, snake-like and obsessed with the physical" (Huerta 1982, 98). *La lagartija* is antithetical to the warm-blooded nurturance that is expected of motherhood. Instead of supporting her man and her children, like *la jefita,* she literally gives birth not to the husband's offspring but, rather, to herself, and, even more blasphemous, she celebrates her liberation. Furthermore, the lizard-poet teases with the edges of sexual propriety by lying "belly to the sun," implying a sexually available pose that makes her open to violation by the "dagger." The lizard-poet, however, has demystified the dagger, representing penetration, and realizes that it is not sexual intercourse that "entangled [her] eyelashes" but, instead, the "imperfections" that she internalized and that blindfolded her. She no longer eats those "flies," or dictums of who she is. By disentangling herself, she can remain a lizard but not consider herself cold-blooded because now she celebrates who she is by "showing off scales of earthen copper from head to tail." The lizard-poet's focus on herself, her sexual availability, and her refusal to eat flies are defiant acts that embrace all those images that have been used against Chicanas to dispute that they are worthwhile women. The lizard-poet is not hard at work like *la jefita;* she does not "hunger for herself" as the narrator in *"Mother May I";* she simply is—with the placid abandonment of a lizard lying in the sun enjoying itself.

But even the femme-macho's power is constructed with built-in limitations, because femme-machos still are at the mercy of most Chicanos' conception of Chicana womanhood, which is highly restricted according to women's sexual behavior. Whatever liberation the femme-macho experiences by crossing gender boundaries and appropriating some "masculine" characteristics such as assertiveness, it is only temporary. Furthermore, from a feminist standpoint, the femme-macho social location presents an inherent contradiction—how can resistance by a femme-macho be celebrated when it is based on appropriating the masculine characteristics of domination and assertion of self to the exclusion of the needs of others? It is a dilemma inherent in many writings by Chicana/Latina feminists who try to grapple with both the subjugation and resistance expressed by Chicanas when they are treated as active agents rather than passive objects of study. Again, as Ruth Behar tries to *fully* understand Esperanza, she concludes that:

> Ultimately, Esperanza's transgressions against patriarchal ideology are tied up in paradoxes. That she appropriates culturally male values that oppress her as well as other women in order to liberate and redeem herself is contradictory. Her violence toward other women, and ultimately toward herself, is problematic. Her fascination with Pancho Villa, in light of her experience with male domination, is ironic. . . . Her critique of, and struggle against, the dominant gender ideology, like any such critique, any such struggle, is necessarily ambiguous. But Esperanza's struggle to define herself, through gender and in spite of gender, ambiguously gendered rather than passively gendered, points the way to the possibility of true gender transformation. So does her struggle to make herself whole, to be self and other, "woman" and "man," in the face of the metonymic misrepresentation that would reduce her to the insignificant partness of being only a subjugated female." (Behar 1993, 296)

Similarly, Broyles observes that Socorro Valdez's temporary transgressions in El Teatro Campesino ultimately did not result in giving her the power to fulfill one of her acting dreams.

> Given the extraordinary acting skill of Socorro Valdez, it would be no exaggeration to speak of her as a leading figure in the history of El Teatro Campesino. In the entire history of her work with the Teatro Campesino, however, Socorro Valdez has never played a lead female part, only numerous male leads. This is a startling fact considering not only Socorro's almost legendary talents as a performer but also her yearning to explore more roles. Yet the stereotyped casting within the company eliminated her, and other women who look like her, from

various female lead roles. There is sadness in her voice when she indicates that she never was allowed to play *La Virgen de Guadalupe* in *La
Virgen del Tepeyac:*[30]

> I never even got close to it. They wouldn't let me . . . could
> never have the role . . . because Luis doesn't see me that way.
> They see the *Virgen de Guadalupe* as a soft, demure, peaceful,
> saintly, ingenue type. The really incredible part was when it
> turned out that I have too many teeth. I was told "You got too
> many teeth. The Virgen didn't have that many teeth." It appears
> the Virgen de Guadalupe had no teeth. I thought to myself: "That
> is the stupidest thing I ever heard of!" *Apoco estaba molacha la Vir-*
> *gen de Guadalupe?* [Don't tell me the *Virgen of Guadalupe* was
> toothless!]

Broyles concludes that the truth of the matter was that Socorro Valdez did
not meet Western standards of beauty: she had *indigena*[31] features and very
dark brown skin.[32] Women who looked like Socorro either played male
parts or the allegorical characters who were "sexless" and were usually
played under heavy makeup or under heavy costume, thus hiding the
"real" gender of the actor: "The sexless roles became numerous, and they
were pursued as a creative outlet for women to escape the confinement of
female roles" (Broyles 1986, 178).

The restricted definition of Chicanas' sexuality—and therefore of their
womanhood—within El Teatro and within Chicano communities stems
from many men's inability to conceive of women as fully human. But, as
Broyles points out, a more complex aspect of that narrowness in the perception of Chicanas by Chicanos is linked to the narrowness of mostly
men's self-perceptions; she quotes Socorro Valdez: "He [Luis] can't experience women any other way except as a man. And no one else can do that
either, unless they are willing to *stretch their own image of themselves*" (ibid.,
168). Therefore, it was no coincidence that Luis Valdez could only write
plays casting women as "types," because to describe women characters
that are fully human would require that he also expand what it is to be a
man. The gender liberation of Chicanas is intertwined with the gender liberation of men within Chicano culture. Therefore, it would require the
restructuring of deeply held values about sexuality, family, and community.

The Community as *Familia:* What Binds Chicanas to the Stage

Chicano/Mexicano culture is a communal culture with deep historical roots in the tending of and caring for the land, and the division of labor between women and men is an integral part of the social arrangements sustained by the culture (Mirandé and Enriquez 1979). Chicanos' colonization, however, gave way to a devaluation of the work performed outside the home, mostly by Chicano men, and a focus on interpersonal relationships as a source of nurturance and validation of personhood. Social events such as *bailes, bautismos, loteria, bar-b-ques, fiestas de cumpleaños, misa, posadas, quinceñeras, velorios*[33] all became central to Chicano men and women in valuing themselves as human beings because of the enormous economic and social constraints they faced as a result of white racism. Many Chicanos as well as Chicanas came to fear the public sphere and to avoid it at all costs. The Chicano community became a refuge from the harshness of the outside world (Barrera 1991, 122). Valdez has described Chicanos' complex feelings about their barrios:

> The barrio is not a ghetto, though there are ghettos in the barrio. It is a microcosm of a Chicano city, a place of dualities: a liberated zone and a prison; a place of love and warmth, and place of hatred and violence, where most of *La Raza* live out their lives. So it is a place of weddings, *bautismos, tardeadas, bailes, velorios,*[34] and patriotic enchilada dinners. It is a place of poverty and self-reliance, of beloved *ancianos* [the old ones], of *familias,* of *compadres* [godparents]. (1972, 145)

For Chicanos the basic unit of community organization has been the family (Zavella 1988). *La familia,* which is patriarchal in nature, is considered a social support group, a source aiding migration, and a catalyst for political mobilization (Hurtado 1995; Zinn 1975b). *La familia* is the community, and the symbolic head of the family is the father (Zavella 1987; Orozco 1986, 12; Frischman 1982, 264). The family is *la cuna de la cultura*—the cradle where Chicano culture gets reproduced.

El Teatro Campesino's organizational structure is also based on family and on the cultivation of land.[35] Members of El Teatro live and work communally, and the relationship between members of the ensemble is defined as a familial one. In addition, El Teatro moved to San Juan Bautista,

California, a rural community, to farm and raise livestock to underscore their philosophical position that "ultimate freedom for the farmworkers means ownership of the land he [*sic*] works. We are now planting and building and raising animals on our forty acres. . . . Our art grows out of our way of life. We call it AGRARISMO CHICANO" (Bruce-Novoa 1978).[36]

El Teatro Campesino's organization is headed by Luis Valdez, who is its symbolic father as well as a writer and director. The actors in the company are typically much younger than Valdez. He is, of course, a benevolent father who has been very influential in the development of Chicano arts, encouraging and supporting the development of young Chicano artists. He has also tried to portray Chicanos, especially poor Chicanos, with dignity and depth—at least the men in his plays. Yet, however benevolent a father might be, if his authority is based on his privilege as a man, it will result invariably in the oppression of women. For example, as a writer and director, Valdez creates the woman characters and decides which women enact which parts. Broyles's (1986) discussion of how roles are created and assigned in El Teatro Campesino in many ways reflects the scripts that Chicanas have been assigned outside the theater. In Chicano communities the legitimacy of patriarchal power also results in controlling the "acceptable scripts" that Chicanas may live.

Some Chicanas are convinced by Chicanos that group survival is dependent on acceptance of the scripts delineated by the patriarchy. Chicano familism is extended to the group as a whole and is embodied in the notion of *carnalismo*, brotherhood and sisterhood (Zinn 1975b).[37] The collective political commitment to group survival is supposedly threatened if Chicanas refuse to enact their ascribed "roles." This is the essence of the hold that Chicano patriarchal power has on many Chicanas.

Women's roles in El Teatro Campesino have remained fairly constant throughout its history. Women characters typically engage in activities that are accessory to those of men. Never is the world seen through the eyes of women (Broyles 1986, 164). In Broyles's interviews with El Teatro women they placed these limited roles within the context of their own personal development. In the 1970s Chicanas who joined El Teatro inherited the women's stereotyped roles as givens. At that time most did not question these roles, because they themselves were very young. Diane Rodgriguez, who joined El Teatro when she was fifteen years old, states: "Somehow at that point we didn't have the consciousness and we played these cardboard roles. Or maybe we did have some consciousness but we didn't know how to get it on stage" (quoted in Broyles 1986, 165).

The limited roles given to women characters were also a result of a historical factor. Broyles notes that during the 1960s in El Teatro Campesino "the efforts to address *raza*[38] and the reality of *raza* as a *whole* somehow precluded a special consideration of women's roles and problems" (1986, 165). During this time it was a common practice among leftist groups to ignore "women's" issues. What was happening with women's roles in El Teatro paralleled the experiences of Chicana feminists in the 1960s within the Chicano movement (Sánchez 1985, 3–6). Chicano activists used two types of rhetoric to keep Chicana feminists from raising women's issues within the movement: one that focused on the divisiveness that would result from considering them and another that implied that joining the white feminist movement was an act of betrayal (Zavella 1988, 125; Trujillo 1991, 188). The fact that the white feminist movement was middle class in its origins, ideology, and practice convinced some Chicanas that, indeed, it did not speak to their specific position in society. Most Chicana feminists also felt that white feminism did not address itself to political struggles that included race and class (Hurtado 1989). In the 1960s the response of many politically progressive Chicano men to Chicana feminist demands were not unlike that of their white counterparts: appeals to reason ("yes, there are problems, but changes can come only incrementally"), cries of confusion ("what is it that you want?"), requests for a prescription ("tell us what to do"), and, finally, outright anger (*"el problema no es el macho, es el gabacho!"* [The problem is not the macho, it is the white man!]) (Orozco 1986, 12).

The dissatisfaction with women's character roles felt by female members of the group led to one of the longest and deepest struggles in the development of El Teatro Campesino. In El Teatro men met women's challenge to expand their roles on the stage with passive resistance; they perceived this action as an unnecessary provocation instead of as a challenge to expand El Teatro's creativity. Whereas El Teatro as well as the Chicano movement have been at the forefront of progressive political action such as unionization of farm labor, voter registration, and prison reform, both have consistently been unwilling to confront the issue of sexism. The men in El Teatro did not meet the women's challenge and, instead, suggested that women create their own theater company. Eventually, the women did leave and proceeded to write, produce, and act in their own plays. For example, Olivia Chamucero started theater work with children of migrant workers and conducted a program of drama workshops for women in battered women's centers and for youth in drug prevention centers. Yet, as Broyles indicates, "Clearly the collective spirit suffered a collapse when gender roles were questioned. Suddenly an individual solution was suggested for what was a collective problem" (1986, 168).

It is important to understand that Chicanas' loyalty to Chicanos derives not from the hope of economic security but, rather, from their desire to gain *respectable* entry into the Chicano community. The Chicano community is the universe for Chicanos, who encounter hostility outside their segregated barrios. Attachment to a man is not merely for Chicanas' economic insurance but for their very inclusion in social and cultural life. That is the crux of the hold that Chicanos have on Chicanas: the threat of the universe collapsing—in El Teatro's terms, *El Fin del Mundo* (The End of the World), the last play by El Teatro Campesino, which was performed in Europe. The fear is that the Chicano way of life will disappear if Chicanas step outside the boundaries of the narrow stage set for them by Luis Valdez and other symbolic fathers.

Like the women characters in El Teatro Campesino, Chicanas in general are trapped in the theater of life, playing scripts that they have very little responsibility for creating and confined on a narrow stage that spotlights men (Cotera 1977, 24). Chicanas are assigned the task of waiting in the wings to pick men up, support them, and enhance them. Chicanas have always been part of the backdrop, not only on the stage but also in life. To refuse to be the backdrop is to destroy the play. The male actor cannot be the hero if the women refuse their role; there is no play if there is no framework, no backdrop, no extras to highlight the centrality of the main actor. Even if it is only a penumbra, there has to be a background, or there is no universe. As women, Chicanas have carried the burden of knowing that they are essential, *no importa cuanto las maltraten* (no matter how much they are mistreated). Most Chicanas are socialized to believe that men cannot exist without them, and this idea has tied them to a stage that they might otherwise abandon—*esta es la esencia de la madrecita sufrida* (this is the essence of the suffering mother).

When Chicanas in El Teatro Campesino questioned their gendered scripts, the response of the men was to say, "Write your own plays." But, as a group, Chicanas are not socialized to separate from the group in this way (Zinn 1975b), and it is not because they lack strength or skills. Many Chicana feminists and activists have resolved the dilemma by separating only in some areas. For example, Chicana academics created their own professional organization, Mujeres Activas in Letras y Cambio Social (MALCS), Women Active in Scholarship and Social Change, in response to men's domination of the National Association for Chicano Studies (NACS). Yet, many of the MALCS members participate in NACS. Chicana feminists have never proposed to boycott or otherwise disengage from NACS. Instead, there have been a series of confrontations over the exclusion of women and the absence of gender issues in the annual meetings of NACS. Many Chicana feminists do not want to be separate from the group that simultaneously constitutes their community and oppresses them.

El Fin del Mundo:[39] Chicanas Walk off the Stage

In 1980, El Teatro ended as a collective enterprise, and the members of the ensemble went their separate ways. El Teatro still exists under Luis Valdez's direction, but it is now dedicated to "mainstreaming" its productions, and, as La Bamba shows, it even has had an effect on Hollywood.

At the same time that El Teatro Campesino was evolving, so were the writings of feminists of Color. In the 1980s, there was an explosion of Chicana feminist writing that helped women in and out of El Teatro wrest from men the right to invent themselves, and they have done so through many avenues, including creative and academic production. The activist legacy of El Teatro, which many of the female actors had a hand in actively creating, was echoed in feminist academic and artistic productions. In particular, Broyles indicates that

> One must not underestimate the importance of the "context of struggle" of verbal art forms within oppressed communities and of the very real *need* for "verbal and intellectual combat." Combat is usually joined for cultural and physical survival. As such it cannot surprise us that impartiality is out of the question. The Teatro Campesino's militance was a direct response to the needs of the United Farm Workers struggle from which it emerged. There was an urgent need to unionize in the struggle against the multiple abuses of agribusiness, which included large-scale pesticide poisoning of farm laborers, exploitative wages, substandard housing, child labor, and no benefits. At times of lesser political ferment the critical exploration of social experience could assume less explicit—if equally pungent—performance forms. The transmission of knowledge within oral performance forms never feigns neutrality, "objectivity," or detachment. A critique is usually implicit or explicit, lines are drawn, sides are taken, particular forms of social behavior are regarded positively, others viewed askance, solutions to problems are put forth or implied. Critiques within the

Teatro Campesino were often embedded in performance forms involving verbal jousting, which calls into question norms of language and conduct as well as dominant and oppressive paradigms of "correct" speech and meaning. The Teatro Campesino described its work within this very combative style, a style that emanated directly from an intimate relationship to the urban and rural struggles of Chicana/o communities. The performance telos involved a grounding in the community experience of the working class, in a social vision and critique. (1994, 25)

These are the nascent beginnings of what Patricia Hill Collins (1991) came to call *positionality*—the emergence of knowledge from particular social positions previously ignored in knowledge production. The positionality of Chicanas developed in El Teatro came directly from the experience of trying to articulate the *rasquachi aesthetic*. From Broyles perspective, the rasquachi aesthetic "refers to the creation of artistic beauty from the motley assemblage of elements momentarily seized. Performances within . . . El Teatro manifest a shared memory system anchored in working-class history and its arsenal of performance practices" (ibid., 36). The rasquachi aesthetic has some conventional elements that are manifested in most of El Teatro's work, among these are the use of stock characters and most important is the comic underdog character who is simultaneously vulnerable and resourceful in overcoming a difficult environment. The underdog characters were the fertile ground for the femme-macho actors in El Teatro. The underdog's vulnerability is largely the result of their derogated group memberships, such as ethnicity, race, gender, and class. The logic of the performance is how these characters are pitted in a power struggle with other characters representing the dominant social order, and in the end, the underdog is able to outmaneuver the more powerful through wits, humor, and verbal combat. Most importantly, Broyles indicates that "None of these characters consisted of fleshed-out figures, nor did they seek to render the psychological workings of individuals. Instead each character stood for a broad social category. Their archetypal nature facilitated a skeletal portrait of the structure of social relations" (ibid., 37).

I would argue that in learning how to express the rasquachi aesthetic through the improvisation of skits and plays, women in El Teatro were deciphering a tremendous amount about power relationships. Most importantly, because the nature of the endeavor was not to portray in-depth psychological portraits of *individuals* but rather of archetypes, these set the stage for the structural emphasis many Chicana feminists openly claim in their work. Again, while many white feminists gained their gender consciousness out of the analysis of intimate interpersonal relationships, many Chicana feminists like the women in El Teatro, emphasized the archetypal aspect of power relationships, regardless of the individual players (Anzaldúa 1990, 378; Castillo 1995, 163–179). As Emma Pérez poignantly asks and answers: "Am I exploiting anyone, and if I am, how can I change? If we do not challenge our own contradictions, then we only pretend to make a revolution" (1993, 66).

By women participating in El Teatro, in-itself, was an act of resistance to the predominant sexist views in their communities. Even though participation in El Teatro was to bring political consciousness to Chicano communities, many of the women actors were criticized in their families for what they perceived as inappropriate behavior for women. Olivia Chumacero recounts: "It's been eleven years since I left the house . . . but when my parents think of theater they think of loose women. In Mexico if you are into the arts in this way *eres mujer de la calle* [you're a woman of the street]. . . . Women have it harder and they have to be strong" (quoted in Broyles 1989, 222). The women actors, however, persisted because participation in El Teatro, however restricted, provided an outlet for their artistic aspirations and because the experiences that El Teatro provided through travel opened worlds to these women that they may have otherwise not experienced. Their resistance to sexist accusations cannot be underestimated nor their love of freedom undervalued especially when these brave actors juggled the rigors of the road alongside their duties as mothers.

We wanted to have more say in certain decisions. For instance: touring and babies. How about taking babies out on the road? So-and-so couldn't travel because she had a baby. Now that's ridiculous. Olivia was one of them . . . the forerunners of the mothers in the company. They had their babies . . . and they proved it, not only to themselves or to their in-laws or to their parents, but to Luis, that it could be done. They proved that women—even now—with all the pressures of motherhood could be seen performing on the stage and then breast-feeding their kid in the van the next hour. It was possible. It wasn't easy. . . . I use Olivia as an example because she just trudged right through it in the best way she knew how. And it wasn't always easy for her. . . . I

don't have any children but I do know how I want to be now that I've
seen how they could do it. They proved certain things for me. And that
was during the *hard* times when we had to go cross-country to New
York in one van, and the baby diapers and all that. . . . You know, that
was a hell of a point that the women made. It affected me a great deal
to see that. The company had to make it possible for children to go
with us. That's what is had to do. Staying home had to be a matter of
choice and not a matter of having children. That point was very important: the establishment of an acting mother. (quoted in Broyles 1989,
222–223).

Obviously, these heroic acts not only affected the mothers in the company
but the other women actors who saw what a struggle these women fought
and how it was a one-sided struggle: "In the women's or men's testimony
there is no mention of difficulties in the establishment of an acting father"
(ibid., 223). Experiences like these, although not coded as creating gender
consciousness and contributing to feminist thought, indeed began to form
the basis for Chicanas' brand of "no-name feminism."

Humor as Oppositional Tool

Yet Esperanza often found amusing my determined efforts to understand
her story; though she wanted to tell me her story and had, in her perception, a sad story to tell, she refused—and still refuses—to succumb to
self-pity. Her telling of her history was always full of humor, of a
picaresque vitality. The laughter that punctuates all our conversations is,
perhaps, also her critique of my academic pretensions . . . That I should
want to take her life seriously also strikes her as comical in terms of the
inversions of social position and hierarchy that it suggests: an educated,
obviously middle-class gringa asking an unschooled Mexican street peddler to tell her life story. In a society where privilege and power are the
monopoly of the fair-skinned, Esperanza is acutely aware of her dark
skin, and of her Indianness.

—Behar 1993, 7–8

Another conventional element of the rasquachi aesthetic is the underdog's
use of humor as one of his or her most powerful weapons against the social
order. Broyles indicates that "as a group, the *pelada/o*, or underdog, characters were bawdy, bold, gutsy, hilarious, thoroughly unpretentious, usually
irreverent, and determined to survive" (ibid., 37). Furthermore, the

Performance elements characteristically aimed to produce laughter. These elements included the wildly exaggerated and broadly mimetic acting style; the archetypal stock characters, such as the hilarious *peladito/peladita* (underdog); or the witty and irreverent attitude toward language and norms of propriety conveyed through a general spirit of *picardía* (ribald humor). Yet in essence this humor was dead serious. It provided the means of exploring and commenting on social oppression and life's day-to-day struggles. The relationship between laughter and human necessity, between slapstick and tragedy is expressed by Luis Valdez (1972b: 360): "Our use of comedy originally stemmed from necessity—the necessity of lifting the strikers morale. We found we could make us very close to the underlying tragedy—the fact that humans have been wasted for generations" (ibid., 27).

Broyles goes on to elaborate how laughter is an oppositional tool used to resist a sense of futility and to conceive of alternative social arrangements:

> Bakhtin conceptualizes laughter as a patently oppositional tool of the popular masses. He illustrates how the culture of laughter in its many forms and manifestations has traditionally opposed the authoritarianism and protective seriousness of the ruling class. Through the ages laughter has for the oppressed functioned as a rehearsal of freedom. (ibid., 30)

Ultimately the "rehearsal of freedom" is the underpinning of the rasquachi aesthetic (often referred to as rasquachismo). Put more succinctly by Tomás Ybarra-Frausto:

> Rasquachismo is brash and hybrid, sending shudders through the ranks of the elite, who seek solace in less exuberant, more muted and purer traditions. In an environment always on the edge of coming apart (the car, the job, the toilet), things are held together with spit, grit, and movidas. Movidas [moves] are the coping strategies you use to gain time, to make options, to retain hope. Rasquachismo is a compendium of all the movidas deployed in immediate, day-to-day living. Resilience and resourcefulness spring from making do with what is at hand (hacer rendir las cosas). This use of available resources engenders hybridization, juxtaposition, and integration. (qtd. in Broyles 1994, 49)

Casualties and Survivors of the Rehearsal of Freedom

Undoubtedly, oppression always results in casualties, but one of its by-products is that some of its survivors go on to further the group's collective consciousness. The ability of some Chicanas to move between many worlds and many perceptions has resulted in the creation of a new consciousness about gender relations that is class and race specific—the result of the cultural and historical evolution of Chicanos.[40] In Maria Lugones's words:

> the liberatory experience lies in this memory, on these other people one is and have intentions one understands because one is fluent in several "cultures," "worlds," realities. One understands herself in every world in which one remembers oneself. This is a strong sense of personal identity, politically and morally strong. The task of remembering one's other selves is a difficult liberatory task. Mystification is one of the many forms of control of our memory of our other selves. All oppressive control is violent because it attempts to erase selves that are dangerous to the maintenance of domination over us. (1990, 7)

The crossing over into many social realities results in recognition of the arbitrary nature of social categories as well as the arbitrary nature of the authority that creates them. As Gloria Anzaldúa puts it: *"Soy un amasamiento,* I am an act of kneading, of uniting and joining that not only has produced both a creature of darkness and a creature of light, but also a creature that questions the definitions of light and dark and gives them new meanings" (1987, 81). Chicana feminists theorize practically and academically from their position as part of the background for the play. Having been part of the penumbra gives Chicanas an advantage. They have seen men while men were not seeing themselves (Lugones 1990, 6–7). As Lugones notes, Chicanas inhabit the limen, meaning they stand "betwixt and between successive lodgments in jural political systems . . . aside not only from [their] own social position but from all social positions . . . formulating unlimited series of social arrangements" (13–14).[41] Inhabiting the limen provides the potential for liberation because it furnishes the social, psychological, and philosophical space in which to conceive of alternatives to oppression—alternatives that are inconceivable in structured social worlds in which oppression is essential to the maintenance of the social and economic order. To inhabit the limen and understand its liberatory

potential is to experience oneself as multiple; therefore, these "limen creatures" are extremely threatening to any world that requires "unification,
either psychologically, morally, politically or metaphysically" (9). Chicana
poets have been especially powerful in delineating the contours of the liberatory potential of the limen:

> To live in the Borderlands means you
>   are neither *hispana india negra española*
>   *ni gabacha,*[42] *eres mestiza,*[43] *mulata,*[44] half-breed
>   caught in the crossfire between camps
>   while carrying all five races on your back
>   not knowing which side to turn to, run from;
>
> To live in the Borderlands means knowing
>   that the *india* in you, betrayed for 500 years,
>   is no longer speaking to you,
>   that mexicanas call you *rajetas,*[45]
>   that denying the Anglo inside you
>   is as bad as having denied the Indian or Black;
>
> *Cuando vives en la frontera*[46]
>   people walk through you, the wind steals your voice,
>   you're a *burra, buey,*[47] scapegoat
>   forerunner of a new race,
>   half and half—both woman and man, neither—
>   a new gender;
>
> To live in the Borderlands means to
>   put chile[48] in the borscht,
>   eat whole wheat *tortillas,*
>   speak Tex-Mex[49] with a Brooklyn accent;
>   be stopped by *la migra*[50] at the border checkpoints;
>
> Living in the Borderlands means you fight hard to
>   resist the gold elixir beckoning from the bottle,
>   the pull of the gun barrel,
>   the rope crushing the hollow of your throat;
>
> In the Borderlands
>   you are the battleground
>   where the enemies are kin to each other;

you are at home, a stranger,
the border disputes have been settled
the volley of shots have shattered the truce
you are wounded, lost in action
dead, fighting back;

To live in the Borderlands means
the mill with the razor white teeth wants to shred off
your olive-red skin, crush out the kernel, your heart
pound you pinch you roll you out
smelling like white bread but dead;

To survive the Borderlands
you must live *sin fronteras*[51]
be a crossroads.

(Anzaldúa 1987, 195)

Anzaldúa uses the term *borderlands* (*la frontera*) to denote that space in which antithetical elements mix, not to obliterate each other or to get subsumed by a larger whole but, rather, to combine in unique and unexpected ways. The limen/borderland is where individuals can put chile in their borscht and speak Tex-Mex with a Brooklyn accent. It is a space that some women of Color, specifically Chicanas, can inhabit because of their ability to maintain multiple selves without feeling incoherence. In the limen it is possible to develop a "forerunner of a new race, half and half—both woman and man, neither—a new gender."

The Embodiment of Mestiza Consciousness: A New Gender

. . . there is something inside us that makes us different from other people. It is not like men and it is not like white women.
—Parker 1979; interview with Toni Morrison

Su Cuerpo Es Una Bocacalle. [Her Body Is A Crossroads] *La mestiza* has gone from being the sacrificial goat to becoming the officiating priestess at the crossroads.
—Gloria Anzaldúa 1990, 380

Many Chicana feminists have written about a new Chicana consciousness stemming from many of these women's ability to "cross borders" (Anzaldúa 1991, 377–89; Espín 1995, 230–31), to perceive "multiple realities" (Alarcón 1990), to develop an "oppositional consciousness" (Sandoval 1991), and to accomplish "a state of *conscienticización*" [feminist conscious-ness] (Castillo 1995, 171). Other feminists of Color have also written elo-quently about women of Color's *positionality*—that is, their structural posi-tion because of their race/ethnicity, class, and gender gives them access to knowledge that allows them to actively resist their structural positions (Zavella 1991a, 1991b; Lamphere et al. 1993, 7). Many Chicanas *embody* this consciousness in their daily lives and in their intellectual work.

Many women of all ethnicities and racial backgrounds also have access to multiple realities. White feminist theorists, in particular, have written extensively about white women's capacity to perceive social reali-ties inaccessible to [white] men (Spender 1980). Chicanas' multiple reali-ties, however, are not the same as that of many white women's. Although white feminist writings have been very helpful in breaking new theoretical ground (ibid.; Henley 1986; Frye 1983), they have not been as helpful in deconstructing many white women's "blind spots" *in relationship* to women of Color. It is in *este sitio* [this space] that Chicanas' *lenguas* [lan-guages] can be most helpful.[52] El Teatro also created *un sitio y una lengua* to articulate the realities and concerns of Chicano communities in the United States.

Chicana feminist writings have been very important in identifying those *sitios* [spaces] where Chicanos and white women converge and in which they have significant differences (Alarcón 1990; Lamphere et al. 1993, 274–97; Segura and Pierce 1993). In identifying the differences, Chi-cana feminists have pushed forward our consciousness about oppression to include its relational nature and how even those who are victimized can occupy the role of oppressor within specified social contexts. For example, Lugones describes the interaction between a white woman and her maid:

In the case of people who dominate others, they may not remember the person they are in the reality of the dominated. For example, many times [white] people act in front of their maids as if there were no one in the room. They say things and behave in ways that one can only imagine as said or done in private. When people behave this way, they do not see themselves as the maid sees them and they do not want to remember or recognize the person who is seen by the maid, of whom the maid is a witness. The maid can only testify in the world of the dominated, the only world where that testimony is understood and recognized. The employers do not remember themselves as maids know them for many reasons. One of these reasons concerns their own sense of moral integrity since as they are witnessed by the maid they lack it. So phenomena such as self-deception become very important in this way of seeing things.[53]

Obviously, not all white women have maids, and not all maids are Chicanas. But this description shows how women can objectify other women. The hope for a comprehensive theory of liberation lies in delineating the different *limen* that are possible and, from those interstices, theorize about potential solutions for oppression. As Lugones proposes: "Merely remembering ourselves in other worlds and coming to understand ourselves as multiplicitous is not enough for liberation: collective struggle in the reconstruction and transformation of structures is fundamental" (1990, 10).

To be sure, there is overlap between the perceptions of different oppressed groups, but it is not complete. This fact is what has only recently been recognized by white feminists (Spelman 1988; Hurtado 1989; West and Fenstermaker 1993). One possible solution is to increase "dialogue among multiplicitous persons who are faithful witnesses of themselves and also testify to and uncover the multiplicity of their oppressors and the techniques of oppression afforded by ignoring that multiplicity" (Lugones 1990, 10). For example, Chicana theorists are struggling to claim their independence and to challenge traditional definitions of what is culturally appropriate for women. Much of Chicana feminist writing tries to redefine the virgin-puta dichotomy, since "virginity (mental, physical, or whatever it may mean . . .) is more an obsession created by and for the use of men than an actual feminine state of being" (Del Castillo 1974, 144). The sweeping redefinition of Chicana womanhood includes the erasure of negative views of homosexuality, of conventional familial roles for women and men, and of Chicanos' own racism in rejecting their Indian heritage:

> Over the years, the confines of farm and ranch life began to chafe. The traditional role of *la mujer* was a saddle I did not want to wear. The conceptions "passive" and "dutiful" raked my skin like spurs and "marriage" and "children" set me to bucking faster than rattlesnakes or coyotes. I took to wearing boots and men's jeans and walking about with my head full of visions, hungry for more words and more words. Slowly I unbowed my head, refused my estate and began to challenge the way things were. But it's taken over thirty years to unlearn the

belief instilled in me that white is better than brown—something that some people of color *never* will unlearn. And it is only now that the hatred of myself, which I spent the greater part of my adolescence cultivating, is turning to love. (Anzaldúa 1987, 202)

To love oneself as a woman is a revolutionary act. The reclaiming of self has come for Chicana feminists through self-love—not narcissistic, selfish involvement but as a political act of valuing what patriarchy has devalued. Chicana feminists proclaim that redemption does not come through men but, rather, comes from giving up the illusion of security and safety that results from being chosen by a man. It is, as Gloria Anzaldúa writes, "Letting Go":

Nobody's going to save you.
No one's going to cut you down
cut the thorns around you.
No one's going to storm
the castle walls nor
kiss awake your birth,
climb down your hair,
nor mount you
onto the white steed.

There is no one who
will feed the yearning.
Face it. You will have
to do, do it yourself.

                                        (Anzaldúa 1981, 200)

Chicana feminism does not advocate separatism from Chicano men or from the Chicano community. Chicana feminists, like other feminists of Color, are struggling to develop a truly inclusive political consciousness that embraces all who have been rejected and does not lead to the abandonment of hope, even in those who reject it. To refuse to separate from Chicano men and to understand their oppression does not mean excusing their brutality (Anzaldúa 1987, 83). What Chicana feminists advocate is a head-on engagement with Chicanos and with other members of their communities to achieve positive change for all parties involved.

Recently, Socorro Valdez was asked by Luis Valdez to return to El

Teatro Campesino to play in his award-winning television special "Corridos." Socorro Valdez agreed under the condition that she play the woman lead for the first time in her career. In her words:

> I didn't want makeup on my face. I didn't want lipstick. I didn't want false eyelashes or fake boobs or nothing. I just wanted to be myself up there, just wanted to be the Indian person that I am. . . . I came back to him [Luis Valdez], but I said: "That's it. No more masks, no more calavera face [skull mask], no more calavera bones on my face. None of that shit. I'll go out there in a plain cotton dress and I'll have those people going." (quoted in Broyles 1986, 182)

Just as Socorro Valdez wanted to keep her home in her theater community, Chicana feminists also want to remain in their communities and make their struggle as women part of the struggle that affects all oppressed peoples. Like Socorro Valdez, their presence will have to be on their own terms.

CHAPTER 3

An Invitation to Power: The Restructuring of Gender in the Political Movements of the 60s

As part of that struggle was the need to speak the truth as he viewed it even when that truth alienated rather than justified, upset minds rather than calmed hearts, and subjected the speaker to general censure rather than acclaim.

—Derrick Bell

If there were a time for this country to be proud of its commitment to democratic ideals, it was during the tumultuous 1960s. It was a time when social justice was the currency of the day and right and wrong were discussed on street corners. There was open debate over racism, and individuals took stands on righteous issues to the detriment of their own individual privilege. These were social movements led by the young, educated elite who joined forces with those outside the circles of power to sabotage their inherited privilege. It is therefore difficult, to say the least, to dissect the regressive currents within them, which are inherent in all progressive movements. It is necessary, as Derrick Bell admonishes, "to speak the truth as he [or she] viewed it," even when it will not necessarily lead to acclaim.

Why focus on the Black Civil Rights movement and the Chicano movement rather than some other progressive social movements? Principally, because I see these social movements as contemporaneous with the massive political mobilization around the ending of the Vietnam War, at the core of which was the redefinition of manhood for white, upper-class men. The changing definitions of manhood (or masculinity) are not a recent phenomenon.[1] What may have been unique, historically, however, is that educated white men, the inheritors of the power structure, questioned the most essential requirement of their manhood: going to war for

The epigraph is taken from Bell 1992, xv.

their country (and, therefore, for their privilege). Their refusal, in substantive numbers, rocked the very foundation of the distribution of power in this country (inheritance laws through biological ties). Furthermore, the refusal to go to war was allied to other progressive causes as exemplified in the Black Civil Rights movement, the Chicano movement, and white Women's Liberation movement. Women of Color participated in all of these social movements but their specific concerns were not central to any of these groups' political agendas. The central problematic I address in this chapter is the question of why women activists in the Chicano and the Black Civil Right's movements were unremittingly in solidarity with these male-dominated movements. At the same time, these women were very skittish about joining the white Women's Liberation movement. Even though there have been eloquent testimonies and analyses of the political movements of the 1960s, almost all have been from men's perspectives, with a few from white women's perspectives and even fewer from women of Color.[2] A better understanding of all the actors and political interests involved in these exciting and dramatic times will allow us to see clearly our potential for coalitions in the present.

In the struggle to understand the relational nature of women's gender subordination, it also becomes important to examine those social spheres where other kinds of subordination have been addressed. Are progressive movements more or less likely to address women's issues when their project has been to dismantle the dynamics of subordination based on class and race/ethnicity? Furthermore, has the scrutiny of subordination in these restricted spheres provided the political and theoretical aperture for scrutinizing women's issues, and if not, how have women in these spheres reacted to this erasure? I address the Black Civil Rights Movement and the Chicano Movement to attempt to answer these questions.

The Eternal Masculine

From feminist analyses since the 1960s, there have been eloquent critiques showing how the state is male and its mission, in part, is not only to protect the privileges of the existing power structure but also to protect women and children—and that the protection of the state is a gendered activity in which both white men and white women are essential.[3] Prior to a feminist movement the notion that women needed protection from men was critical in "legitimating women's exclusion from some spheres of human endeavor and confinement within others." (W. Brown 1992, 9). Of course, certain women are considered more worthy of protection than others, codes of protection are largely based on race and class privilege: "Protection codes are thus key technologies in regulating privileged women as well as in intensifying the vulnerability and degradation of those on the unprotected side of the constructed divide between light and dark, wives and prostitutes, good girls and bad ones" (ibid.).

For educated white feminists the protective function of the state has posed a serious dilemma: should they organize to demand formalized, institutional protection from the state with the accompanying by-product, the right of the state to regulate its subjects, or should they fight for equal inclusion in a state that by its very masculinist nature will place women at a disadvantage? This dilemma pervades all arenas of social life: Who should pay for child care and care for the elderly, when it is mostly women who are charged with these responsibilities; for equal pay for equal work, when in fact there is a highly segregated labor market in which most low-paying, low-prestige occupations are held by women; for due process laws, when by definition certain crimes suffered by women (e.g., rape and battery) are *by law* punished less than other equally serious crimes?

Wendy Brown argues that the origins of this tension can be traced to how the liberal state is conceptualized. First, according to liberal ideology, the polity is divided into autonomous spheres of family, civil society (economy), and state. The family and civil society are perceived as natural, whereas the state is an unnatural arrangement developed for the protection of the first two spheres. In Brown's words: "In classic liberal accounts, the state is the one conventional and hence fully malleable part of this tripartite arrangement; it is constructed both to protect citizens from external danger and to guarantee the rights necessary for commodious commerce with one another" (ibid., 17).

At the core of classical social theory, from Thomas Hobbes and John Locke through Karl Marx, Max Weber, Emile Durkheim, and Sigmund Freud, there are several underlying currents about the state's gender:

All proclaim "man" as his own maker . . . men's ability to give birth to themselves. This man exists originally outside society . . . he has to be brought into society through socialization. This passage—from the state of nature into civil society—is a gendered creation myth. It is about men's power to give birth to society. . . . Originally, there was chaos, but men created society to get out of this chaos. . . . "The conventional understanding of the 'political' is built upon the rejection of physical birth in favor of the masculine creation of (giving birth to) social and political order." Just like John Locke made a distinction . . . between "labor of our body and the work of our hands," so too did social theorists claim a difference between labor that produces no lasting product because its possessor is dependent, and labor that transforms nature into something of value, the work, which is independent of the producer's survival needs and may outlast him. Labor, as in women's work, as in "going into labor" does not count; what counts is work. (Kimmel 1993, 31)

In fact, man's masculine identity is derived from successful homosocial competition in the marketplace (ibid.). The process of becoming a man is a process of striving for power. Because power is in limited supply, not all men will accomplish masculinity successfully. And, because white hegemonic masculinity is power driven, there has to be a counter construction to define who the dominated should be—those who exhibit in the marketplace dependency, cooperation, caring, and tenderness, mostly women and "failed men" (Ramazanoglu 1992, 340).

Feminists have done an excellent job of problematizing this conceptualization. If the family is "natural" and women are the primary workers within this sphere, then their work is natural and outside the regulation of the state, where "unnatural," and therefore "real," work is defined and regulated. Concomitantly, if most of women's work transpires in the "private" sphere, their involvement in the public sphere is severely limited in comparison with men. Men, therefore, have unlimited access to women in the privacy of their families, because relations within this sphere should be out of the state's reach. Again, as Wendy Brown observes:

> For the most part, rights do not apply in this sphere; rather this realm is formally governed by norms of duty, love, and custom, and until quite recently, has been largely shielded from the reach of law. Indeed, the difficulties of establishing marital rape as rape, wife battering as battery, or child abuse as abuse, pertain, *inter alia*, to the liberal resistance to recognizing personhood inside the household; in the liberal formulation, persons are rights-bearing individuals pursuing their interests in civil society. (1992, 17–18)

In classical liberal theory "women have no civil personality—they exist only as members of households while personhood is achieved in civil society" (ibid., 18). From a liberal perspective men's power within the family is a natural prerogative, while his rights in the public or civil sphere have to be obtained through an elaborate set of rules agreed upon and codified by the state. Of course, the liberal subject not only has a say-so in the construction of these rules and obligations but also has participatory power in modifying them if they oppress him.[4] The family sphere should "buttress" rather than limit his civil rights. It is exactly the opposite case for women, because the division of labor places limits on her participation in civil society. And, even though women now have roughly the same civil rights as men, they are of limited use to them and have different substantive meanings than for men (18–19), because they are the rights fashioned by a masculinist state.

Inherent to the prerogative masculinist power of the state is the threat of violence to women if they are not protected by a man or by specific arms of the state such as the police or the welfare system. According to Weber, "male household authority is rooted in its provision of protection from institutionalized male violence" (quoted in ibid., 19). Brown concludes that "the gendered character of liberalism is partly determined by the gendered character of prerogative power in which women are cast as requiring protection from the world of male violence while the superior status of men is secured by their supposed ability to offer such protection" (25).

Brown's analysis is a powerful one but one that she clearly admits suspends, for strategic theoretical purposes, the burgeoning literature on "the specific mores and mechanisms through which state power is systematically rather than incidentally racist" because she does not want to "develop their speculations" (ibid., 17).[5] I contend that, from the vantage point of Blacks and Chicanos in this country, the liberal vision of the polity with the separation of the other three spheres and with the progressive spin of the war movement in the 1960s, was a much more palatable state of affairs than what these groups had experienced historically. The recognition of privacy for people of Color would mean that the state could not intervene in their private lives,[6] which would work to their advantage; if men of Color were recognized as legitimate civil subjects who could negotiate with the state, their entire families could accrue benefits; if there were true separation between citizens of Color and the state, they could start building their communities and negotiating with the state by exercising their voting rights—as all other citizens do.

The liberal vision of the state highlighted the effects of how gender has been differentially constructed according to race. These differences also underscore the relational character of gender. In Connell's words, "Differential masculinities are constituted in relation to other masculinities and femininities—through the structure of gender relations" (1987, 175–88).

Varying Definitions of Masculinity

Only recently has there been a serious intellectual questioning of what constitutes masculinity, or, more correctly, masculinities.[7] For the better part of this century masculinity (or manhood) has been conceptualized "as a psychological essence [that] obliterates questions about social structure and the historical dynamic of gender relations" (Connell 1993, 599). Masculinity, in its cultural forms, also cannot be extracted from sexuality, "which is an essential dimension of the social creation of gender" (602). Gender has been differentially constructed for different ethnic/racial groups in this society. People of Color's gender, whether masculine or feminine, has accentuated their sexuality (West 1993, 83–91)[8] and their capacity for physical work, whereas for white people, especially educated white people, it has emphasized their intellectual abilities and their capacity to lead.[9] Masculinity is also intertwined with power—mostly with the power to dominate others for the accumulation of material resources. The greater the power to dominate, the greater the value of a particular man. The ability to dominate is also related to a man's ability to provide and protect. Because men are household representatives in civil society, their ability to compete in the "dog-eat-dog" economic arena also determines the strength of their manhood (Kimmel 1993, 31). Therefore, real men are competitors throughout their lives, usually developed through ritualistic participation in sports (Connell 1992, 741), who protect their families (products of serial monogamy) and are actors in civil society. But, because not all men are created equal, Chicano and Black men have had different historical antecedents than white men, which affect the manifestation of their masculinities.

Chicano and Black Manhood

"Machismo" has been a central concept in the description of Chicanos' masculinity (Perez 1991, 163). In its most popularized form by the media and social science research, *machismo* refers to excessive masculinity based on the need to compensate for deep insecurities through the extreme dominance of women. Alfredo Mirandé indicates, however, that the mainstream popularized version of Chicanos' masculinity is not what men themselves perceive. In his research, based on oral life histories with Chicano men, the majority rejected the concept as a caricature, one that was detrimental both to men and women. But an essential part of machismo was the positive aspects of the masculinity it implied—honor, respect, responsibility, dignity, and bravery. Rather than machismo, the men aspired to *hombría*—manhood. In the words of the respondents interviewed by Mirandé:

> What it [machismo] means is that the person is responsible, helps to provide for the family and well-being of the family. . . .

> It's a man responsible for actions, a man of his word. . . . I think a *macho* does not have to be a statesman; just a man that's known to stand by his friends and follow through. A man of action relative to goals that benefit others, not himself.

> To me it refers to a code of ethics that I use to relate values in my life, and to evaluate myself in terms of my family, my job, my community. My belief is that if I live up to my code of ethics, I will gain respect from my family, my job, and my community. *Macho* has nothing to do with how much salsa you eat, how much beer you can drink, or how many women you fuck! . . . They have self-pride, they hold themselves as meaningful people. You can be *macho* as a farmworker or judge. It's a real mixture of pride and humility. Individualism is a part of it; self-awareness, self-consciousness, responsibility. (1988, 80–81)

While Chicano men have been characterized as acting domineering toward women and suffering from "macho extremis," Black men are portrayed, on the one hand, as being emasculated by their women and, on the other, as extremely violent, especially as they are represented in the "myth of the black rapist" (A. Y. Davis 1981, 172–201).[10] Whatever the distortions, both Chicano and Black men, as described in mainstream social science and the media, are sorely lacking in the characteristics of hegemonic (white) masculinity. In particular, they lack the ability to be respected civil subjects who can successfully navigate in the civil sphere and negotiate with the state to procure resources for their households:

> Under conditions of manhood confined to the ability to secure and guarantee economic well-being for self and family, Black men are for-

ever condemned to something less than "true manhood." Nor can blackwomen be "true" (private sphere) women, fulfilling images of female dependency, since the economic, political and social system is grounded on Black men and women's marginalization, denying well-being and security to all. The problem then is not what black women are saying, but what race, gender and class oppression are doing to all of us. (C. I. Harris 1993b, 787]

I contend that Chicano and Black men's masculinity is sabotaged to mute, in fact, their prerogative to power as men within a civil sphere. The state has incapacitated Chicano and Black men so that they cannot properly provide for their families (within a liberal conception of what constitutes legitimate social arrangements for productive participation in civil society). The imprisonment and undereducation of these men of Color effectively subverts their gender privilege and any trickle-down effects it may have on women from their respective groups. The crippling of these men's masculinist power further disenfranchises women in these ethnic/racial groups and puts their children at risk of genocide.[11] The latest toll is clearly documented in these youths' rates of incarceration, homicide, and death by drugs (Morganthau 1992, 20).[12] Even though there is a man in the state, that man is not brown or Black; it is a white man who is punishing brown and Black men more severely than any other group in this society.

The Derogation of Chicanas and Blacks' Womanhood

Supposedly, slavery and conquest (Castillo 1991, 34)[13] resulted in the emasculation of Black and Chicano men, which implies that the worst thing a man can be is like a woman.[14] This is not surprising given that what Chicana and Black women have endured historically is nothing to be desired. The derogation of the womanhood of Chicana and Black women resulted primarily from their men's inability to protect them, which left them vulnerable to sexual violence. A man's ability to rape without consequence is a measure of his power. Rape, within the slave culture and during war, was among the weapons of terror used by white men to remind Chicano and Black men of their inability to protect their women. As Robert Staples writes: "The rape of the slave woman brought home to the slave man his inability to protect his woman. Once his masculinization was undermined in this respect, he would begin to experience profound doubts about his power even to break the chains of bondage" (1973; quoted in hooks 1981, 22).

Chicano and Black women have, historically, been available to white men for the satisfaction and experimentation of their sexual violence. At the same time, these women are not valued as white women are because of their inability to produce white offspring[15] and because of their enormous value as laborers.[16] Consequently, their womanhood, from the dominant group's perspective has always been oversexualized, to the point of being portrayed as animalistic.[17] That is one of the reasons that interracial coupling between white men and women of Color has been seen as so abhorrent—it is seen as being cross-species, not cross-racial, coupling.[18]

Again, bell hooks points out that the emasculation of Black men during slavery (which continues to this day) has been overemphasized in historical accounts, in which women's experience is *never* as important as that of men. In fact, she argues that Black men were not so much emasculated as Black women were masculinized and perceived as "surrogate" men by white slave owners (1981, 23).[19] This is also true for large number of Chicanas who, because of economic necessity, have been forced to work in the fields picking crops and in canneries (Zavella 1987). hooks points as evidence to the fact that male slaves were not castrated in large numbers, nor were they made to perform "female" tasks or made to wear women's clothing—all of which were within the slave owner's prerogative and definitely would have decimated man's masculinity. The point to be made here, however, and that hooks does not pursue, is that Black men were indeed emasculated *in comparison* to white men's masculinity, which at its core is built around the protection of their women and offspring and, therefore, of their privilege. Black and Chicano men were not emasculated *in relationship* to women in their groups, but this point is irrelevant because such humiliation is beyond the acceptable realm of oppression.

The history of slavery and conquest made it impossible for Black and Chicano women to participate in the "cult of true womanhood" as defined by white hegemonic standards—in which a white woman was seen as fragile and in need of being taken care of by an able man. In fact, during Reconstruction (1867–77) Black women tried to dispel the stereotype that they were sexually loose by emulating the dress, conduct, and mannerisms of white women. They were accosted in public streets, subjected to lewd comments, and even physically assaulted by white men to remind them that "in the eyes of the white public she [they] would never be seen as worthy of respect" (hooks 1981, 55). The vilification of the womanhood of Chicanas and Black woman served the purpose of instilling terror in white woman by reminding them what could happen to them if they violated hegemonic standards of white femininity while simultaneously highlighting their privilege. bell hooks also indicates that the notion that Black women were masculinized, subhuman creatures was a necessary creation to avoid the question of how Black "women" could perform hard slave labor and remain "women" without white women eventually questioning the biological frailty of their sex. Therefore, the only viable explanation was to assert that Black women were not women and, therefore, not human (hooks 1981, 55).

The political movements of the 1960s provided an opportunity for these women to participate *as women* if the men in their groups could in fact be considered men by the dominant white political liberals who were redefining the boundaries of manhood.

Challenges to the Traditional Definitions of Manhood
in the 1960s

The challenge posed by educated white men in the antiwar movement precipitated a series of crises, many of them through violent encounters with authority figures, which provided what Janet Hart calls "political space" in which

> new resources, information, and ideological support from strategically placed allies are now available to groups to change their positions in the political hierarchy and, in some cases, to gain access to the political system for the first time. Whether or not new political space actually allows groups to fully realize their potential, political space makes the acquisition of power and prestige *possible*. . . . [W]ars and other apparent disasters may in retrospect provide a *narrative* opening for the political system: an opportunity for new political stories to be told featuring new plots and nontraditional characters acting in hitherto inconceivable settings. (1992, 640)

What these young white men were offering Chicano and Black men was an invitation to privilege. However, it was an invitation to a preestablished party in which the rules of conduct were already well set. The invitation was to a liberal vision with its masculinist underpinnings that, by its very nature, implied the subordination of women. Yet it was the best invitation these groups have received to date. And, indeed, it might have been the only true invitation that has ever been extended to these groups in the history of this country. There has never been any doubt about the sincerity of many of these young white men's dedication to social change and to the sincerity of their belief in their vision. There were other failures of this vision, but authenticity was not the main one.

At the time of the Civil Rights movement many educated white men rebelled against hegemonic white society and began to redefine manhood as consisting not merely of brute aggressive force used to impose their will on the rest of the world but perhaps of power that can be used to "lead," "direct," and "guide" the world into a more enlightened state in which (white) justice would prevail. The model of leadership was exemplified in the idealization of John F. Kennedy as a humane, cultured, masculine, compassionate, rational, and, above all, intelligent, young, and good-looking leader.[20]

At the core of the 1960s Civil Right's movement was a modernist vision of justice. Justice would be the result of equal participation by all people in society—hence, the emphasis on voting, election of officials, and procedural issues within the justice system. (An example was the emphasis placed on fighting the irregularities of police conduct in dealing with people of Color.) There were other variations in the political movements that advocated revolution and the overthrow of the government, but even these movements advocated a Marxist government that has as its core a modernist vision of the utopian society in which resources are allocated on a more rational basis—from each, according to his or her ability, to each, according to his or her need. There were rules to be followed that would result in a just society.

In a modernist view of justice the hard facts of life, such as class and race, are central to the analysis of oppression. They are tangible individual/group characteristics that can be seen as the basis for subordination. Other kinds of oppression were not as credible because they seemed to be natural categories of social life, such as gender, and in fact the biological functions of women overrode other kinds of considerations. Therefore, the reproduction of children and the chores that followed simply seemed the natural domain of all women. In fact, psychologizing oppression was contradictory to the aims of the political movements in the 1960s, in which "objective" oppression was the core of its analysis. Under this paradigm, therefore, it was impossible to interject an analysis that questioned the very categories on which the analysis was premised. There was a further safety valve when the pressure of the analysis grew unbearable—other concerns were perceived as detracting from the "main" struggle and as a regression to a romantic (and therefore bourgeoisie and corrupt) vision of society (Navarro 1991, 117; Echols 1992, 21). Under these circumstances women's complaints about the allocation of household chores were trivialized, and women of Color's desire for more leadership within their various movements was perceived as an imitation of the dominant (and unjust) existing political order.[21]

I argue that the 1960s political movements were basically modernist movements that aspired for liberation from archaic notions of conventionality and exalted the rights of individuals as human beings. Janet Hart argues that, further,

> Like any cultural system, modernism contained silences, blind spots, vanities, conflicts, hypocrisies. It was paradoxical in striving simultaneously for both freedom *and* limitation. Ironically, it was accused of being too revolutionary by the orthodox and not revolutionary enough by its various hard-liners (see Dolar 1991). Uncritical conceptions of gender, race, class, and the meaning of power took their toll. Like its Enlightenment model, the Eurocentric, androcentric, modernist impulse sometimes actually thwarted the advance of those it might logically have united with. Through neglect, snobbery, bigotry or even ruthlessness, it sometimes based its actions on discriminatory moral "imperatives." Driven by a philosophy of manifest destiny, it was often motivated by self-interest, sanctimony, and the desire to dominate rather than the avowed altruism. (1996, 45)

The 1960s movement toward Black liberation explicitly delineated roles for Black men and women. As bell hooks indicates: "Black male activists publicly acknowledged that they expected black women involved in the movement to conform to a sexist role pattern. . . . Black women were told that they should take care of household needs and breed warriors for the revolution" (1981, 5). The justification for the delineation of roles was to bolster the manhood of the men in these groups, which had been systematically decimated through economic and social oppression. Nonetheless, women in these movements were deeply aware of their inherent contradiction:

> Invariably, I hear from some dude that black women must be supportive and patient so that black men can regain their manhood. The notion of womanhood, they argue—and only if pressed to address themselves to the notion do they think of it or argue—is dependent on his defining his manhood. So the shit goes on. (Cade 1970, 107–8)

Women in the Chicano and Black Civil Rights movements were not silent about the restrictions that the men imposed on them (Fernández 1994, 30; Davis 1974, 159–60, 179–80, 374). Simultaneously, however, they came from a long line of political resisters who understood well the consequences of breaking ranks when they were so severely under attack by powerful institutions and repressive organizations such as the FBI and the local police (Davis 1974, 95). Their protests took place mostly within the group and many times took the form of artistic productions such as poetry and song, perhaps not so much to soften the blow but, rather, to camouflage the critique from the constant surveillance of the state. Take, for instance, the poetry written by Chicanas contemporaneously at the height of the Chicano movement. Evangelina Vigil directly addresses the men within Chicano communities:

para los que piensan con la verga
(with due apologies to those who do not)

lost cause:
ya no queda energía mental
y ni siquiera señas
del sincero deseo
de tratar de aliveanarle la mente
al hombre bien perdido
en el mundo de nalgas y calzones

se trata de viejos repusilvos
tapados con cobijas de
    asqueroso sexismo
agarrándose los huevos
a las escondidas
with brain cells
displaced/replaced
by sperm cells
concentrating:
pumping away

ya no queda energía mental

for those who think with their dick
(with due apologies to those who do not)

lost cause:
There is no mental energy left
and not even a trace
of sincere desire
to try to enlighten the mind
of the man lost
in the world of asses and
    underwear

it is a matter of repulsive men
covered with blankets of
    nauseating sexism
grabbing their balls
secretly
with brain cells
displaced/replaced
by sperm cells
concentrating:
pumping away

there is no mental energy left
(1982, 47)

Sexual liberation was an essential part of the political movements in the 1960s for white upper-middle-class students and for many white youth. For Chicanos, however, sexual liberation, although an undercurrent, was not as central. Sexual liberation was not central primarily because it was not seen as the root of Chicanos' social problems—economic issues were—and because culturally there were strong sanctions against indiscriminate sexual activity for women. Carlos Muñoz (1989, 7–8) defines the Chicano movement as encompassing the unionizing efforts of César Chávez with the farmworkers, the militant efforts of Reies López Tijerina to recapture the lands taken from Chicanos in the southwestern United States, and the political mobilization of Chicano students on university campuses across the United States:

> I define the Chicano student movement and the larger Chicano Power Movement as a quest for a new identity and for political power. The movement represented a new and radical departure from the politics of past generations of Mexican American activists. It called for new political institutions to take possible Chicano self-determination. As such it was a counter-hegemonic struggle and held certain of the characteristics of the New Left as defined by George Katsiaficas: it opposed racial, political and patriarchal domination and economic exploitation; it called for freedom from material deprivation and the freedom to create *La Nueva Raza*, a new people proud of their Mexican working-class culture; it called for the expansion of the democratic process and individual rights for Mexican Americans; and it emphasized direct political action.

Furthermore, most Chicanos involved in the Chicano movement, whether they were students or not, were from working-class backgrounds in which sexuality had not been repressed in the same way as it had been in white middle-class homes (Castillo 1991, 26–27).[22] The "unfettered" expression of sexuality by Chicano men in their communities took the manifestations of extreme harassment and interference with women becoming leaders. Consequently, "sexual liberation," although certainly occurring among many Chicano activists, also had its underside, as expressed in Vigil's poem—an underside that verged on what we later learned to call sexual harassment.

Even among highly politicized men, an overemphasis on seeing Chicanas as sexual providers also interfered with their full participation in the

Chicano movement. The same issues voiced by Evangelina Vigil echo in Lorna Dee Cervantes's poem "You Cramp My Style, Baby":

You cramp my style, baby
when you roll on top of me
shouting, "Viva La Raza"[23]
at the top of your prick.

You want me como un taco,
dripping grease,
or squeezing maza[24] through my legs,
making tamales for you out of my daughters.
You "mija"[25]
"mija" "mija" me
until I can scream

and then you tell me,
"Esa, I LOVE
this revolution!
Come on Malinche,[26]
gimme some more!"

In the first poem, by Vigil, the perpetrator ("the man lost in the world of asses and underwear") appears to be the older, and perhaps less politicized, male member of the Chicano community; in the Cervantes poem the perpetrator is obviously one of the in-group leaders of the movement. Cervantes effectively uses the political slogans of the Chicano movement to highlight the contradiction between the perpetrator's noble political goals for his community and his crass and somewhat brutal treatment of his female lover. Again, the critique is particularly effective because it is directed at those within the movement who are likely to understand the subtlety of the language and its ironic juxtaposition to the political goals all members of the Chicano movement are fighting for. The last sentence "Come on Malinche, gimme some more!" is an open indictment of the male's hypocrisy, since he reduces the female lover to a traitor for no apparent reason other than her sex.

Women in these political movements, aside from voicing their critique of the sexism in the groups, also opted for forming parallel organizations that would specifically address the concerns of women. Even then, however, these parallel organizations made explicit their commitment to the larger organizations and their solidarity with men. Take, for example, the women's group called La Federación de Mujeres del Partido Raza Unida, formed in 1975 as a parallel organization of the Raza Unida Party.[27] Their preamble states:

> *La Federación de Mujeres del Partido Raza Unida* does not view the men as the enemy but the system as being the oppressor. Our struggle is not a battle of the sexes but a common struggle for the true liberation alongside the men. The purpose of the Federación is to develop *La Mujer* into leadership position at A-1 levels of the *Partido*. . . . *La Federación* shall not be limited to only women but shall make every effort to involve men as well as educate them to the issues and needs of *La Mujer*. *La Raza Unida Party* is opposed to the domination of one sex by another and recognizes no distinction between men and women in the common leadership. Both women and men of *La Raza* must provide leadership. [Muñoz 1989, 117]

White women had similar tensions around gender issues in the political movements of the New Left. But, unlike many white feminists who opted, eventually, for splitting off from the men, most Chicana and Black women, with a few individual exceptions, never contemplated leaving their group, regardless of their dissatisfaction with the men's behavior. Instead, most have stayed and have continued to struggle through the gender issues that persist in most progressive groups.

Why Nationalism?

The political movements of the 1960s, including the Black Civil Rights movement and the Chicano movement, fit Janet Hart's description of a "leftist populism," in which charismatic leaders or social movements "seek to mobilize the political participation of strategic groups—some of them latent—in society" (1992, 646). An essential part of this strategy is to include people who traditionally have not been included in political mobilization—for example, women, children, and the elderly. The new actors go beyond the traditionally defined politicians, which reinforces the movement's claim that it is the "people" who should rule, not professional politicians. Political populism "is almost always ideologically linked by its exponents to nationalist appeals." The conception of nation, however, is "purposely kept indeterminate." In Hart's words:

> Leaders construct narrative frames creatively employing history and pithy cultural symbols to attract a cross section of the population while seeking to divert attention away from particularistic identities such as class, gender, region, ethnic group, or religion. Paradoxically, then, at the same time that influential "authors" are emplotting narratives based on inclusionary principles, localized concerns are viewed with suspicion. A generic "progressive person" is invented, to use Hobsbawm's term, or imagined, to use Anderson's, as an entity whose ultimate orientation is toward a slightly blurry utopian future. (1992, 646)

Both the Chicano movement and the Black Civil Rights movement did a magnificent job of fully creating the generic "progressive person" completely enculturated with the symbols of each of these groups' history, language, and culture. For activists in the Black Civil Rights movement it was finding the Black within the Negro,[28] as illustrated by Malcolm X's remarks:

> But the white man is misjudging the times and he is underestimating the American so-called Negro because we're living in a new day. Our people are now a new people. That old Uncle Tom-type Negro is dead. Our people have no more fear of anyone, no more fear of anything. We are not afraid to go to jail. We are not afraid to give our very life itself. And we're not afraid to take the lives of those who try to take our lives. We believe in a fair exchange.
> [*Applause*]
> We believe in a fair exchange. An eye for an eye. A tooth for a tooth. A head for a head and life for a life. If this is the price of freedom, we won't hesitate to pay the price.
> [*Applause*] (quoted in Perry 1989, 68]

The imagined person constructed by these groups exalted a preconquest, preslavery past, and also underscored the unimagined future in which conquest and slavery had not only been overthrown but in which the very elements of the conquerors' culture had been alchemically transformed.[29]

For Chicanos the concept of Aztlán, the mother land, and the creation of the Raza Cósmica represented this philosophical development built around political mobilization.[30] During the National Chicano Youth Liberation Conference in March 1969 participants drafted *El Plan Espiritual de Aztlán*. Its preamble states:

> In the spirit of a new people that is conscious not only of its proud historical heritage, but also of the brutal "Gringo" invasion of our territories, we, the Chicano inhabitants and civilizers of the northern land of Aztlán, from whence came our forefathers, reclaiming the land of their birth and consecrating the determination of our people of the sun, declare that the call of our blood is our power, our responsibility and our inevitable destiny. . . . Brotherhood unites us, and love for our brothers makes us a people whose time has come and who struggle against the foreigner "Gabacho" who exploits our riches and destroys our culture. . . . We are Bronze People with a Bronze Culture. . . . We are Aztlán. (Muñoz 1989, 77–78)

Muñoz goes on to define Aztlán as

> the name used by the Aztecs to refer to the place of their origin. Since the Aztecs had migrated to central Mexico from "somewhere in the north," Chicano activists claimed that Aztlán was all the southwestern United States taken from Mexico as a result of the Mexican-American War. This included California, Texas, New Mexico, most of Arizona, large parts of Colorado, Nevada and Utah, and a piece of Wyoming. (1989, 77)

In addition to it being a geographical region, "Aztlán symbolizes the spiritual union of the Chicanos, something that is carried within the heart, no matter where they may live or where they may find themselves" (Leal 1981, 18).

Essential in creating this imagined person were music, poetry and art; in fact, it was through the arts that the imagined person was presented to the folk, absorbed by them, and became part of the popular ethos. There was a constant effort in the Chicano and Black Civil Rights movements to incorporate community people in the intellectual developments of its mobilization efforts. For Chicanos El Teatro Campesino and offshoots of smaller *teatros* were very effective in communicating to working-class people why political mobilization was important and how to interpret their subordination to lead them to feeling more empowered. In fact, in many of these regional *teatros* the actors and members of the audience often changed roles throughout a play's development. The themes of these productions ranged from labor organizing and welfare rights to ending barrio warfare (Xavier 1983, 27). But the imagined person, by its very definition, was gendered in such a way that it reproduced the existing man-woman hierarchies existing in society at large. This was not unusual. Male domination of ethnic/racial movements was the result of existing patriarchal structures in all ethnic/racial groups but with cultural and historical specificity. The white political movements of the 1960s also had an imagined ideal that was gendered: for many white leftist men it was embodied in the persona and work of the sociologist C. Wright Mills, and for many white feminists it was embodied in the writer Simone de Beauvoir, for her work and her unconventional relationship with the philosopher Jean-Paul Sartre (Echols 1992, 23). Tom Hayden explicitly states Mills's influence on his own political development:

> Here I fell under the powerful influence of the heretic sociologist C. Wright Mills. . . . Mills defied the drabness of academic life and quickly became the oracle of the New Left, combining the rebel lifestyle of James Dean and the moral passion of Albert Camus, with the comprehensive portrayal of the American condition we were all looking for. Mills died in his early forties of a heart attack during the very spring I was drafting *The Port Huron Statement*, before any of us had a chance to meet him, making him forever a martyr to the movement. (1989, 77–78)

The imagined person for Chicanos and Blacks embodied what the political activists perceived as their groups' most valuable characteristics. Consequently, it is not surprising that nationalism was a strong undercurrent in their political mobilization efforts. Although the nationalist argument has enormous appeal among the working class, ironically, its essence pulls at the heartstrings of those who grew up in a barrio, who had parents who were farmworkers, and who have "made it" in the white world—precisely, those who are likely to pose a challenge to its logic. The nationalist rhetoric appeals to the most educated in these groups because the promise of the American dream rarely comes without an enormous psychic cost.[31] The nationalist rhetoric is full of passion, love, and idealism in a modern framework in which the "hard" facts of life like food and having a roof over one's head are the primary basis for political solidarity. It is precisely because of its appeal that it is blasphemous for a group member to dissect a nationalist rhetoric outside the confines of the group. It is not out of paranoia but, rather, group survival that criticism of the group is confined to its members. But for an outsider it is difficult to understand the intoxicating effervescence of a nationalist perspective without a small sampling of its enervating logic. Although there is a strong intellectual and philosophical basis for a nationalist argument, much of the undergirding of its rhetoric is full of emotion and religion—religion both in its traditional sense (e.g., as a universal system to guide individual behavior) and as a spiritual quest for the restoration of the humanity of the oppressed. A prime example of this perspective is Malcolm X, whose conversion to Islam represents both a spiritual quest and a political commitment to fight racism:

> Somebody's got nerve enough, some whites have the audacity, to refer to me as a hate teacher. If I'm teaching someone to hate, I'm teaching them to hate the Ku Klux Klan. But here and in America they have taught us to hate ourselves. To hate our skin, to hate our hair, to hate our features, hate our blood, hate what we are. Why, Uncle Sam is a master hate-teacher, so much so that he makes someone think he's teaching law when he's teaching hate. When you've made a man hate himself, you've really got it and gone. (Malcolm X 1970, 181)

Both the Black Civil Rights movement and the Chicano movement have a strong religious tradition that put them at odds with other secularly based political movements of the 1960s such as the New Left and the white Women's movement.[32] To be sure, there was diversity of commitment to religious goals among Black and Chicano activists; nonetheless, there was almost a universal sense of commitment to the spiritual and moral fight against racism.[33]

The religious underpinnings of most mobilization efforts by Blacks and Chicanos still remain. Consequently, women in these groups may still be at odds with the current white feminist movement because of its modern origins, especially with its secular emphasis on women's individual rights as human beings. The clash between a religious and secular core in political mobilization is especially salient around women's reproductive rights. Whereas for white feminists control over their bodies has been central to a feminist agenda, for feminists of Color curtailing reproduction has been filled with contradictory desires. On the one hand, feminists of Color recognize that having fewer children frees women to realize their potential in various arenas; on the other, they are keenly aware of their history of genocide and forced sterilization (Hernández 1976; Del Castillo 1980). Furthermore, religious commitment as part of cultural history (not necessarily religious dogma)[34] makes feelings about abortion extremely complex. It also brings up contradictions around extended family issues because, for racial/ethnic groups of Color, the entire community is family, not just their immediate nuclear family (Davis 1974; Muñoz and Barrera 1982). The Chicano movement and to a certain extent the Black Civil Rights movement were based on the notion of familial solidarity. As Zavella indicates:

> In contrast to the women's movement, the Chicana movement placed a high value on families. *La familia* and *"carnalismo"*—the generic male brotherhood—were central values of Chicano movement ideology. Important struggles within the Chicano movement, such as the union-ization drive by the United Farm Workers recruited women who became strong leaders and encouraged participation in the union by the entire family. Chicano movement ideology used the family to sym-bolize our need for unity, strength, and struggle within adversity. Some Chicanas did feel ambivalent about the implicit male dominance within the symbolism of *la familia*. But the fervor of nationalist ideol-ogy guiding the Chicano movement precluded attempts by Chicana activists to denounce sexism within the movement or to point out Chi-canas' subordination within Chicano families. . . . Thus, during a time when white feminists were recognizing the tyranny of the traditional family, Chicana activists were celebrating the unity of traditional Chi-cano families. Moreover, at a time when white feminists were demanding reproductive rights, including the right to abortions, Chi-cana activists were fighting forced sterilizations and defending the right to bear children. (1988, 124–25)[35]

Therefore, historically, white women have been encouraged to procreate,[36] while women of Color have been encouraged to become sterilized[37] and their children are seen as expendable—most recently in the drug and gang wars.

Nationalist movements' primary tactic for political mobilization is to use cultural production to stir the populace into action (Alurista 1975, 23). Of course, the Chicano and Black movements did not have precisely engineered principles. Instead, mobilization strategies emerged from the folk, and the resulting utopia exalted the characteristics of the working-class *in comparison* to the characteristics of the better-off dominant whites. A prime example within the Chicano movement was El Teatro Campesino, led by its founder, Luis Valdez:

> What is Chicano theater? It is theater as beautiful, rasquache,[38] human, cosmic, broad, deep, tragic, comic, as the life of *La Raza* itself. At its high point Chicano theater is religion—the huelguistas [strikers] de Delano praying at the shrine of the *Virgen de Guadalupe*, located in the rear of an old station wagon parked across the road from DiGiorgio's camp #4;[39] at its low point, it is a cuento [tale] or a chiste [joke] told somewhere in the recesses of the barrio, puro pedo.[40] . . . Chicano theater, then, is first a reaffirmation of LIFE. That is what all theater is supposed to be, of course; but the limp, superficial, gringo seco[41] productions in the "professional" American theater (and the college and university drama departments that serve it) are so antiseptic, they are antibiotic (anti-life). The characteristics and life situations emerging from our little teatros are too real, too full of sudor [sweat], sangre [blood], and body smells to be boxed in. Audience participation is not cute production trick with us; it is a pre-established pre-assumed privilege. "Que suenen la campanita!"[42]

Unlike the New Left and the white Women's movement, the leaders of the Chicano and the Black movements were not predominantly from the educated elite.[43] Consequently, their imagined person emphasized the working-class characteristics of these ethnic/racial groups. Even the students who participated in these movements came from working-class backgrounds and many times were the first in their families to attend higher education.[44] The political rhetoric that developed in the Chicano and the Black Civil Rights movements reflected these historical and structural underpinnings. Also, the rhetoric not only emerged from the folk, but it had to make sense to the folk. The pedagogy used to reach them relied on analogies and political fables. The result was some of the most brilliant deconstruction of racist rhetoric, which had an overwhelming logic and vehemence that moved working-class communities to the core. It was not surprising, then, that many of the educated elite, both of Color and white, were similarly moved and mobilized like never before. A particularly effective strategy in this type of political mobilizing was to take an accusation from the dominant group and turn it on its head to high-light the illogic of the accusation to begin with. Malcolm X was a master-ful user of this technique, as in his response to the accusation from some whites that he was an *extremist* unlike Martin Luther King, who was "rea-sonable":

> My reason for believing in extremism, intelligently directed extrem-ism, extremism in defense of liberty, extremism in quest of liberty, is because I firmly believe in my heart that the day that the black man takes an uncompromising step and realizes that he's within his rights, when his own freedom is being jeopardized, to use any means neces-sary to bring about his freedom or put a halt to that injustice, I don't think he'll be by himself. I live in America where there are only 22 mil-lion blacks, against probably 160 million whites. One of the reasons why I'm in no way reluctant or hesitant to do whatever is necessary to see that blacks do something to protect themselves is I honestly believe that the day they do, many whites will have more respect for them, and there will be more whites on their side than are now on their side with these little wishy-washy love-thy-enemy approaches that they've been using up to now. (1970, 177)[45]

Despite the cultural and historical specificity of each of these move-ments, there were several political and social issues on which all of them intersected. One of them was the adamant opposition to the Vietnam War; second, the commitment to a more equitable distribution of wealth; and, third, the conviction that the existing power structure was illegitimate. There were also some core differences—for example, about the importance of personal freedom, the means by which to accomplish their goals, and the prioritizing of these goals. For example, the Chicano movement, like the New Left, rejected war as a viable mechanism for reinforcing manhood and acceptance into the white mainstream. El Teatro Campesino, as a voice of the militant Chicano community, produced several plays that denounced participation in the Vietnam War as nothing more than brainwashing by the dominant society. (Frischmann 1982, 262–63)

> The war in Vietnam continues, asesinando familias inocentes de campesinos. Los Chicanos mueren en la guerra, y los rancheros se hacen ricos, selling their scab products to the Pentagon. The fight is here, *Raza! En Aztlán.* [The war in Vietnam continues to kill innocent

farmworker families. Chicanos die in war, and the ranchers get richer, selling their scab products to the Pentagon. The fight is here, Raza! In Aztlán.] (Valdez 1971, 130)

Also noteworthy was the Chicano Moratorium organized in Los Angeles on 29 August 1970, which drew over thirty thousand to protest the war in Vietnam and the disproportionately high rate of Chicano war casualties. The protest turned violent, and three people were shot by Los Angeles police (Gómez-Quiñones 1990, 124–28).

Despite these political movements' similar goals and devotion, there was very little collaboration and formal coalition building from which a stronger and more integrated movement could emerge.[46]

The Reconstitution of Manhood in the 1960s: Redefinition for White Men and Restitution for Men of Color

Oddly enough, the political movements of the 1960s provided educated white men the opportunity to redefine their manhood away from "the domesticated, attenuated sort of masculinity critiqued by William Whyte in his book, *Organization Man*," to an "untamed masculinity—one which took risks and dared to gamble," as embodied in Black men (Echols 1992, 16). Black men's masculinity was perceived as "unencumbered by domestic constraints, and therefore somehow more authentically masculine" (17). The appropriation by educated white men of "a 'black' style, may also have helped destabilize racial boundaries in the United States" (12).

On the other hand, Chicano and Black men were trying to appropriate that aspect of hegemonic masculinity that allowed them to exert power and responsibility on behalf of their families and communities. Manliness was intimately tied to fighting for justice on behalf of the oppressed and against the rich and powerful. César Chávez explicitly tied manhood with morality and the commitment to fight for family, religion, and community within a specifically Chicano framework. After his twenty-five day fast in which he attracted national attention, and which was broken in the presence of Robert Kennedy, his public statement read:

Our struggle is not easy. . . . Those who oppose our cause are rich and powerful, and they have many allies in high places. We are poor. Our allies are few. But we have something the rich do not own. We have our own bodies and spirits and the justice of our cause as our weapons. . . . I am convinced that the truest act of courage, the strongest act of manliness is to sacrifice ourselves for others in a totally non-violent struggle for justice. To be a man is to suffer for others. God help us to be men! (Levy 1975, 286)

This cross-genderizing was also happening with women in these political movements. Alice Echols (1992, 18) explores Sara Evans's *Personal Politics* in concluding that "while ERAP [Economic Research and Action Projects] women were attracted to the self-sufficiency and assertiveness of neighborhood women, the men were often drawn to the renegade and antidomestic masculinity of the most marginal men"[47] (1992, 17). Echols rightly points out that the cross-genderizing emulation was based on what each group imagined the other group to be and not based on actual in-depth knowledge based on intimate cross-racial social interaction.

Regardless of the motivation of these white men, I do not want to demean in any way their ideals. In fact, these white men were traitors to their inherited privilege and ideologically (if not in practice) supported ethnic/racial movements, which were also male dominated. I say white men because we still have not fully grasped the significance of white women's participation or the participation in these political movements of other ethnic/racial groups (Martínez 1989; Echols 1992). As gendered as the student and Civil Rights movements were, everybody, both men and women, behaved in extraordinary ways. In fact, one of the factors that made these times extraordinary is the renunciation of privilege that many of these people willingly submitted themselves to for the sake of collective goals. The renunciation, of course, was not entirely selfless, especially for white men, as the definition of manhood require that they not be soldiers but leaders, and, if soldiers, they were generals in waiting.[48] Nonetheless, as illustrated in Tom Hayden's autobiography, these white men tried to live by their ideals. They actually moved into the communities they were trying to organize and experienced some of the deprivation that their constituencies had to endure all their lives. So, like Kennedy, who could have lived a life of luxury, Hayden too renounced his inherited privilege for the sake of public service (Bailey 1993).

The redefinition of manhood around progressive political mobilization also entailed the liberalizing of sexual attitudes for both men and women. In theory everybody was a human being ("all men are created equal") with a right to his or her own body and mind and the right to the pursuit of happiness. Women, or white women, were also included in this category in theory, but in practice it was another matter. In theory white women could and did participate in political activity and became sexually liberated, though in practice they were still responsible for "women's work" (Echols 1989), which now included activities related to political mobilization but those that had always been done by women—for example, typing, cleaning up, and child care. Thus, the redefinition of white manhood did not include a radical restructuring of gendered labor in practice, although there were some promising starts in theory, some of which were written down.[49] The modernist vision of justice was appealing to white men and women because, potentially, all human beings would have equal rights. In practice the gendered understructure of that vision ultimately destroyed the potential alliance between white men and white women and spun off one of the most powerful political movements of this century—the white Women's movement. Meanwhile, the nationalist appeal for Blacks and Chicanos had a strong emotional pull because at its core it advocated empowerment for historically oppressed communities and, at least theoretically, for both men and women and, most important, for future generations (Davis 1974; Fernández 1994, 25). But, again, the masculinist underpinnings of nationalism prevented men activists in the movements from addressing gender issues, and, ultimately, the movements were unable to develop and grow into a more sophisticated analysis. Women of Color, however, did not leave their respective movements but, instead, built pockets of mobilizations around gender issues[50] and continued to struggle with men on behalf of their communities.

At the same time that the student and Civil Rights movements were sweeping the country, there were other groups mobilizing; among them were Chicanos, predominantly in the southwestern United States, with such leaders as César Chávez, Reies López Tijerina and Rudy Acuña. They, too, were adhering to this radical redefinition of manhood. The redefinition of white manhood provided an aperture for men of Color to claim they could lead their own communities. Unfortunately, they adopted models of leadership similar to that of white men, which entailed maintaining the gendered division of labor. In fact, the gendered division of labor and the coalition between progressive white leftists and student organizers lifted men of Color to positions of leadership equal to them, in practice, making the composition of political movements at the national scale more integrated than ever before.

This was a radical change. By being leaders of their own communities, becoming visible at the national level, and negotiating with the highest levels of government, men of Color were validated as men and, by implication, as human beings. In fact, President Kennedy, an icon of the 1960s, started this history-breaking gesture in 1960 when he declared his candidacy and soon after called for help from Ralph Guzmán and other Mexican American leaders and professionals. As Carlos Muñoz points out:

> The Kennedy campaign thus marked the entry of this leadership into national politics. They [Mexican American leaders] played an important role in the campaigning through the Viva Kennedy Clubs and they became visible as well in middle-class organizations. Most important, it marked the beginning of a new era of politics that was to eventually produce the Chicano Generation: Mexican American student activists who would embark upon a new quest for identity and power characterized by a militant and radical politics. (1989, 50)

An essential part of this definition as men was that women of Color enact their womanhood as defined by hegemonic standards, which at the time were predominantly white. To question the sexism of men of Color in public would have been to tear down not so much their manhood but their chance to be fully human, perhaps for the first time in the history of this country. The possibility of being human was also very attractive to women of Color because hegemonic definitions of gender roles entailed that men take care of women and children, at least financially. This would have relieved an enormous burden from women of Color, who did not only have to work a second shift but actually have been perceived historically as beasts of burden—exploited for their labor as well as for their sexuality. Therefore, that they would be considered women brought them a step closer to being human beings, with the privileges and considerations that entailed. Yet many women of Color were not enticed by the potential privileges of seduction and questioned these gendered arrangements within their own communities, either through political action or in the form of artistic productions such as poetry, whose influence would not be widespread nor likely to be picked up by the mainstream media.

Thus, the solidarity between women of Color and men of Color was based on, and continues to be, a common fight for the recognition of their humanity, not only by the dominant group but by each other. The tension between men of Color and women of Color has resurfaced recently as white feminists and feminists of Color have formed alliances and as women of Color's intellectual production has been recognized and cele-brated[51]—and as women of Color scholars have broadened the topics of their inquiry to include gender subordination within their own communi-ties. At times this intellectual production has been perceived by both men and women of Color as treason, not so much as we conceive of treason in the conventional sense but as an act that may lead to the demise of their communities or, worse yet, to erode the little advancement ethnic/racial groups have made in convincing others, and perhaps ourselves, that indeed we are human.

Conclusion: Implications for Political Mobilization

The Failure of the Eternal Masculine

However extraordinary the political movements of the 1960s were and how much their aura continues to haunt us, especially for those of us who believed in their magic to transform society, they were doomed to fail. Masculinist politics insure failure because of their overreliance on domina-tion. Masculine-based politics are also exclusionary by definition because the absence of testosterone is always perceived as an unmendable flaw that condemns women to an inferior status on the basis of biology. Their essen-tialist definition of gender makes even masculinized women not good enough and gay men not masculine enough.[52] As Kimmel points out, "immigrant men, homosexual men, and black men were all tainted with the same problem: they were not properly manly. Some were unable to exercise manly self-control over primitive impulses, others were overly refined and effeminate; both effeminacy and primitivism were indications of insufficient manhood" (1993, 32). Put more directly, Connell asserts that hegemonic masculinity (a public model of masculinity that may not be what most men are but is generally a model consented to) is constructed in opposition to homosexuality and also prevents other subordinated masculine identities from gaining cultural definition.[53] Ultimately, the exclusionary nature of masculinist politics makes them reactionary and conservative.

Masculinist politics, however, are not the only politics that are conservative; the problem is not the exclusive domain of only one dominant group. Rather, if oppression is relational rather than an inherent character-istic of well-defined social groups, then all members of society have the potential for enforcing their privilege within a particular context. The ques-tion is how to theorize about oppression, and therefore about liberation, in a relational manner that takes the theorizer's privilege into account.

The solidarity between Black and Chicano men and women during the political movements of the 1960s—a solidarity that persists to the present—has to be understood in the context of these historical dynamics based on relational oppression. Otherwise, it is not clear why men and women in these groups have not experienced the same political splits as white men and women in the New Left. Furthermore, if these exciting and humane times are going to teach us a lesson for the future, the participation of all the groups involved has to be fully documented for the lessons to apply. Of utmost importance to this project will be the future documenta-tion and analysis of other ethnic/political movements, such as those of Native Americans and Asian Americans, that were also integral to political mobilization of this era.

The 1960s as Linkage

Unfortunately, the studies of the 1960s have not analyzed, in depth, the linkages among the political mobilization activities happening during that time. Ironically, the existing analyses have inadvertently reproduced the class and race hierarchies present in U.S. society. Even though it is the rad-icals of the 1960s who have written these accounts, both white men and white women have excluded other ethnic/racial groups from their analy-ses;[54] Black and Chicano men have excluded women of Color;[55] and women of Color have minimally documented their presence in these movements (E. Brown 1992; A. Y. Davis 1974; among a few others).[56] These are not motivated biases but simply a testimony to the strength of struc-tural hierarchies. For example, Elizabeth Martínez asserts that the reason leaders of the Chicano movement have not written their accounts, in com-parison to say Tom Hayden and Todd Gitlin, is because the main leaders of the movement, the Big Four, as she calls them—Chávez, "Corky" Gonzalez, Gutierrez, and Tijerina—(Gutierrez being a notable exception) lack formal education, knowledge of English, "an adequate self-image, and the contacts to get a book published . . . all of them [handicaps] with roots in racism" (1989, 51). And even when the Black Civil Rights movement is discussed extensively in white-authored books about the 1960s, the discussion of the Movement is not presented as central to the era but, rather, as happening *along with* the white student movement. In Martínez's words, it is "pigeonholed, not germane to society as a whole; by implication it is separate and unequal" (49–50).

Whether the studies of the 1960s covered all of the political mobilization activities occurring during the time or not, the fact remains that these were extraordinary times with extraordinary actions happening on a daily basis (Davis 1974). Martínez offers a small but rich sampling of the events: the Puerto Rican Socialist Party's stand against the Vietnam War; the 1968 massive walkouts by high school Chicano students in Los Angeles; the Filipino farmworkers' strike in 1965, even before the Chicano strike in Delano, California; the Chinatown-Manilatown draft counseling project; the "Yellow Identity movement" of Chinese and other Asian students at universities in California and New York City; the Red Guard community-based youth organization; the eight-year struggle to save the International Hotel for elderly Asians in San Francisco; the Third World student strikes in 1968–69; the occupation of Alcatraz in 1967–69, which dramatized the Indian land struggle; the American Indian movement, which resulted in framing Leonard Peltier; and the armed occupation of Wounded Knee (ibid., 49–50). This is a sampling, not an exhaustive list, of events and actors in direct confrontation with oppressive structures. And yet their lessons and their worldviews remain mostly undocumented and therefore fail to inform our present struggles.

In spite of the simultaneous mobilization that took place in the 1960s, and the similar goals and struggles, the lack of direct contact between different ethnic/racial groups has resulted in the persistence of stereotypes among them. Martínez points out that Mexicans are still perceived as some form of debased white who is happy "snoozing next to a cactus, eating greasy food, always late and disorganized, rolling big Carmen Miranda eyes, shrugging with self-deprecation 'me not speek good engleesh,' perhaps engaged in petty theft" (ibid., 51). The social consequence is that Chicanos have been psychologically *invisibilized*.

The political consequence has been that they ignored the lessons that these "debased whites" can offer around mobilizing their communities. Instead, the model of political analysis that persists among progressive whites is one of extreme ethnocentrism and sexism that automatically excludes the knowledge of ethnic/racial struggles. It is so ethnocentric that, when white progressives fail to mobilize nonwhite ethnic/racial communities, it leads to a nihilist position of "nothing can be done." In the meantime there are successful community efforts that remain outside the lens of the progressive mainstream; consequently, they do not exist. John Brown Childs documents the successful Justice "Gang Truce" Summit that met in Kansas City in 1993 (1994, 50). The summit brought together gang members, community activists, and spiritual leaders from Latino, African American, and indigenous communities with the goal of promoting peace and justice across ethnic/racial lines. This event went largely unnoticed by the mainstream media, and its spirit of cooperation was barely highlighted on television or print reports; instead, the usual images presented to us are of warring gangs with no possibility of peaceful cooperation (Hurtado 1993, 47–57).

The reality of the political movements of the 1960s is that whether the different movements had formal and planned interaction between them was irrelevant because simply existing within the same period, with intense media coverage, resulted in a shared osmosis of political tactics. That is, although the mutual influence has been left largely unexamined, the fact remains that political movements have learned a great deal from one another. For example, as Martínez points out, white radicals learned concepts and tactics from Blacks, who learned from Asians (Gandhi), and from white workers of an earlier era (1989, 52). In addition, Native Americans borrowed tactics from Blacks, and so did Chicanos, who copied breakfast programs from the Black Panther Party. Asian Americans, in turn, were inspired by Puerto Rican activists.

What would a nonmasculinist multicultural politics look like? We do not know. The apartheid that has persisted in the analysis of the 1960s means there is much still to be mined from these extraordinary times; however, feminist deconstructions of masculinity provide some cornerstones of what these new politics would entail (Ramazanoglu 1992, 345). First, we have to fully analyze the *power* basis of masculinity (Rausing 1991), rather than emphasizing the deconstruction around identity and the disadvantages and interpersonal pain of masculinity. Second, the analysis of power has to lead to a radical politics of dismantling privilege, not of reconstituting manhood while leaving its privilege untouched but simply renewed and improved (Canaan and Griffin 1990). Third, subordinated masculinities, including homosexuality, have to be an integral part of the analysis for the "new man" to be fully representative of the diversity that already exists but is submerged by a hegemonic white masculinity (Ramazanoglu 1992, 346). And, finally, of foremost importance will be the active engagement with culturally diverse groups *at an intimate level* so that the mutual lessons are the result not of what each ethnic/racial groups imagines the other to be but, rather, of what they are. How will this be accomplished? Nobody knows, because it has not been done before on a mass scale. There are, however, already grassroots efforts to work across ethnic/racial lines to develop "transcommunality," which John Brown Childs conceptualizes as the highest stage of multiculturalism (1994, 49). Transcommunality is the ability of individuals to communicate and work across ethnic/racial lines without obliterating their own ethnic/racial distinctiveness. What can frighten dominant groups the most are potential alliances between grassroots movements across national or racial lines. As soon as we move away from feeling that racism and sexism (as well as other *isms*) are "interest group" politics, the sooner we can see them as "lethal poison(s) in the spirit and the body of our entire society" (Martínez 1989, 52). Egalitarian collaboration among progressive and politically engaged groups will be the greatest challenge—perhaps as great a challenge as those experienced by political mobilization movements in the 1960s.

CHAPTER 4

On a Reflexive Theory of Gender Subordination

My work requires me to think about how free I can be as an African-American woman writer in my genderized, sexualized, wholly racialized world. To think about (and wrestle with) the full implications of my situation leads me to consider what happens when other writers work in a highly and historically racialized society. For them, as for me, imagining is not merely looking or looking at; nor is it taking oneself intact into the other. It is, for the purposes of the work, *becoming.*

—Toni Morrison*

The Problem

Toni Morrison writes that, in reading literary works, the reader not only becomes engaged but also *watches* what is being read all at the same time. As a reader, she had been struck by how pervasive the use of Black images and people was in expressive prose and "in the shorthand, the taken-for-granted assumptions that lie in their usage . . . the sources of the images and the effect they have on the literary imagination and its product." She goes on to explain that the main reason this matters to her is because she, as an African American woman, does not have the same access to these traditionally useful constructs of blackness. She says:

> Neither blackness nor "people of color" stimulates in me notions of excessive, limitless love, anarchy, or routine dread. I cannot rely on these metaphorical shortcuts because I am a black writer struggling with and through a language that can powerfully evoke and enforce hidden signs of racial superiority, cultural hegemony, and dismissive "othering" of people. . . . My vulnerability would lie in romanticizing blackness rather than demonizing it; vilifying whiteness rather than reifying it. The kind of work I always wanted to do requires me to learn how to maneuver ways to free up the language from its some-

---

* The epigraph is taken from Morrison 1992, 4.

times sinister, frequently lazy, almost always predictable employment of racially informed and determined chains. (Morrison 1992, xi)

The intrinsic racism in our language is not completely conscious, and therefore, it requires our watching what we read while simultaneously being engaged. The use of a language, which by its very nature racializes, is not the only thing that limits our imaginations in conceiving of nonracist worlds; how we write about race also restricts what may be possible in the world if we could redistribute power.

In this chapter I contend that we have not integrated privilege in our explorations of racializing processes. We have explored and meticulously documented the effects of oppression on its victims. The victims of racism and sexism have borne powerful testimony to their injuries and their resilience, but we have yet to chronicle how those who oppress make sense of their power *in relationship* to those they have injured. We are all potentially in the oppressor category, because whether we have power over others varies from context to context and is primarily determined by race, class, and gender. Yet we do not even have the language to speak about how those who oppress—how they feel about, think about, react to, make sense of, come to terms with, maintain privilege over, and ultimately renounce the power to oppress. The missing part of the puzzle in dismantling domination is integrating at the core a reflexive mechanism for understanding how we are all involved in the dirty process of racializing and gendering others, limiting who they are and who they can become.

Precedents for a Reflexive Theory of Oppression

> Feminists have stakes in a successor science project that offers a more adequate, richer, better account of a world, in order to live in it well and in critical, reflexive relation to our own as well as others' practices of domination and the unequal parts of privilege and oppression that make up all positions. . . . So, I think my problem, and "our" problem, is how to have *simultaneously* an account of radical historical contingency for all knowledge claims and knowing subjects . . . a no-nonsense commitment to faithful accounts of a "real" world, one that can be partially shared and that is friendly to earthwide projects of freedom, adequate material abundance, modest meaning in suffering, and limited happiness.
> —Haraway 1988, 579

A cornerstone of a feminist paradigm is the importance of experience in the definition and acquisition of knowledge. Although there are a variety of feminist methods, and varying points of view on what constitutes feminist paradigms, valuing women's experience of their social reality is most important. Feminist paradigms and methods are not uncontested, but their critique takes place within a feminist epistemology that emphasizes listening to women's experience as a basis for remapping social reality. The same is not true of a Western, positivist (masculinist) tradition. Unlike Western male traditions, in which the acquisition of knowledge is based on the reification of others' experience with very little disclosure on the part of the writer, a feminist epistomology makes the narrator, the generator of knowledge, central to understanding that knowledge. In fact, it is the other's experience that constitutes knowledge. Furthermore, there are no fixed hierarchies in terms of whose experience is more valid; if an actor believes it is significant, then it is. A linear Western tradition would argue that this leads to an intellectual cul-de-sac in which nothing can be known because we cannot generalize across diverse experiences.[1] But the intention of a feminist epistomology is quite the opposite. The guiding assumption is that disclosure and validation lead to a unity of experience that constitutes women's ways of knowing (Belenky et al., 1986). Women's condition is so similar because of their gender that many other barriers will melt away as a result of this unconditional listening to one another's experiences. Feminists as diverse as Catherine MacKinnon, Annie Oakley, and Adrienne Rich advocate the validation of women's experiences. In Christine Littleton's words: "Feminist method starts with the very radical act of taking women seriously, believing that what we say about ourselves and our experience is important and valid, even when (or perhaps especially when) it has little or no relationship to what has been or is being said *about* us" (1989, 764).

A further development in feminist epistemology is Haraway's assertion that listening to different women's experiences does not result in chaos but in a more egalitarian and textured view of reality:

"All these pictures of the world should not be allegories of infinite mobility and interchangeability but of elaborate specificity and difference and the loving care people might take to learn how to see faithfully from another's point of view, even when the other is our own machine. That's not alienating distance; that's a *possible* allegory for feminist versions of objectivity. Understanding how these visual systems work, technically, socially, and psychically, ought to be a way of embodying feminist objectivity" (1988, 583)

What is appealing about a feminist epistomology, whether it is built by white women or women of Color, is the struggle to focus on the sanctity of life and the recognition that humans should not be oppressed. Whereas a Western intellectual tradition specifies the conditions under which privilege should be allocated, a feminist epistomology assumes that oppression is unnecessary. As Donna Haraway reminds us "What money does in the exchange orders of capitalism, reductionism does in the power mental orders of global sciences. There is, finally, only one equation. That is the deadly fantasy that feminists and others have identified in some versions of objectivity, those in the service of hierarchical and positivist orderings of what can count as knowledge. That is one of the reasons the debates about objectivity matter, metaphorically and otherwise. Immortality and omnipotence are not our goals" (1988, 580). Furthermore, within a Western tradition the assumption is that the oppressed should be the object of pity for the more enlightened, more educated folk. The notion that these "others" may have their own subjectivity and, in fact, see the privileged as deserving of pity (or ridicule) is inconceivable (Hurtado 1996).

From a competitive, masculinist Western perspective where equality regardless of "difference" is inconceivable, any group-based political mobilization is perceived as interest group politics, rather than sincere investment in having a better world for everybody, not just for particular groups. There is a reluctance to deconstruct privilege—it is almost a psychological impossibility. A Western male intellectual tradition cannot theorize from a position of privilege but, rather, one of victimhood, because paternalism is the only viable political solution that leaves the status quo untouched. Superior groups remain superior, and victims are inferior and therefore have to be rescued out of the benevolence of the dominant group, whose power remains unquestioned and therefore superior.

A case in point is white men's studies. The white Men's movement has usurped the language of victimhood. The questioning of manhood by Robert Bly (1990) and others exalts the drawbacks of power, which produces indescribable wounds unbeknown to subordinates, who do not have to deal with its burdens. There are also those, more progressive than Bly, who question manhood's privileges in the subordination of others, including other men who do not adhere to its rules, but their reference point is other (mostly white) men (Stoltenberg 1993). It is a dialogue among the powerful, not a dialogue *with* the recipients of that power—women and some men of Color. In this analysis there is a necessary suspension of the relationship between those with power and those without it, in order for the internal questioning to take place.

Analyses of manhood from this progressive perspective often focus, however, on manhood "as an act" or an "enactment" (ibid., 2–3). Such an approach is valuable in documenting the contours of behavior and values that have become so natural that they are invisible. Yet the deconstruction of enactment does not address the ultimate purpose of manhood: to maintain privilege over others—privilege not only in terms of enhancement, if not exaltation, of self but also material privilege, which allows men to earn more money, have more choices, and have less tedious and less monotonous work than women (for whom it is often unpaid work). Enactment, although interesting to study in an evolutionary kind of way, is irrelevant to power. It alone does not bring power; power has to already have been allocated to this particular group of people, men, before the enactment of manhood can have any meaning. It is also why men are attracted to the enactment of manhood—because there are enormous tangible rewards that go beyond the enhancement of oneself through the subordination of others. Another outcome of this analysis is that men learn to become accountable *interpersonally* to those around them for their transgressions (ibid., 16–18), and in many ways the prescription given for this accountability is a throwback to when manhood also implied chivalry, justice, and wisdom.[2] All of these prescriptions are commendable but leave unexamined the dynamics of power and its redistribution. Their main outcome are modifications of interpersonal relationships, but they leave structural forces largely unexamined; they are part of a benign humanism that is badly needed but that will be insufficient for a revolutionary change in the distribution of power.

The part of this analysis within men's studies that does relate to power has to do with the intrinsic competitiveness of manhood, which feels threatened by the assertion of self by others (ibid., 201–5). The assertion of self by others is experienced by many men as self-diminishing, even when the others include other men. Dominance is essential for the assertion of manhood. Dominance, of course, occurs in relationship to others in the immediate environment as well as symbolic others. Sports is a quick enactment of the thrill of dominance and subordination (not of victory) over others, who in the final contest one hopes are weaker. The socialization into a physiological high from having dominated and subordinated the other is a necessary precursor for the internalization of the need for power. Without the ability to subordinate others manhood cannot exist; thus, the man without manhood is nothing (ibid.), and manhood, by its very definition, because it involves the ability to subordinate, cannot exist without power. The deconstruction and obliteration of manhood, therefore, is not possible without the deconstruction of power through its more equitable distribution.

Yet, within the core of the essential need for subordination in order for manhood to exist, there are elaborate rules among men about how privilege and domination works throughout their ranks. This is the core of power and what will not be revealed. These rules vary within each socioeconomic class and racialized/ethnic group. They are socialized, mostly through ritual and nonverbal communication, and once internalized become so natural as to be unutterable—and the same is true of subordination. How and why different groups endure subordination is just as mysterious and has been the focus of progressive scholarship mainly in ethnic studies and women's studies. Dominated groups have been much more candid about examining these cloaked dynamics, and dominant groups have also reveled in putting in their two cents' worth about what motivates the victims of their privilege to take it. The elites have remained unexamined; they are not yet saying how it is that they are socialized to enforce their privilege on others.[3] These revelations should be the core of a feminist reflexive theory of subordination. The white Men's movement does not theorize about how it feels not to be women—not to belong to a derogated group or to fear physical violence, to be free of the drudgery of housework, which allows them the freedom to create, and ultimately the fear of not living up to their own expectations. What are the unspoken rules of privilege? Almost nobody who is a member of privileged groups has violated the silence so that members of oppressed groups will learn to defend themselves. Unlike a Western masculinist paradigm, feminist paradigms require the disrobing of self; feminists writers have documented the testimony of how women perceive themselves at their worst—about bulimia, anorexia, rape, incest, sexual harassment, confessions of abortions—and in this disrobing women have acquired strength through collective nakedness. Although the pain and shame at times becomes unbearable, and at times there is even cannibalizing of one another, feminists writers have continued.

The lack of disclosure by those with power maintains their privilege and reflects the interactional standards in the classic relationships in which there is power asymmetry—between master and slave, between master and servant, between men and women, between employer and employee

(Henley 1986). The interest on the part of the powerful to "know" the subordinate is only to manipulate through the acquired knowledge, including enhancing their sense of self by getting to know *exactly* the oppressive conditions they do not have to experience. For the most part most participants in an asymmetrical power interaction know the rules that guide disclosure (Romero 1992, 115–17). Rollins cites one of her informants as clearly understanding that conversations with her employer were merely designed to reinforce inequality: "They want to know all your business so they know just where you're coming from. They tell you some of their problems so that you'll tell them your business. It's knowledge for control they want. They're uneasy if they don't know enough about you, if they don't know what you're thinking" (1985, 116). The privilege to make certain people nonpersons and therefore invisible also has its historical roots in the master-slave relationship:

> A Virginian gentleman told me that ever since he had married, he had been accustomed to have a Negro girl sleep in the same chamber with himself and his wife. I asked for what purpose this nocturnal attendance was necessary. "Good Heaven!" was the reply, "If I wanted a glass of water during the night, what would become of me." (Goffman 159, 2)

The privilege to relegate *physically* to nonperson status to this extreme may have been limited by the outlawing of slavery, but the *psychological* privilege still remains. The powerful have the privilege to ignore and therefore make invisible those with less power. Using Morrison's words, "My project is an effort to avert the critical gaze from the racial object to the racial subject; from the described and imagined to the describers and imaginers; from the serving to the served" (1992, 90). I agree with Toni Morrison that the focus in most intellectual work has been a

> pattern of thinking about racialism in terms of its consequences on the victim—of always defining it asymmetrically from the perspective of its impact on the object of racist policy and attitudes. A good deal of time and intelligence has been invested in the exposure of racism and the horrific results on its objects. . . . The scholarship that looks into the mind, imagination, and behavior of slaves is valuable. But equally valuable is a serious intellectual effort to see what racial ideology does to the mind, imagination, and behavior of masters. (11–12)

It takes psychological work to maintain privilege; it takes cognitive training not to empathize or feel for your victims—how individuals get socialized to accomplish the abnormal should be at the core of a reflexive theory
of subordination.

The Site for Theorizing

> How do you tell people who do not get it in the first instance that it is
> only out of the arrogance of white privilege and/or male prerogative
> that they assume that it is an honor for a black woman to be proclaimed
> their black mother or their black friend or their black guardian or their
> black conscience?
>
> —duCille 1994, 618

Toni Morrison describes the discomfort that many literary critics feel in
integrating race into their analysis. In the social sciences, in which race has
been the focus of many a career, the same discomfort exists when stepping
outside the paradigm of how race has been studied. Morrison attributes the
lack of materials that integrate race into the reading of literary texts to the
fact that,

> in matters of race, silence and evasion have historically ruled literary
> discourse. Evasion has fostered another, substitute language in which
> the issues are encoded, foreclosing open debate. . . . It is further com-
> plicated by the fact that the habit of ignoring race is understood to be
> a graceful, even generous, liberal gesture. To notice is to recognize an
> already discredited difference. To enforce invisibility through silence
> is to allow the black body a shadowless participation in the dominant
> cultural body. According to this logic, every well-bred instinct argues
> *against noticing* and forecloses adult discourse. (1992, 10)

The ignoring of race results in the peculiar situation of whites assuming they are like a person of Color because they share some significant
characteristics (profession, gender, geographical residence, similar family
structure, similar artistic interests). The reality of a racialized society is that
this is a false assumption. Even brushing one's teeth is experienced differently when a person has been raised in a society with a historical legacy of
slavery that is still present in every molecule of every cell of all physical
and social structures in U.S. society. Or, as Angela Davis points out,
"racism, like an ancient plague, infects every joint, muscle and tissue of

social life in this country" (1974, 37). Professor duCille calls this the "*Driving Miss Daisy* Syndrome," in which, through "an intellectual slight [sic] of hand that transforms power and race relations to make best friends out of driver and driven, master and slave, boss and servant, white boy and black man" (1994, 615). That is why the discourse on race has been so limited: the assumption of race solidarity because a person ignores racism is so pervasive that even those scholars who have dedicated their lives to the dismantling of race privilege end up feeling a false chumminess with those who live with the burden of their color—a burden that will not be fully understood by those who do not share the stigma. Adherence to racial etiquette, however, does not result in obliterating race as an essential core of all social interactions in this country. In fact, it is the polite ignoring of race in interethnic/interracial social interactions that is responsible for the assaultive feelings that many people of Color feel when there is a lapse in the maintenance of the racial etiquette because it reminds all involved of the persuasiveness of racism. Morrison quotes an article written in 1936 about the use of Black dialect in Edgar Allan Poe's work as an example of this lapse in racial etiquette:

> (A short article clearly proud of its racial equanimity) opens this way: "Despite the fact that he grew up largely in the south and spent some of his most fruitful years in Richmond and Baltimore, Poe has little to say about the darky.". . . Although I know this sentence represents the polite parlance of the day, that "darky" was understood to be a term more acceptable than "nigger," the grimace I made upon reading it was followed by an alarmed distrust of the scholar's abilities. If it seems unfair to reach back to the thirties for samples of the kind of lapse that can occur when certain manners of polite repression are waived, let me assure you equally egregious representations of the phenomenon are still common. (1992, 10–11)

Even when there is no mention of race, there is racializing; even when there is no mention of gender, there is gendering. In Morrison's words:

> I assumed that since the author was not black, the appearance of Africanist characters or narrative or idiom in a work could never be *about* anything other than the "normal," unracialized, illusory white world that provided the fictional backdrop. . . . I came to realize the

obvious: the subject of the dream is the dreamer. The fabrication of an Africanist persona is reflexive; an extraordinary meditation on the self; a powerful exploration of the fears and desires that reside in the writerly conscious. It is an astonishing revelation of longing, of terror, of perplexity, of shame, of magnanimity. It requires hard work *not* to see this. .... What became transparent were the self-evident ways that Americans choose to talk about themselves through and within a sometimes allegorical, sometimes metaphorical, but always choked representation of an Africanist presence. (16–17)

The discussion of racism by white liberals and radicals alike has been from the perspective of appropriation of experience; the degradation and possession of the other is not necessarily motivated by feelings of hate and vindictiveness (duCille 1994).[4] And even Morrison recognizes that the degradation of others is one of the primary ways of boosting one's self-esteem and identity—a basic psychological mechanism that is wholly documented in social psychology—but there is something deeper going on than that. Self-aggrandizement may always be with us, and there will always be ways to adorn ourselves physically as well as psychologically so we feel that we are better than others. What is at stake here is the physical and psychological confinement of a whole group of people largely based on skin color and gender. The purpose of the confinement is the regulation of privilege—mostly of concrete material resources and of ways of constructing the world that do not disturb existing strategies for the allocation of privilege. Much of the contemporary progressive writing by white authors tries to dissect the mechanisms by which this is accomplished without these authors ever *putting themselves, their group, and their history* into the process of resolving this problematic. As Emma Pérez indicates:

Within capitalist patriarchal ideology, there is no place for the sensitive human being who is willing to transform the world. "If I am the world, and I heal myself, then I heal the world." These are personal private revolutions, each member of the collective taking responsibility for her/his contradictions within the collective, willing to grapple with the question, "Who am I exploiting?" (1991, 173)

In a liberatory theory of subordination the study of the other is not undertaken to find out who the other is but, rather, what we can learn about ourselves by studying the other (hooks and West 1992, 33).

The Method for Theorizing

The notion of a reflexive theory of subordination that will also lead to a reflexive theory of liberation is slowly emerging in ethnic studies and women's studies (Behar 1993; hooks and West 1992; Haraway 1988, 580; Harding 1987; Keller 1984). These fields of study have also been at the forefront of inventing new methods to obtain social knowledge that subvert the myth of objectivity and allow researchers to go beyond the surface of both subordination and privilege (Haraway 1988). Although there are several paradigms proposed for these new methods (some of which I explored in chap. 2), one particular method that may be especially helpful in documenting the dynamics of power is a new school of legal thought called "critical race studies" proposed by Derrick Bell and his colleagues. As described by Bell, its "practitioners, often through storytelling and a more subjective, personal voice, examine the ways in which the law has been shaped by and shapes issues of race." Here I use a device often used by critical race theorists[5] of constructing my own fable to explore the unspoken rules of power.[6]

The Trickster Treaty: A Play of Power

Trick Number 1: The Center of the Universe
If I am not the center of the universe, you do not exist. If I am not the central actor in whatever drama, I will not listen to you, I will not acknowledge your presence, and I will remove myself from the situation. My absence will highlight my centrality to all actions. I will not acknowledge your presence; my ability not to *see* you is my power. If I do not see you, you do not exist. If you only exist at my will, you are nothing without my attention. I am, therefore, the one that controls who is *real* and who is not.

Trick Number 2: Special Needs Population
I will claim my right to be central to all action by claiming my special needs as a (white) child, a man with important work/ideas/artist/genius, a (white) woman with special demands that supersede the needs of anybody else involved in the situation. If you claim your own needs, I will proceed as if I did not hear you and will reassert my initial claim. The more you push, the more I persist in my claims, with no reference to yours. Unless I want you to exist, you do not.

Trick Number 3: Special Games

I will engage in pseudo-actions that are related to my special population and claim their superiority/necessity to your needs and actions. All rituals/games that involve me are life affirming and enhancements for the soul, even if it is at the expense of your *essential* needs of food and clothing. I will build great stadiums and pay enormous amounts of money for players to enact the rituals/games that glorify me and my group. I will make my rituals/games the center of our national identity at the same time I exclude you from having anything to do with the administration/ ownership of these rituals/games. Entire academic departments will be dedicated to the perfection of my rituals/games at the expense of finding ways to solve the most pressing social problems that will benefit your communities—homicide, drug abuse, child abuse, spousal battery. Instead, I will develop the perfect football, the most advanced athletic shoes, the most perfect regiment to play my rituals/games. All of this will only highlight my importance, including my leisure, at the expense of your survival. This will show the world how important I am, and, simultaneously, it will diminish you to the point of nonexistence. I will also use these games to train my people to love and exercise power. The lifetime socialization through my games will provide the framework for teaching the dynamics of power and domination, all in the guise of "having fun." My games are the boot camp of military training and teach the might of sheer physical domination.

Trick Number 4: The Pleasing Game—Boosting, Stroking, and Silence

I will make it impossible to please me. I will make request upon request, one after another in rapid succession, making it impossible for you to fully comply and barring you from thinking of anything else but me. I will rob you of time and energy so you cannot develop your own subjectivity and identity independent of my needs. I will not allow you even to conceive of a world independent of pleasing me. I will not be belligerent when you do not please me, but I will be dejected so you will feel not only guilt, but, most important, you will feel incompetent, which will increase my centrality to your life, and you will feel empty without my presence. My centrality and my unwillingness to be pleased will subvert your belief that you are able to exist outside the parameters of my presence. You are nothing when I am not around. I am the master and creator of the universe, and you will have nowhere to exist if I am not present.

Trick Number 5: Power Solidarity

I will be a rabid individualist unless the power of my group (based on gender, superior social class, and white race) is threatened. If it is, I will use all of my capacities to think of alternative, benevolent explanations for ruthless and abusive behavior for members of my power group. If a member of my power group is attacked, we will close ranks without a single word being spoken. "You, as woman, don't understand what a burden it is to be a (white) man—the incredible responsibility and courage it takes to fight all these obstacles that society places before you."

Trick Number 6: The Pendejo Game

When you, the outsider, come close to subverting my power through the sheer strength of your moral arguments[7] or through organized mass protest, I will give you an audience. I will listen to you, sometimes for the first time, and will seem engaged. At critical points in your analysis I will claim I do not know what you are talking about and will ask you to elaborate ad nauseam.[8] I will consistently subvert your efforts at dialogue by "claiming we do not speak the same language."[9] I will assert that many of our differences, if not all, are due to our different ways of communicating. I will ask you to educate me and spend your energies in finding ways of saying things so that I can understand. I will *not* do the same for you. Instead of using your resources to advance your causes, I will see you like a rat in a cage running around trying to find ways to explain the cage to me, while I hold the key to open the door. At the same time, I will convince you that I have no ill intentions toward you or those like you. I am simply not informed. The claim of ignorance is one of my most powerful weapons because, while you spend your time trying to enlighten me, everything remains the same. The *"Pendejo* Game" will also allow me to gain intimate knowledge of your psyche, which will perfect my understanding of how to dominate you.

Casting the Play: The Use of Whiteness to Maintain Structural
Privilege and to Promote Racism

I will develop elaborate pseudorules that will allocate how much power every person and child will have in my play, and I will call it "merit." Merit will be defined by me (or those like me) and will have the semblance of objective rules of achievement. When I am questioned about how the rules were developed, I will claim exclusive wisdom for their origins. I will develop extensive mass testing techniques that will be skewed in favor of knowledge available only to those I have determined belong to my group. Everybody will have access to the tests, but few will have access to the knowledge in the test. When a sizable number of nongroup members are successful, I will change the test and the rules of the game. If my people are failing or do not meet the objective standards I have set, I will find exceptions to the rule that will leave our privilege untouched.[10]

The casting of the play is inherited. Those most like me are determined through family ties of race and class. White women will have a special category because they are necessary to reproduce more people like me. They will be accessories to my power, but rarely will I allow them to be even close to full participants. They are essential, however, and I will treat them well if they comply and punish them if they do not.

Epilogue: Audience Participation

The play is actually a *pastorela*,[11] in which the skeleton is written, but the particulars have to be flexible so that the purpose of the play does not get subverted. I invite those like me to hone the skills of domination and invent new rhetoric that will leave our privilege intact and will insure our children's future reign. I also caution you against those traitors who will divulge our tactics and those impostors who will divulge whatever knowledge they gain about domination when they are able to rule in limited contexts. Traitors and impostors are the only two ways the play can be deconstructed to subvert our most perfect mechanisms of production.

Studies of Whiteness

Is there evidence for *The Trickster's Treaty*? Indirect evidence comes from recent (and unprecedented) studies of whiteness.[12] The importance of studying whiteness is to see how it deconstructs the primary way that unspoken "race" privilege is allocated. Unlike other social characteristics used to allocate subordination that have been extensively scrutinized (e.g., being a woman, poor, or of Color), only recently has the primary characteristic used to assign privilege been subjected to scrutiny by social scientists and essayists through the study of whiteness.

No clear paradigm and method has emerged to study whiteness, although the few studies that address whiteness directly give us more than the expressed knowledge that the mostly white authors purport. The unintended outcomes of these studies on whiteness are the revelations of the researchers themselves, thus making the results multilayered; that is, they tell us more than the authors intended and more than the respondents knew they were revealing. With this perspective in mind I use the best contributions to document the trickster's play.

Trick Number 1:
The Center of the Universe—Naturalizing Whiteness

If I am not the center of the universe, you do not exist. If I am not the central actor in whatever drama, I will not listen to you, I will not acknowledge your presence, and I will remove myself from the situation. My absence will highlight my centrality to all actions. I will not acknowledge your presence; my ability not to see you is my power. If I do not see you, you do not exist. If you only exist at my will, you are nothing without my attention. I am, therefore, the one that controls who is real and who is not.

For whiteness to be the "center of the universe" it has to be considered a "natural" unmarked racial category. Indeed, the recurrent finding in the study of whiteness is the fact that white respondents do not consider their "whiteness" as an identity or a marker of group membership per se. Most feminist theorists also assume whiteness is the norm. As duCille writes:

> The colonial object is furthered not only by the canonical literature of the West, as Spivak suggests, but also by a would-be oppositional feminist criticism whose practitioners continue to see whiteness as so natural, normative, and unproblematic that racial identity is a property only of the nonwhite. Unless the object of study happens to be the Other, race is placed under erasure as something outside immediate consideration, at once extratextual and extraterrestrial. Despite decades of painful debate, denial, defensiveness, and color-consciousness-raising, "as a woman" in mainstream feminist discourse all too often continues to mean "as a white woman." (1994, 607)

That is, whiteness is a natural identity because it has not been problematic and therefore salient to most respondents in these studies or to most feminist theoreticians. In particular, most white respondents are hard-pressed to define whiteness and the privileges that it brings to those who own it. Interestingly enough, whiteness becomes much more definable when the privilege it accords its owners is lost. For example, Michelle Fine, Lois Weis, and Judi Addelston (1994) document white-working class men's frustrations as they see their jobs "being taken" over by people of Color. It is in the loss of their way of life, which includes their jobs, that they begin to articulate what it means to be white. That is, whiteness begins to matter when it is decentered and its privileges threatened. Beverly Tatum (1992) and C. A. Gallagher (1995) describe how students in multicultural college classrooms similarly, and painfully, "discover" their whiteness.

Another way to naturalize whiteness is to ignore its significance in the subordination/domination process. Toni Morrison (1992) appropriately notes, however, that even in this nonmention the racialization process continues. Morrison's point (made in reference to U.S. literature) is also well documented in Frankenberg's (1993) research on what their race means to white women from all walks of life. Almost all her respondents mention having been socialized not to "see" people of Color.[13] Yet, not seeing is an integral part of their identity formation because the privilege of "whiteness" is based on the availability of "surrogate, serviceable Black bodies for her [their] own purposes of power without risk, so the author[s] employs them in behalf of her [their] own desire for a safe participation in loss, in love, in chaos, in justice" (Morrison 1992, 28). People of Color are the serviceable others who are the blank slates on which white people can project all those fears, emotions, and attitudes, thus giving whiteness purity and centralness because there are others to live out that which would taint whiteness. Norma Klahn makes a similar point about how, historically, the (temporary) crossing of the border by whites into Mexico was an integral part of building identity, of testing identity, and ultimately of experimenting with all those taboos that were unacceptable in the United States. In her words:

> The voyages are, finally, quests for self-definition, self-indulgence or self-affirmation. Some are evasions, flights from the law or from unspoken societal codes: searches for spaces where rules can be broken. For others, the displacements become rites of initiation, crossings of thresholds toward the unexplored. . . . [T]he other side became the last frontier, a place where the Anglo hero could be tested and prove his strength, usually against the weakly constructed Mexican. (1994, 35)

These temporary transgressions almost always conclude with the traveler crossing back to the U.S., the site of normality; the traveler "returns to the safety of his [or her] home, initiated and transformed, but secure in his [or her] identity and place in the world" (38). If whiteness is never articulated, then it is people of Color, as a group, who can be scrutinized and blamed in order to exalt the perfection of that which is natural and left unexamined.

For whiteness to be the center of the Universe, it is necessary for whiteness to be not only an unmarked category but also an *inherently* superior category. The articulation of exactly what whiteness constitutes is difficult for most respondents in these studies. What is not as difficult for them to articulate, however, is the superiority they feel in comparison to nonwhite people. For example, Peggy McIntosh (1992) tries to articulate precisely what white privilege provides for her, giving us insight into the superiority that most white people come to expect in almost all social contexts. Because white privilege is perceived as the natural state of affairs, by definition it embodies an attitude of superiority: "whites are taught to think of their lives as morally neutral, normative, and average, and also ideal, so that when we work to benefit others, this is seen as work that will allow 'them' to be more like 'us'" (1992, 73). In other words, even though McIntosh does not see herself as oppressing anybody, the list of privileges she was socialized to expect in almost all daily interaction have trained her to feel and act superior to nonwhite people.

Susan Ostrander (1984) similarly finds in her sample of upper-class women a feeling of unquestioned superiority that is their birthright. Because they do not feel they had much to do with constructing the structure of inequality, these women feel that their superiority is natural. Furthermore, these women are very conscious of the pleasures that their material privilege affords, which is intertwined with their feeling of superiority, yet at the same time they don't see how it is related to whiteness. The legitimacy of their superiority because of their birthright allows them not to question their class position. Many of these respondents proudly announced that "the door opens for position" and that access to every sphere is "just a phone call away" (Ostrander 1984, 29).

The pleasure these women feel in their superiority prevents them from challenging the class and race legitimacy on which it is based. In Ostrander's study the upper-class women do not challenge their husbands because they recognize that these men "know how to rule and are masters of the exercise of power" (ibid., 151). Furthermore, if they are not likely to be shaken from their positions of power outside the home, how likely are they, really, to be successfully challenged as heads of their households? Ostrander astutely points out that, in the unlikely event that these women successfully challenged their husbands on their gender superiority, they might be putting their own class status in peril. Therefore, these women submit to their husbands: "They will do so perhaps in part because the gains of *gender* equality would not be enough to balance the losses of class equality" (151–52).

Trick Number 2: Special Needs Population—The Relationship between Privilege and Subordination in Defining White Identity

I will claim my right to be central to all action by claiming my special needs as a (white) child, a man with important work/ideas/artist/genius, a (white) woman with special demands that supersede the needs of anybody else involved in the situation. If you claim your own needs, I will proceed as if I did not hear you and reassert my initial claim. The more you push, the more I persist in my claims, with no reference to yours. Unless I want you to exist, you do not.

A special needs population is defined through social comparison with other populations that are *not* considered to have the right to claim special needs within a specified context. By definition, then, some populations can claim that their special needs deserve priority and therefore are privileged needs. Other populations' needs have been forfeited and are either not articulated or are part of the background and subsumed to meet the needs of the special population that has been privileged. This process is especially salient in the ethnographies on women of Color maids and their employers. For example, Mary Romero (1992) demonstrates how a sixteen-year-old maid in El Paso, Texas, is perceived as a full adult in the service of the entire family, though the employers have a sixteen-year old child themselves. Whereas the "needs" of the employer's child are perceived as special and deserving of full attention, the sixteen-year-old maid actually gets sexually harassed by the father of the sixteen-year-old in the household. In one case, the special needs of the privileged sixteen-year-old are perceived as not only legitimate but, of necessity, to be met, whereas the sixteen-year-old maid's needs are either nonexistent, or she is categorized primarily as a maid and not as a sixteen-year-old.

Many of the studies focusing on whiteness explicitly use social comparison between whites and nonwhites to delineate white identity. In the U.S. national identity has been constructed as white (C. I. Harris 1993a, 1790) because whiteness is the natural state of affairs, or mainstream, and nonwhites are the outsiders, or the marginalized. To be nonwhite is to be non-American. This country's national identity, normality, and superiority are not independent, however, of the existence of nonwhites. An integral part of defining free Americans is by contrast to those who are non-

American and unfree. White identity, constructed through social comparison, supersedes other identifications—poor white people at least have the
consolation that they are not Black. A white woman at least has the consolation that her status is above nonwhites—at least she is not a woman of
Color.

McIntosh, in her brutally honest essay on whiteness, lists the nonconscious "privileges" that whiteness brings her on an everyday basis. Perhaps, not surprisingly, the list is shaped by *comparisons* to people of
Color rather than being an introspective focus on herself and her group.
(McIntosh is not alone in this practice.) As a result, the list is an account of
privileges based on what people of Color do *not* have, rather than what
whites possess in the absence of the presence of people of Color. The element of superiority comes through because people of Color in this paradigm have no subjectivity, and the dominant individual assumes that what
he or she wants and has is exactly what all people desire. The notion that
people of Color may have a different "list" of what a good life is, or what a
good person is—that is, that they have their own special needs—is not
acknowledged in a paradigm in which whiteness reigns supreme (McIntosh 1992, 73–74). As A. duCille so poignantly queries: "Why are black
women always already Other? I wonder. To myself, of course, I am not
Other; to me it is the white women and men so intent on theorizing my difference who are the Other" (1994, 591–92). McIntosh is fully aware of this
contradiction between how the other perceives herself in contrast to how
whites perceive her, and her essay is an attempt to deconstruct the privileges of whiteness. Again, her honesty, which may be perceived as betrayal
by some whites and offensive to some people of Color, is the beginning of
reimagining whiteness and, by definition, the inferiority assigned to nonwhites.

The use of people of Color for the exaltation of whiteness, although
itself gendered, still occurs by both men and women. Whiteness and maleness are defined in opposition to "color" and "femaleness": the other has to
exist to exalt the centeredness of the subject. If the other refuses to be the
other, it creates chaos in the subject, because this person has to reconstitute
him- or herself (Fine, Weis, and Addelston 1994, 2). The presence of nonwhites creates a "humanity" scale in which white men represent the pin-
nacle of human development: they are rational, logical, unemotional,
industrious, adventurous, in control, creators (C. I. Harris 1993b)—and all
of these characteristics, or special (privileged) needs, would be difficult to
judge if it were not for the presence of nonwhites. Even the gender relations

among whites are more "human" because of the presence of people of Color. Morrison illustrates this when discussing Hemingway's novel *To Have and Have Not*. In the novel Harry and his wife, Marie, are making love. Marie asks her husband, "Listen, did you ever do it with a nigger wench?"

> "Sure."
> "What's it like?"
> "Like a nurse shark."

Morrison goes on to remark that for Hemingway the Black woman is

> the furthest thing from human, so far away as to be not even mammal but fish. The figure evokes a predatory, devouring eroticism and signals the antithesis to femininity, to nurturing, to nursing, to replenishment. In short, Harry's words mark something so brutal, contrary, and alien in its figuration that it does not belong to its own species and cannot be spoken of in language, in metaphor or metonym, evocative of anything resembling the woman to whom Harry is speaking—his wife Marie. The kindness he has done Marie is palpable. His projection of black female sexuality has provided her with solace, for which she is properly grateful. She responds to the kindness and giggles, "You're funny." (1992, 84–85)

It was in the owning of people of Color, historically through slavery, not through their labor, that white men's manhood was transformed in the New World and that his special, privileged needs were created. As Morrison points out: "whatever his social status in London, in the New World he is a gentleman. More gentle, more man. The site of his transformation is within rawness: he is backgrounded by savagery" (44). Similarly, Gutiérrez (1991, 194) indicates that the Spanish colonizers in seventeenth century New Mexico thought of society as composed of conquerors and conquered where ". . . The Indians were vanquished heathens engulfed in satanic darkness" and they were "Christians, Spaniards, 'civilized,' and white." The presence of people of Color and the potential threat of their darkness and their concomitant "savagery" open the gateways for white people to assume their color burden and to protect the "civilized world" through the use of brutality, which by definition is uncivilized. This tautology leads to the most brutal acts, such as the imprisonment and execution of more poor Black people than in any other country—all done in the name of civilization.

Morrison argues that the use of people of Color, historically, to give whiteness its identity emerged largely because there was no "royalty" in the U.S., as there was in Europe, from which to draw a counterdistinction:

> Americans did not have profligate, predatory nobility from which to wrest an identity of national virtue while continuing to covet aristocratic license and luxury. The American nation negotiated both its disdain and its envy in the same way Dunbar did: through the self-reflexive contemplation of fabricated, mythological Africanism. For the settlers and for American writers generally, this Africanist other became the means of thinking about body, mind, chaos, kindness, and love; provided the occasion for exercises in the absence of restraint, the presence of restraint, the contemplation of freedom and of aggression; permitted opportunities for the exploration of ethics and morality, for meeting the obligations of the social contract, for bearing the cross of religion and following out the ramifications of power. (47)

Morrison quotes sociologist Orlando Patterson's observation that "we should not be surprised that the Enlightenment could accommodate slavery; we should be surprised if it had not. The concept of freedom did not emerge in a vacuum. Nothing highlighted freedom—if it did not in fact create it—like slavery" (38). Similarly, in Ramón Gutiérrez's study of 18th century New Mexico, he notes that

> The presence of Indian slaves in New Mexico society gave meaning to honor-status. Much of what was considered Spanish culture in this northern frontier of New Spain gained its meaning in opposition to and as an exaggeration of what it meant to be an Indian or *genízaro*.[14] What the Puebloans and *genízaros* were, the Spanish were not. What the Spanish were, the Puebloans and *genízaros* were not. Negative stereotypes of the other, that is, of the defeated and fallen Indian within Hispano society and outside of it, defined the boundaries between "them" and "us," between the dishonored and the honored. (1991, 180)

The significance of white identity, however, is still in reference to the presence of dark others as are the definitions of social issues. For many whites the passion that propels their lives stems from the need to "help" save and, by default, indirectly control the dark others. In Morrison's words: "Africanism is the vehicle by which the American self knows itself as not enslaved, but free; not repulsive but desirable; not helpless, but licensed and powerful; not history-less, but historical; not damned, but innocent; not a blind accident of evolution, but a progressive fulfillment of destiny" (52).

In sum people of Color are the experimentation ground upon which real lives get hurt, trashed, dumped, and disposed of, while whites' psyches remain intact. Because people of Color are not human, they are not entitled to special needs, which are the provenance of white human beings. Because oppression is relational, special needs will be defined in reference to those present in the environment, with a fairly stable set of rules about whose superiority takes precedence.

Trick Number 3:
Special Games—The Documentation of the Dynamics of Power

I will engage in pseudo-actions that are related to my special population and claim their superiority/necessity to your needs and actions. All rituals/games that involve me are life-affirming and enhancements for the soul, even if it is at the expense of your essential needs of food and clothing. I will build great stadiums and pay enormous amounts of money for players to enact the rituals/games that glorify me and my group. I will make my rituals/games the center of our national identity at the same time I exclude you from having anything to do with the administration/ownership of these rituals/games. Entire academic departments will be dedicated to the perfection of my rituals/games at the expense of finding ways to solve the most pressing social problems that will benefit your communities—homicide, drug abuse, child abuse, spousal battery. Instead, I will develop the perfect football, the most advanced athletic shoes, the most perfect regiment to play my rituals/games. All of this will only highlight my importance, including my leisure at the expense of your survival. This will show the world how important I am, and simultaneously it will diminish you to the point of nonexistence. I will also use these games to train my people to love and exercise power. The lifetime socialization through my games will provide the framework for teaching the dynamics of power and domination all in the guise of "having fun." My games are the boot camp of military training and teach the might of sheer physical domination.

The socialization into power for white men happens primarily through the rituals of organized sports—either through viewing or playing them (Connell 1995). Sports have often been identified as an important arena of informal decision making that has historically excluded women and men of Color. In fact, some claim that this is where the *real* decisions get made in industry as well as in politics.

Many of these "games" get viewed and played in exclusive private clubs with written and unwritten rules maintaining white racial exclusivity. It is through a network of friendships, many of which are sustained mainly through club memberships, that economic and social advancements happen in industry. Lawrence Graham interviewed professionals of Color at more than six hundred U.S. corporations and found that they "were unable to build networks, find mentors, or even attract business opportunities because of their exclusion from private clubs that white peers were joining" (1995, xv). At a more personal level, Graham remarks that even though he grew up in affluence, received a bachelor's degree from Princeton and a law degree from Harvard, the color of his skin kept him from ever joining the inner circles of power:

> Today, I'm back where I started—on a street of five- and six-bedroom colonials with expensive cars and neighbors who all belong somewhere. Through my experiences as a young lawyer, I have come to realize that these clubs are where businesspeople network, where lawyers and investment bankers meet potential clients and arrange deals. How many clients and deals am I going to line up on the asphalt parking lot of my local public tennis courts? . . . My black Ivy League friends and I know of black company vice presidents who have to ask white subordinates to invite them out for golf or tennis. We talk about the club in Westchester that rejected black Scarsdale resident and millionaire magazine publisher Earl Graves, who sits on *Fortune* 500 boards, owns a Pepsi distribution franchise, raised three bright Ivy league children, and holds prestigious honorary degrees. We talk about all the clubs that face a scandal and then run out to sign up one quiet, deferential black man who will accept a special "limited-status" membership, remove the taint, and deflect further scrutiny. . . . I wanted some answers. I knew I could never be treated as an equal at this Greenwich oasis—a place so insular that the word *Negro* is still used in conversation. But I figured I could get close enough to understand what these people were thinking and why country clubs were so set on excluding people like me. (ibid., 2–3)

Graham goes underground as a busboy in one of these private clubs to figure out how privileged white people think in order to answer his question of why he is excluded—he finds no other answer except racism.

Communal view of sports is also where working-class white men build camaraderie and bond in male solidarity (often excluding men of Color and women). Ironically, although many professional sports are played by men of Color, these men are often not in the decision-making positions of constructing them or in the organized rituals of watching them with those in power. The recent work on whiteness begins to document how the activities of participating in or watching ritualized sports are used to socialize individuals of privilege to the dynamics of power.

The power that whiteness holds for its owners has not been explicitly documented (C. I. Harris 1993a); it is a birthright that is socialized from generation to generation in the largely racially segregated living arrangements that exist in the United States (McIntosh 1992, 77). Like the construction of manhood through a lifetime of socialization in sports (Kimmel 1993; Connell 1995), the process is largely hidden, unless one has been admitted to this exclusive club. The current research on whiteness begins the process necessary for understanding the power of whiteness as well as the beginning of its deconstruction. It can draw from research on social class that has already identified some of the mechanisms used to pass along class privilege. This is not to suggest that race and class can or should be collapsed but, rather, that the mechanisms used to conceal and perpetuate one kind of institutionalized privilege may have counterparts in the analysis of other kinds of institutionalized privilege. It is important to note, though, that the intersection of privilege and subordination will always complicate things. Thus, the mechanisms associated with race privilege will be affected by its co-occurrence with poverty or wealth, maleness or femaleness, etc. Nevertheless, we must begin to identify and define the mechanisms so that we will be able to recognize them in the many forms in which they appear.

Trick Number 4:
The Pleasing Game—Boosting, Stroking, and Silence

I will make it impossible to please me. I will make request upon request, one after another in rapid succession, making it impossible for you to fully comply and barring you from thinking of anything else but me. I will rob you of time and energy so you cannot develop your own subjectivity and identity independent of my needs. I will not allow you even to conceive of a world independent of pleasing me. I will not be belligerent when you do not please me, but I will be dejected so you will feel not only guilt but, most important, you will feel incompetent, which will increase my centrality to your life, and you will feel empty without my presence. My centrality and my unwillingness to be pleased will subvert your belief that you

*are able to exist outside the parameters of my presence. You are nothing when I am
not around. I am the master and creator of the universe, and you will have nowhere
to exist if I am not present.*

Boosting. Ostrander, in her study of upper-class women, gives us an
intimate portrait of how the upper crust of U.S. society makes sense of its
class privilege. The upper-class family has a well-established script, with
the woman as the "booster," the man as the provider. As one woman told
Ostrander: "You have to be your husband's biggest booster. You have to
make him feel good. He does not appreciate it if he comes home and I'm
exhausted. I've got to be ready to find out what his week was like. He
comes first, and I have to bend my life to fit his" (1984, 39). Ostrander sees
this as serving the function of wives—showing solidarity, giving help,
rewarding, agreeing, understanding, and passively accepting most of their
husbands' actions. The husband wants a "sounding board" for his business
strategies, *not* an active participant (46). Also, the wives have to be available to travel with their husbands—a request they comply with but also
find tiring. Boosting gives these women privilege through proxy; that is,
their husbands' money or privilege protects them from the "mundane"
chores that have been assigned to them by gender. They have the economic
authority to tell others to do their cleaning as well as other unpleasant
responsibilities. In Ostrander's words, "Wives run the households for men
who essentially run the nation's business" (42).

Stroking. As part of their "jobs" of running their households, these
women are also responsible for maintaining a network of "congenial" people, further pleasing their husbands by having their social needs met (ibid.,
45). The creation and maintenance of acceptable social networks for the
entire family is an integral part of maintaining whiteness. In addition to
maintaining lateral social relationships, they also smooth the social relationships between their group and their subordinates. Lateral relationships
are almost exclusively between whites, whereas relationships with subordinates exist both with whites and nonwhites. The upper-class women
entertain not to enhance their husband's careers but, rather, to express grat-
itude to their employees for a job well done. As with their charity work,
they are coconspirators in the subordination of workers. Although these
women speak of volunteer work as a way to justify their privileged status
or as a way to pay back society for their privilege; their work is also a way
to appease subordinates and to diffuse structural opposition; because of it,
it becomes much more difficult to see the entire class as being made up of
"devils" (129). A by-product of these women's "charity work" is the main-

tenance of power over nonwhites, thus an affirmation of the inherent superiority of whiteness. Another by-product is that the white family structure
appears "normal," "desired," and the "correct" way to be a family. The fact
that mostly whites can afford this arrangement is treated as a historical
accident or perhaps as a result of an unspoken social Darwinism in which
the "good" families with "lineage," and a history of superiority, just happen to be white.

Silence. One of the major rules of solidarity is first and foremost the
code of silence to hide imperfections (ibid., 30). The women in Ostrander's
study are not passive recipients of their class privilege but, instead, actively
participate in maintaining it. The code of silence is intricately related to
what these women refer to as "social graces," which defines their class (and
race) status (see Domhoff 1983; Ryan and Sackrey 1984). Ostrander
observes that "these social graces are not just optional amenities of upper-
class life; they are essential to the ways in which the upper-class persons
are able to control—with great civility and charm—virtually any social situation in which they find themselves" (89). Similarly, David Wellman
argues that "European Americans have advantages that come from their
social location in the racial hierarchy, and . . . they explain, or ignore, their
privileged position in socially acceptable terms" (1993, 26).

Further probing reveals that, even though these women enjoy tremendous privileges as a result of their race and class, they also pay a high cost.
There is a structural paradox in that, the higher the socioeconomic status of
the husband, the more rigid the division of labor. This has led to a recurrent
regret expressed by many of these upper-class white women of not having
"tested" their abilities or whether they can make it "on their own." They
had restricted their own development in the service of their husbands.
Oddly enough, all of these women had inherited wealth independent of
their husbands', and yet they still submitted themselves to their husbands'
will; the "need" for a husband was obviously separate from their economic
needs (Ostrander 1984, 51). That is, the need to please is independent of
their economic survival. The closeness of these women to the centers of
power through intimacy with their husbands did not result in personal
empowerment. When they were asked to be sounding boards, there was a
potential for them to participate and learn the dynamics of the inner sanc-
tum of power. But this subversion of the "wife" role is only possible if these
"opportunities" are provided to someone who has an independent subjectivity, someone who has an identity and an agenda *apart* from the husband.
These opportunities are data to be made sense of from the subjectivity of

the subordinate. What is tragic about these women is that, despite their class and race privilege, they are denied their subjectivity and therefore human agency. They have opportunities but have absolutely no idea what to do with them apart from their husbands' agenda. Nevertheless, these negative observations were mostly undercurrents. Most of the women experienced their class position as desirable and their inherited privilege as a right they enjoyed. They dispensed their social responsibility through charity work and the raising of their families. They saw very little wrong with their class status and were oblivious to their active role in the construction of whiteness.

Trick Number 5: Power Solidarity—Whiteness Is a Family Affair
I will be a rabid individualist unless the power of my group (based on gender, superior social class, and white race) is threatened. If it is, I will use all my capacities to think of alternative, benevolent explanations for ruthless and abusive behavior for members of my power group. If a member of my power group is attacked, we will close ranks without a single word being spoken. "You, as woman, don't understand what a burden it is to be a (white) man—the incredible responsibility and courage it takes to fight all these obstacles that society places before you."

Ultimately, white privilege depends on its members not betraying the unspoken, nonconscious power dynamics socialized in the intimacy of their families. White solidarity may on first sight appear to be an oxymoron. Yet many of the respondents and essayists covered in this review reveal a tacit understanding of white solidarity. Although whiteness to them is natural and although few can articulate the privileges that whiteness brings, most can detect when whiteness is being questioned and its privilege potentially dismantled. Therefore, solidarity on the basis of whiteness will have to be fully understood and dismantled for the deconstruction of race privilege to continue.

The mechanisms of power employed in the exercise of whiteness are both daily practices and psychological processes that simultaneously support and reflect the position-justifying beliefs Wellman (1993) and others find that whites hold about race. Thus, these mechanisms are geared to the maintenance of structural power for white people as a whole. Whether individual whites use these mechanisms or not is irrelevant to the outcome of the white group's superiority, and certainly the studies conducted so far suggest that most whites are socialized to employ them, whether or not they actually do.

Ironically, given the potential for "race" retaliation in the current arrangements of power, whiteness gets recreated within families, making it a very important element in the maintenance of whiteness. Women's prominent roles within families, therefore, are also immensely important in reproducing white privilege. For example, in Ostrander's ethnography of upper-class women, her respondents were particularly concerned that their children maintain power solidarity by *not* marrying outside their race and class. As one of her respondents states: "I certainly wouldn't abandon them if they married someone I didn't approve of, a Black person or whatever, but it would be difficult. It is easier to marry somebody near your own interests and background. It makes for compatibility" (1984, 88). Upper-class women, thus, considered it part of their role as mothers to maximize opportunities for same-class marriages for their children. Frankenberg (1993, 95) also found that even among women professing belief in "common humanity stumble over the question of marriage and procreation." Moreover, even though the number of black-white interracial marriages has nearly quadrupled since 1970 when there were a total of sixty-five thousand black-white interracial couples, a large number of whites still remain strongly opposed to miscegenation (Graham 1995, 34). For example, a 1992 Gallup Poll indicates that only 10 percent of whites would approve of a family member marrying outside the race and the approval for interracial unions only goes slightly up (15 percent) when the "survey participant was neither related to nor acquainted with the individuals being married" (ibid., 34).

According to Ostrander's work, the upper class has well-established normative familial arrangements that perpetuate and support white (as well as class) privilege. Oddly enough, most of the respondents in her study readily acknowledged their class privilege, but white privilege remained unexamined. Instead of recognizing their race privilege, they spoke of their lineage as the capital they bring to their marriage. In fact, when asked what made them upper class, they did not use their husband's income or education as evidence but, rather, their own family ancestry and the prestige that this accorded the marriage (ibid., 34). If privilege is ultimately conferred through lineage, then by definition people of Color will always be outside the confines of assigned privilege. The maintenance of whiteness, then, is inextricably intertwined with class maintenance. As part of class maintenance, upper-class families create the hegemonic standards that most families, both nonwhite and white, are judged by. Although upper-class women have the resources to have a lifestyle not accessible to working-class white families, they represent almost a purified form of the internal dynamics that white families generally use to maintain whiteness. In fact, Roediger (1991) shows how working-class whites (such as Irish-American workers) elaborated anti-Black ideologies—including a horror of miscegenation—gradually, as they found that this construction served complex economic, social and psychological purposes. Thus, he shows how different rationales were developed to support the claim of white superiority at different times and in different social class groups, but for my purposes the important point is that they always end up being developed in white families (see Wellman, 1993, for contemporary examples that cross social class lines). The particular rationales and dynamics that have been identified in upper-class white families provide an understanding of how families construct racial privilege when they are unconstrained by class subordination.

The resources that Ostrander's respondents possess exempt them from housework, which allows these women to concentrate on raising their children. These mothers inculcate the norm of whiteness, thus increasing power solidarity. Upper-class families have more children than middle-class families largely because they want to increase the numbers of their class. As Beth Vanfossen states: "Children are valued as carriers of the family's elite status, and, accordingly, the number of children per family is considerably higher than in the middle class" (1979, 296). Upper-class mothers try to be available to their children because they are too precious to leave their raising to hired caretakers. Ostrander summarizes this view: "The proper development of the next generation of privilege is far too important to be left to hired hands. This is confirmed by Mrs. Wainwright, who said: 'We don't have someone else taking care of our children. You've got to raise your own children if they're going to succeed'" (1984, 71). Every member of the white upper class is valuable, and mothers, especially, are in charge of not letting a single member fail, regardless of whether they are poor students, for example, or otherwise not performing well (84).

One way that upper-class mothers insure that their children will not fail is by constructing an environment in which desires and wants are congruent with what is possible and available for them—thus creating solidarity. The women are very much aware of this function. In Ostrander's words: "For upper-class children, doing what they want to do for personal happiness and doing what they should do to construct and maintain a social class are especially consonant with one another. And their mothers are primarily responsible for creating and upholding this consonance and the expectations and activities to which it leads and which it, in turn, creates" (ibid., 96).

Power solidarity is also socialized through feelings of belonging. A sense of belonging can be communicated in a variety of ways. Susanna Sturgis (1988), in her autobiographical essay, discusses beautifully how the unmarked history she was taught in school provided a direct measure of her importance as a descendant of "founding fathers" and of the importance of those who *can* make history. The historical lessons she learned about whites' (mostly male) accomplishments gave her a sense of their centrality and their belonging to the mainstream of life. Not to belong, because of race and/or class, is a way to control and diminish those who are outside this well-defined mainstream. Again, when the sense of belonging is taken away, white respondents immediately "see" how belonging is an integral part of their whiteness, and they openly complain about being robbed of their comfort by the invasion of minorities tainting their neighborhood or demanding equal participation in the mainstream (Fine, Weis, and Addelston 1994, 8–9). It is clear, then, how dependent this sense of belonging is on processes of exclusion. C. A. Gallagher quotes a white student whose sense of belonging was being threatened: "We can't have anything for ourselves anymore that says exclusively White or anything like that. But everyone else can" (1995, 177).

Trick Number 6: The *Pendejo* Game—Distancing and Denial

When you, the outsider, come close to subverting my power through the sheer strength of your moral arguments or through organized mass protest, I will give you an audience. I will listen to you, sometimes for the first time, and will seem engaged. At critical points in your analysis I will claim I do not know what you are talking about and will ask you to elaborate ad nauseam. I will consistently subvert your efforts at dialogue by "claiming we do not speak the same language." I will assert that many of our differences, if not all, are due to our different ways of communicating. I will ask you to educate me and spend your energies in finding ways of saying things so that I can understand. I will not do the same for you. Instead of using your resources to advance your causes, I will see you like a rat in a cage running around trying to find ways to explain the cage to me, while I hold the key to open the door. At the same time, I will convince you that I have no ill intentions toward you or those like you. I am simply not informed. The claim of ignorance is one of my most powerful weapons because, while you spend your time trying to enlighten me, everything remains the same. The "Pendejo Game" will also allow me to gain intimate knowledge of your psyche, which will perfect my understanding of how to dominate you.

Distancing. Again, Ostrander's study of upper-class women not only provides documentation of the dynamics of how the upper crust of U.S. society makes sense of its class privilege but demonstrates, in this particular instance, that class privilege is inextricably tied to race privilege because Ostrander's definition of her sample required them to have had wealth in their families for multiple generations, as measured by their membership in registered clubs. The women interviewed consistently distanced themselves from the origins of their race/class privilege by claiming that it was based on an accident of birth and that they had nothing to do with creating it. Their class and race membership was not borne out of a conscious intention on their part; therefore, they do not take any responsibility for the costly consequences for others of their privilege. That is, they claimed "not to know" how exactly they were fortunate enough to receive their privileged position. The respondents in Ostrander's study *distanced* themselves from the phenomenon as if it were a natural disaster they had nothing to do with creating and which they resent having to clean up. Even though these women recognize their privilege, most feel it is the natural arrangement of things, and they do their personal best to help those less fortunate through their charity work.

Denial. Many researchers have documented the psychological strain involved in "passing" from a subordinate group to a dominant group, say fair-skinned Blacks passing as whites (C. I. Harris 1993a). The same strain has been documented for those individuals who become conscious of racism and perceive the omnipresence of its effects in all areas of social life. This is one reason that individuals resist acquiring a "double" consciousness, because becoming conscious of power and domination creates enormous psychological stress and pain (Du Bois 1973; C. I. Harris 1993a, 1711; Tatum 1992). It is not surprising, then, that many of the white respondents in these studies claim that whiteness does not bring unearned privileges— that is, that whatever privileges are accorded to whiteness are earned through merit because whites, as a group, perform better than people of Color in all kinds of arenas. In fact, denial of white privilege is only fully documented once it is lost. It is in the process of being dislocated and making sense of that dislocation that white respondents begin to fully acknowledge the privileges they previously denied that whiteness had brought them (Fine, Weis, and Addelston 1994; Gallagher 1995).

Another form of denial is to assert ignorance of practices that exclude groups from certain privileges. Lawrence Graham documents how this was done at Princeton when it came to excluding Blacks from admission from the beginning of Princeton's history until 1944:

> Founded in 1746 as the College of New Jersey, Princeton's antiblack policies very quickly began to stand out as an aberration among the top colleges in every segment of the United States except the South. . . . Princeton pursued a three tier strategy to ensure that blacks would not enroll, and was so successful that it accepted a black student exactly a hundred years after Harvard and eighty years after Yale. First, Princeton strictly enforced an unwritten rule of rejecting all black applicants; second, it denied having such a rule in the face of growing criticism; finally, it utilized "deflection" rejection letters directing high-profile black applicants to apply to other schools rather than explicitly denying admission; this was designed to deter those who might publicly protest their rejection by the school.
>
> Reflecting Princeton's obsession with decorum, these polite letters of deflection were written in a uniform format developed by Princeton's thirteenth president, Woodrow Wilson, just three years before he was elected president of the United States. The University Archive in the Seeley Mudd Library reveals a letter that begins, "Regret to say that is altogether inadvisable for a colored man to enter Princeton. . . ."
>
> In an impressive display of early-twentieth-century political maneuvering, Wilson never signed these letters, but instead had his secretary send them out with his own signature with the polite closing line, "I would strongly recommend you to secure your education in a Southern institution . . . Yours Very Truly. (1995, 191)

Princeton University was not integrated until 1944 when the U.S. Navy began an ROTC program on campus and, unbeknownst to Princeton, four Black students were part of the program (ibid., 192). The unwritten practice of not admitting Blacks continued for the next twenty years with virtually no Blacks admitted in the classes of 1950 to 1959 "and only seven Blacks were on the 3,500-student campus by 1962" (ibid., 193). Princeton has to this day denied that such a policy ever existed and has refused any official comment on the outcome of its unwritten practices.

Princeton University is not unique in maintaining its privilege through unwritten practices that are officially denied although practically applied to exclude those that should not be part of the Trickster's Play.

Casting the Play: The Use of Whiteness to Maintain Structural Privilege and to Promote Racism

I will develop elaborate pseudorules that will allocate how much power every person and child will have in my play, and I will call it "merit." Merit will be defined my me (or those like me) and will have the semblance of objective rules of achievement. When I am questioned about how the rules were developed, I will claim exclusive wisdom for their origins. I will develop extensive mass testing techniques that will be skewed in favor of knowledge only available to those I have determined belong to my group. Everybody will have access to the tests, but few will have access to the knowledge in the test. When a sizable number of nongroup members are successful, I will change the test and the rules of the game. If my people are failing or do not meet the objective standards I have set, I will find exceptions to the rule that will leave our privilege untouched.

The casting of the play is inherited. Those most like me are determined through family ties of race and class. White women will have a special category because they are necessary to reproduce more people like me. They will be accessories to my power, but rarely will I allow them to be even close to full participants. They are essential, however, and I will treat them well if they comply and punish them if they do not.

The objective of the mechanisms of power described in the research on whiteness is to maintain the very real structural privilege of whiteness. Racism—the belief that whites are superior to other nonwhite "races"—is an integral part of this process. The superiority of whiteness is codified into law as a form of property whose value has not been thoroughly articulated (C. I. Harris 1993a). In fact, law professor Cheryl Harris claims that whiteness has been an exclusive club that has been protected by the courts, more than any other kind of property (1736). Whiteness, codified in law, by definition coerced nonwhites into denial of their identity to insure survival (see Williams 1995); therefore, it makes no sense to study race as if the mechanism of construction were the same for all groups (C. I. Harris 1993a, 1744).

But how exactly are the dynamics of whiteness used for the maintenance of structural privilege? In a society that prides itself on being a race-blind democracy, how can the trickster's play be cast without referring to race in order not to sabotage its legitimacy? It is especially pressing to find answers when its possessors are apparently so oblivious to its effects and some of its nonpossessors seem to agree that it is not whiteness per se that confers privilege as they strive to climb into the (white) mainstream wagon (Chavez 1991). The answer may lie in the different functions groups serve in the domination/subordination process as outlined by Erika Apfelbaum (1979). In her theory of intergroup relations the formation of groups in industrialized society is not independent of the process of enforcing power. The dominant group de-emphasizes its function as a group and, instead, portrays its existence as the "norm," or as natural, to mystify how its members obtain power by their group membership. Apfelbaum names this as the universal rule, in which supposedly *anybody* that "acts" according to prescribed standards is meritorious and deserving of societal and economic rewards. The universal rule, in theory, is open to everybody and, in fact, applies primarily to those who possess whiteness and secondarily to those who act as white as possible. An unspoken double standard gets set up in which, as Cheryl Harris (1993a) points out, democracy and rules are exclusively for whites (or those who act as white as possible), while tyranny is justified for Blacks. This double standard is not dictated by the democratic state but, rather, by the "inherent" difference between Blacks and whites. This inherent difference is biological race, which is codified into law through the one-drop rule—those individuals with at least one drop of Black blood are legally cast as Black. Belief in a biological basis for whiteness insures that it will take many generations of intermarriage with "pure" whites before individuals can *legally* possess the privileges of whiteness; meanwhile, they are without its property (ibid.).

On the other hand, the subordinate group is marked, or stigmatized. The value attached to being white and the devaluation of being nonwhite makes group membership in a nonwhite ethnic/racial group problematic for its members. In effect, the nonwhite ethnic/racial group is (de)grouped and cannot serve the usual positive functions that groups serve—providing a basis for positive social identity, group solidarity, a sense of belonging, and empowerment (Apfelbaum 1979). At the same time, whiteness does serve those functions for its possessors (Sturgis 1988; McIntosh 1992). Degrouping as a basis for group subordination is also a very effective means of sabotaging resistance to domination. While ethnic/racial membership is not supposed to matter in the United States, all privilege and power is distributed according to race, class, and gender: "In effect, the courts erected legal 'No trespassing signs'—passing, therefore, is largely a phenomenon from subordinate to dominant group rather than the other way around" (C. I. Harris 1993a, 1741, 1761). This is reminiscent of a movie *La Cage aux Folles II,* in which a gay man passes as a woman in Italy, and, having to do grueling woman's work, he looks up from the floor he is scrubbing and states, "I want to be a man!"

Apfelbaum argues that a critical stage in overthrowing domination is when the subordinate group, which has been degrouped, begins to use its own norms and standards for positive identity formation and political mobilization. When a previously degrouped group begins to fight back, the dominant group steps up its restrictive controls. Thus, it is not surprising that, when there are increasing numbers of people of Color in the United States, as well as increasing awareness of how race is socially constructed and therefore not about inherent merit—that is, at the very moment when race is on the verge of taking center stage in the analysis of oppression—all of a sudden race does not matter and we should be colorblind (C. I. Harris, 1993a, 1768). In fact, the deconstruction of white privilege has brought a backlash of countercharges of reverse racism. The often openly expressed response to charges of racism is the assertion that whiteness is a legitimate criterion of resource allocation because merit is colorblind and that it is a coincidence (or inherent superiority) that most meritorious persons happen to be white and male.

Nowhere are the unmentioned assumptions of the inherent merit of whiteness more clear than in the legal battles on reverse discrimination. For example, in the now famous Bakke case, where a white male student claimed and won a legal suit of reverse discrimination when he did not get admitted to medical school at the University of California, Davis. The defendant only claimed discrimination on one criterion, whiteness. Other selection criteria, such as that applicants were the offspring of wealthy donors, went unchallenged, largely because these hierarchies are perceived as legitimate. Whiteness as property is possessed by all members of the defined group and lends itself to race solidarity. Wealth is possessed in varying degrees and does not lend itself to being a sound criterion for solidarity; it is not universal enough. In fact, whiteness may be the only uniformly unifying characteristic of the dominant group. In Harris's words, "Bakke expected that he would never be disfavored when competing with minority candidates, although he might be disfavored with respect to more privileged whites" (ibid., 1773). That is, competition among whites is *fair* because they are racial equals.

The inherent right for whiteness to serve as valuable property is based on biology; it is property therefore that groups of Color cannot possess immediately, and this results in a priori structural privilege. When whiteness, because of its natural order and its elusive nature, remains unquestioned, we have *racial realism,* leaving no room to question whiteness or privilege (ibid.).

Epilogue: Audience Participation

The play is actually a pastorela *in which the skeleton is written, but the particulars have to be flexible so that the purpose of the play does not get subverted. I invite those like me to hone the skills of domination and invent new rhetoric that will leave our privilege intact and will insure our children's future reign. I also caution you against those traitors who will divulge our tactics and those impostors who will divulge whatever knowledge they gain about domination when they are able to rule in limited contexts. Traitors and impostors are the only two ways the play can be deconstructed to subvert our most perfect mechanisms of production.*

Women's studies, men's studies, and ethnic studies all subvert the play; that is why the backlash occurs—that is, new reactionary rhetorics emerge to co-opt the advancements that progressive scholarship can make on the trickster's play. It is like the Wizard of Oz manipulating those who choose to go down the yellow brick road toward finding the real Oz. At any point in time they can be diverted by the illusions of the trickster pulling levers behind the big screen.

Dismantling Privilege: Beating the Trickster

Precisely because of the "naturalness" of white identity and because of the cloaked secrecy of its manifestation, it is difficult to take the time and energy to "listen" to whiteness. For one thing, it is not viewed as problematic, given that it provides privilege (we are much more passionate about combating injustice, which makes us feel we are doing something worthwhile) and that it is natural and thus difficult to describe. To listen to it also seems like useless "work," like pressing the already ironed dress or putting clean dishes in the dishwasher—since, after all, it isn't a problem and everybody knows what it is, why indulge in introspective angst that leads nowhere? There is the rub; privilege has the semblance of naturalness that in itself defends it from scrutiny. Much of the struggle in the twentieth century has been to problematize "the natural," and progressive scholarship has accomplished an admirable body of research questioning many forms of oppression. But the challenge of the twenty-first century will be to continue the work of the Enlightenment—when royalty was scrutinized and the privilege of lineage was questioned to provide avenues for democracy to flourish. Race privilege has substituted for lineage of royalty in our time. It countervails class, at times, just like "royal blood" did in the past. We believe in its goodness as former subjects believed in the direct connection to God through their kings.

The Solution

I began this chapter by outlining the core of the problem as the absence of an integration of privilege into an analysis of domination and subordination. I hope it has become clear that I am not merely speaking of moving the gaze from the oppressed to the oppressor,[15] which results in the "exchange of dominations—dominant Eurocentric scholarship *replaced* by dominant Afro-centric scholarship. . . . More interesting is what makes intellectual domination possible; how knowledge is transformed from invasion and conquest to revelation and choice" (Morrison 1992, 8). What would power look like if we had a reflexive theory of subordination? And, more to the point, what would be the outcome of a reflexive theory of subordination? Outlines are already being formulated about what elements this paradigm should contain. Most progressive scholarship that has a reflexive undercurrent emphasizes that, in order for power to have a different face, a primary concern is that all mechanisms of decision making have participatory components to them. The notion of separating the leaders from the folk, and the role of leader itself, to convince less enlightened folk to follow, is hierarchical and elitist. Current forms of communication, however, allow for participatory forums:

> We need national forums to reflect, discuss, and plan how best to respond. It is neither a matter of a new Messiah figure emerging, nor of another organization appearing on the scene. Rather, it is a matter of grasping the structural and institutional processes that have disfigured, deformed, and devastated Black America such that the resources for collective and critical consciousness, moral commitment and courageous engagement are vastly underdeveloped. (West, quoted in hooks and West 1991, 25)

The emphasis in a reflexive theory of liberation is not on the qualities of good leaders but, rather, on the types of leadership models that lead to strategic action to accomplish particular goals:

> We need serious strategic and tactical thinking about how to create new models of leadership and forge the kind of persons to actualize these models. These models must not only question our silent assumptions about Black leadership such as the notion that Black leaders are always middle class but also force us to interrogate iconic figures of the past. This includes questioning King's sexism and homophobia and the relatively undemocratic character of his organi-

zation, and Malcolm's silence in the vicious role of priestly versions of Islam in the modern world. (ibid., 25)

Simultaneously, there is an emphasis on appreciating the strengths and struggles of these "iconic Black leaders . . . so that we learn from past struggles how to strengthen and renew ourselves for the future" (ibid., 25).

Reflexivity is happening with Black writers especially in the area of critical race studies.[16] Many of these writers integrate their own privilege and possible bias in the quest to give a more accurate analysis about race. Another characteristic of this reflexive scholarship is its addressing the differences between different constituencies within the Black communities and how different writers/leaders represent different views. For example, bell hooks, a feminist, interviews Ice Cube, a rapper, whose lyrics are not always on the right side of feminist rhetoric and concerns. Hearing their conversation, we are educated in a profound way about how both of these individuals make sense of their privilege and how they bond across their political differences to try to be responsible members of their constituencies. Again, some white feminists have tried to do the same, but we still have not fully developed a paradigm for progressive scholarship to do this consistently and for the outcome to be applied to political action on behalf of a more democratic social arrangement. In other words, how is domination a puzzle that can be understood in order to be dismantled, and how are we all players *in relationship* to one another, with different access to power, much of it contextually based and some of it ever present? Our social existence is intertwined, for better or worse, and, whether we live next to one another or not, we influence one anothers' lives. To be conscious of this *all* the time and to act in relationship to this *all* the time is what will be required to understand fully domination and oppression and to conceive of and construct a world in which race, sexual orientation, and gender will not matter and in which we will not know the meaning of class.

Notes

Preface

1. A word about ethnic labels used in this book. I use *people of Color* to refer to Chicanos, Asians, Native Americans, and Blacks, all of whom are domestic minorities. Therefore, I capitalize *Color* because it refers to specific ethnic groups. I also capitalize *Black* following the argument that it refers not merely to skin pigmentation but also to a "heritage, an experience, a cultural and personal identity, the meaning of which becomes specifically stigmatic and/or glorious and/or ordinary under specific social conditions. It is socially created as, and at least in the American context no less specifically meaningful or definitive than, any linguistic, tribal, or religious ethnicity, all of which are conventionally recognized by capitalization" (MacKinnon 1982, 516). On the other hand, *white* is left in lowercase letters because it refers not to one ethnic group or to specified ethnic groups but to many.

Chapter 1

1. I concur with Catherine MacKinnon's theoretical assertion that "feminism fundamentally identifies sexuality as the primary social sphere of male power.... Gender socialization is the process through which women come to identify themselves as sexual beings, as beings that exist for men. It is that process through which women internalize (make their own) a male image of their sexuality *as* their identity as women.... Sex as gender and sex as sexuality are thus defined in terms of each other, but it is sexuality that determines gender, not the other way around" (1982, 529–31). Therefore, like MacKinnon, I too use *gender* and *sexuality* interchangeably. See Littleton (1989) for a thorough discussion of the implications of MacKinnon's assertions for feminist theory.

2. By *women of Color* I mean nonwhite women, especially Blacks, Latinas (e.g., Chicanas, Puerto Ricans), Native Americans, and Asian Americans (e.g., Japanese, Chinese, Filipina, Vietnamese). I do not include Jewish women because their historical and cultural experience is different from the women of Color I describe. Jewish women merit a separate analysis, perhaps within the context of the discussion of the heterogeneity among white feminists. Women

worldwide share commonalties; however, there are very important cultural and economic differences that should not be ignored. I focus on women in the United States in order to understand the differences between white women and women of Color in this country. What the implications of my analysis are for women elsewhere is for them to decide.

I also do not explore the implications of my argument for men of Color and white men because that would require explicating an entirely different set of relations, which includes the use of repressive force like prisons, blocked economic opportunity, homicide, and drug use. A progressive men's movement and studies will benefit us enormously in discussing these differences between different ethnic/racial men in our society.

3. In discussing these linkages, my language emphasizes differences—those among women but also the different relationships between various groups of women and white men. I do not mean to imply that these groups are thought of as undifferentiated categories. I take Angela Harris's suggestion to "make our categories explicitly tentative, relational, and unstable" (1990, 239). I also acknowledge diversity within them as I examine, for purposes of this study, the more important problem of the differences in relationship that white women and women of Color have to white men. Readers from the social sciences will recognize this problem in analysis of variance terms in which internal diversity must be considered in order to know if two (or more) groups differ from each other. Although differences within groups are intrinsic to the statistical decision about differences between groups, we social scientists can be faulted for using language at times that implies that merely statistically different categories are unitary and universal. This tendency fosters essentialist thinking about social categories when in fact members of categories always vary in the extent to which they possess prototypic features of the category. See Rosch 1973, for a discussion of psychological research on categories, and Scott 1986, for a discussion of the need for feminists to find a way of analyzing constructions of meaning and relationships of power that call "unitary, universal categories into question" (Scott 1988, 33).

4. Asian Americans, as a group, are stereotyped as the "model minority," a group to be emulated by less successful people of Color. Close examination of the statistics of achieved attainment indicates, however, that the structural integration of different Asian groups (e.g., Japanese, Filipino, Vietnamese, Chinese) is at best uneven and at worst deceptive. Scholars in Asian American studies have highlighted the importance of taking into account bases of stratification such as gender, foreign-born versus U.S.-born native, language competency in English, the geographical distribution of the Asian population within metropolitan areas of high-income/high-cost-of-living locales (e.g., San Francisco, Los Angeles, Hawaii, and New York), historical wave of immigration, and number of wage-earning family members. These factors in combination paint a very different picture of Asian American advancement, especially for women. For example, most Asian Americans (especially women) are overqualified, as measured by formal education, and underpaid when compared to their white male counterparts. In fact, once regional variation is adjusted for,

Filipino and Chinese Americans had a median annual income equivalent to African American men in four mainland Standard Metropolitan Statistical Areas (SMSAs)—Chicago, Los Angeles/Long Beach, New York, San Francisco/Oakland (Woo 1992, 177). For presentations of the intricacies of measuring the structural position of Asian Americans, see Susuki 1977; Woo 1985; Cabeza and Kawaguchi 1987.

5. I use the word *Hispanic* only when the source cited uses that label and does not list figures for individual Latino groups. For accuracy I use the ethnic/racial labels used in the original sources. I cite data separately for different groups of women when available.

6. Asian women as a group have an impressive educational attainment record. Yet, while education facilitates mobility among Asian American women, a large proportion of them continue to be in clerical or administrative support jobs. For example, in 1980 close to a third of native-born Filipinas who were college educated continued to be in clerical administrative support jobs. Deborah Woo indicates that for Asian American women: "Education improves mobility but it promises less than the 'American Dream.' For Asian women, it seems to serve less as an opportunity for mobility than a hedge against jobs as service workers and as machine operatives or assembly workers—the latter being an area where foreign-born Asian women are far more likely than their Anglo male or female counterparts to concentrate. The single largest category of employment here is as seamstresses or 'textile sewing machine operators' in garment factories" (1985, 331–332).

7. Again, this newspaper article follows the practice of aggregating all "women" when there is substantial variation in different groups of women's educational achievement.

8. An exception to this are Asian American women, 13 percent of whom are heads of households (Ortíz 1995).

9. For example, at the University of California, the largest public university in the world, of the total faculty of 7,731, 15.4 percent are white women, 0.7 percent are African American, 1.0 percent are Chicanas/Latinas, 1.5 percent are Asian American, and 0.1 percent are American Indian (the remaining 81.3 percent are men, out of which 69.3 percent are white) (Biennial Higher Education Staff Information [EEO-6] Reports 1993).

10. Several authors have provided analysis of how white feminist theory has excluded women of Color and also how white feminist theory has helped understand the condition of all women regardless of race and class differences (Hurtado 1989; Segura and Pierce 1993).

11. hooks (1989) has offered a similar critique by indicating that many white feminists judge the writing of white working-class women and of women of Color as "experiential," while the writings of white feminists are considered "theory."

12. Harris (1990, 238–39), however, notes that even those feminists theorists who are committed antiracists still rely on gender essentialism to argue that gender supersedes other kinds of subordination.

13. The mission statement for MALCS was written collectively by its

members, but it was published in a newsletter edited by Adeljiza Sosa-Ridell, cochair of the organization.

14. Limitations of space preclude a discussion of the relationship between women of Color and men of Color. Women of Color have started to portray eloquently the solidarity as well as conflict between women and men of Color. For an especially insightful analysis on Chicanas, see Pesquera 1986; Segura 1986; and Zavella 1987. Suffice it to say that men of Color are also influenced by the different conceptions of gender that depict women of Color as less feminine and less desirable than white women (see Joseph 1981; and hooks 1984). This problematic is one that I believe has been belabored in the last twenty years. It must ultimately be resolved by men of Color rather than by women (see Memmi 1965; and Cleaver 1968).

15. In Ostrander's (1984) study of (white) women of the upper class, her respondents felt that one of their main functions was to maintain the "lineage" of their families, and therefore their decision to marry a particular man (and vice versa) was based not so much on their material assets (those were taken for granted to a large extent) but, rather, on how much they could contribute to maintaining a way of life by their club memberships, the social circles they could open up for their husbands, and what associations they belonged to—all of them assets that a woman of Color would not contribute to a marriage.

16. MacKinnon rightly points out, in quoting Cade (1970, 168), that "the pain, isolation, and thingification of women who have been pampered and pacified into nonpersonhood—women 'grown ugly and dangerous from being nobody for so long'—is difficult for the materially deprived to see as a form of oppression, particularly for women whom no man has ever put on a pedestal" (1982, 520).

17. An integral part of white women's socialization is to serve as reflective mirrors to white men so that their accomplishments take on a larger-than-life proportion. Ostrander documents this in her ethnography of upper-class white women, in which the women see their function as affirming and stroking their husbands to allow them to feel powerful outside the home. She states: "The upper class [white] women I spoke with centered their lives around their husbands and their husband's work and adapted themselves to the men's needs, performing what Jessie Bernard has called the 'stroking' function. The stroking function, according to Bernard, consists of showing solidarity, giving help, rewarding, agreeing, understanding and passively accepting" (1984, 39). It is, then, very difficult for most white women to turn against most white men, whom they have been socialized to respect and uplift as an integral part of their sense of self (MacKinnon 1983, 645).

18. Classical writings in Marxism and feminism recognize that women's class position in the United States, with their concomitant privileges and restrictions, is derived from their relationship to men (MacKinnon 1982, 521). This analysis, however, fails to take into account the hypodescent rule in the United States, in which the offspring of a race-dominant parent and a race-subordinate parent is assigned the race-subordinate designation (Davis 1991, 5). So, for example, the son of a white man and a Black woman would be *legally*

Black, with all the restrictions that implies, regardless of class. In these circumstances, if a Black women, regardless of class, marries a prominent white man, her class and that of her children would not necessarily be completely related to her legal connection with her husband, but, rather, it would be superseded by her legal designation as Black (Harris 1993, 1738–41).

19. Connell (1985, 56–57) identifies Chodorow 1978 and Mitchell 1971 as examples of feminist theory with implicit biological assumptions about gender.

20. White (1985, 162) concludes from this exchange that it is a metaphor for how Black women were completely unprotected and how only Black women had their womanhood so totally denied. From my perspective it shows how the lack of protection gave Black women the opportunity to develop strengths denied to the white women in the same meeting and the potential to challenge men's power. Angela Davis (1981, 11) makes this same point.

21. Catherine MacKinnon argues that it is women's sexuality that is the marking mechanism for their domination, while gender is the outcome of their subordinated sexuality: "sexuality is the linchpin of gender inequality" (1982, 533).

22. Afrocentric scholarship is beginning to document how gender and all aspects of social life were conceptualized prior to slavery. These labors will educate all of us on the distortion that slavery imposed on the lives of its victims.

23. As the United States expanded to the west by colonizing native people and importing labor, other women of Color experienced similar treatment. Marta Cotera documents that among the martyrs and victims of social injustice were such women as Juanita of Downieville, California, who was lynched in 1851; Chipita Rodriguez, who was the only woman to be executed in Texas; and countless other Chicanas who were killed by Texas Rangers during their raids on Chicano communities (1977, 24).

24. In 1933 Black feminist educator Mary McLeod Bethune gave the following address:

One hundred years ago [the black woman] was the most pathetic figure on the American continent. She was not a person, in the opinion of many, but a thing, a thing whose personality had no claim to the respect of mankind. She was a house-hold drudge—a means for getting distasteful work done; she was an animated agricultural implement to augment the service of mules and plows in cultivating and harvesting the cotton crop. Then she was an automatic incubator, a producer of human live stock, beneath whose heart and lungs more potential laborers could be bred and nurtured and brought to the light of toilsome day. (Lerner 1973, 579–80)

25. West indicates that "throughout the eighteenth and well into the nineteenth century, U.S. women were barred from speaking 'in public'"—so much so that, "when Emma Hart Willard, a white woman, addressed the New York Legislature in 1819, she remained seated to avoid any suggestion that she was engaged in public speaking" (forthcoming).

26. Suzette Elgin writes a futuristic novel in which women invent a new language, Láadan, that expresses the social reality of women rather than that of men (1984, 250). For example, in Láadan there is a word to name the silence that follows after a woman brings up a topic of conversation and the man she is talking to does not want to pursue the topic and simply pauses for so long that other topics either are suggested by the woman or the uncomfortable pause allows him to insert his own topic (29). These "topic extinctions" (West 1992, 141–42, 145) are a way to control conversation, including what topics are engaged in, and in many instances makes the woman in the interaction feel diminished and less competent in the social interaction (ibid.).

27. I owe this insight to Candace West (pers. comm., 25 October 1986).

28. In addition to incarceration rates, a recent newspaper article reported that, although pregnancy-related deaths continue to decline, Black women are still three times more likely to die from complications than white women. The Federal Centers for Disease Control and Prevention attribute this difference in death rates between Black and white pregnant women to the quality of care these women receive. Black women are twice as likely as white women not to receive prenatal care; only about 60 percent of pregnant Black women receive prenatal care, in comparison to three-fourths of all pregnant women (*San Francisco Chronicle*, 13 January 1995).

29. Another way is through spinsterhood, although spinsterhood does not necessarily lead to the rejection and banishment from the nuclear family that often follows the disclosure of homosexuality.

30. Primarily because, as MacKinnon points out, "As the organized expropriation of the work of some for the benefit of others defines a class—workers—the organized expropriation of the sexuality of some for the use of others defines the sex, woman. Heterosexuality is its structure, gender and family its congealed forms, sex roles its qualities generalized to social persona, reproduction a consequence, and control its issue" (1982, 516).

31. In fact, Cuadraz and Pierce argue that working-class position, regardless of race, results in many graduate students of working-class backgrounds needing to develop survival strategies to succeed in the academy. This "endurance labor" is practiced by those who have no control over dominant structures but who develop strengths to struggle against the very structures designed to disempower them. Endurance labor "pushes against these confrontations of power" (1994, 17).

32. bell hooks sees this as one of the reasons feminists of Color and white feminists have had difficulty uniting:

> Increasingly, only one type of theory is seen as valuable—that which is Euro-centric, linguistically convoluted, and rooted in Western white male sexist and racially biased philosophical frameworks. Here I want to be clear that my criticism is not that feminist theorists focus on such work but that such work is increasingly seen as the only theory that has meaning and significance. . . . Academics who produce theory along these lines often see themselves as superior to those who do not. Feminist theory is

rapidly becoming another sphere of academic elitism. . . . Each time this happens, the radical, subversive potential of feminist scholarship and feminist theory in particular are undermined." (1989, 36–37)

33. Personal choices are also scrutinized when they have political implications—for example, the issue of interracial/interethnic couplings (Graham 1995, 66–67).

34. The conservative press has had a field day mocking the outcome of modifying speech to dismantle hierarchies based on group membership. Rather than address the goals of making language more egalitarian, the focus has been on pointing to ridiculous examples of its implementation. It has been a particularly effective strategy to ridicule egalitarian speech to avert the discussion of why we need to modify our language in the first place (for examples of this conservative media see Beard and Cerf 1992; Beckwith and Bauman 1993; Reese 1993).

35. Some may argue that everything is political. Many feminists of Color, however, are reluctant to invade the only recently acquired right to have a private sphere. Also, many people of Color who only recently have had access to material goods find it oppressive to have their personal lifestyles scrutinized— material acquisitions and comforts have a different meaning if, historically, you have never had access to them. Caraway (1991) discusses this point when she addresses the issue of African American women's "vanity," which, she notes, is really the reacquisition of self after their looks have been derogated for so long and the beauty standard has been set by white women. "Vanity," or keeping up one's appearance, has a very different meaning for women of Color; as hooks (1988) points out, the "demeaning" activity of pressing one's hair was turned on it head, so to speak, by the community-building aspects of getting together with other women to talk in the kitchen while they performed this weekly ritual.

36. White feminists, too, have circles of accountability, but they are much more circumscribed because there is such internal diversity, as Alison Jaggar (1983) points out in her book *Feminists Politics and Human Nature.*

37. The Men's movement is a perfect example of not understanding the existential and therefore dialectical nature of power. Their project has been to voice the downside of power, the responsibilities, the burdens, and constant competition, which entail the denial of emotion, constant belligerence, and rugged individualism. Unfortunately, they do not incorporate into their critique the enormous satisfaction and material privilege that their masculine (and sometimes race) privilege brings them. Consequently, much of the writing in the Men's movement does not lead to a liberatory politics.

38. Caraway 1991, in particular see chap. 5, " 'Now I Am Here': Black Women and the First Wave of Feminism."

39. In fact, radical feminists do not see this collusion of the personal/experiential as undesirable but, rather, as what *should* be cultivated in a feminist community (Jaggar 1983).

40. I do not wish to engage the modernist underpinnings of much of the writings of women of Color and compare it and contrast it to the postmodernist

critique. Caraway (1991) does an excellent analysis of how both theoretical positions can benefit from each other. I'm more interested in what feminists of Color can offer in our understanding of subordination and its implications for political mobilization—political mobilization on behalf of what there is for all of us, collectively, to find out.

41. See Haney and Hurtado 1994, for how merit is racially constructed and to a large extent male.

42. Angela Harris makes this point in analyzing Catherine MacKinnon's and Robin West's work on feminist jurisprudence: "First, my argument should not be read to accuse either MacKinnon or West of 'racism' in the sense of personal antipathy to black people. Both writers are steadfastly anti-racist, which in a sense is my point. Just as law itself, in trying to speak for all persons, ends up silencing those without power, feminist legal theory is in danger of silencing those who have traditionally been kept from speaking, or who have been ignored when they spoke, including black women" (1990, 238).

43. The Latino population in the United States uses different ethnic labels—Chicana, Mexican American, Cuban American, Puerto Rican American, Central American, and so on. Most recently, however, the ethnic terms *Latina* and *Latino* are used as the most inclusive. They refer to any person of Latin American ancestry residing in the United States (female and male, respectively). They also connote identification with the Indo American heritage rather than a Spanish European identification.

44. Caraway elaborates this analysis: "The elevation of white womanhood to the nonthreatening space of ornamental powerlessness, the 'pedestal,' completed the structure of southern patriarchal racism and intensified interracial antagonism between women" (1991, 77).

45. Sandoval reminds us that "Althusser lays out the principles by which humans are called into being as citizen/subjects who act—even when in resistance—in order to sustain and reinforce the dominant social order" (1991, 2).

Chapter 2

1. Lamphere et al. 1993 rightly point out that there is a great deal of internal variation and diversity in how women negotiate structural restrictions. Many ethnographies give us valuable information of variation in how Chicanas negotiate the gender ideologies imposed on them (see ibid. chap. 1 for a review of this literature).

2. For a summary that communicates the purpose and spirit of the beginnings of the Teatro Campesino, see Valdez (1971, 115–19).

3. Several scholars have highlighted the function of characters as archetypes in the representations of the Teatro Campesino. For example, see Morton 1974; Ramirez 1974; and Frischmann 1982, 260.

4. Several analyses of the Teatro Campesino indicate that Valdez explicitly wanted his plays to highlight what in his fiction he saw as the reality in Chicano communities. As Manuel de Jesus Vega states: "El Teatro Campesino es a la vez 'afirmación de la vida' y 'espejo de la realidad.' . . . Si la obra del Teatro

está ligada estrechamente a la vida, esto quiere decir que hemos de encontrar allí una visión total de la misma; tanto el presente como el pasado y el futuro deben aparecer reflejados en la obra" (El Teatro Campesino is at the same time the 'affirmation of life' and 'the mirror of life.' . . . If the project of El Teatro Campesino is intimately tied to life, this means we should find in it a complete vision of it; not only the present but the past and the future should be reflected in the plays) (1983, 350).

5. These characters appear in the play *La Carpa de los Rasquachis* (The Tent of the Underdogs).

6. This definition of femininity is highly influenced by hegemonic definitions in the United States.

7. The only celebrity that comes close to this adaptation in the United States is Madonna; she exhibits all the characteristics of a femme-macho, and that is why cultural theorists have been intrigued with her blasting of sexual, gender, racial, and class boundaries. The main difference, however, between Madonna and Chicana/Mexican femme-machos is the fact that in the United States there is no cultural space for her that fits into our conception of womanhood, whereas for Chicanos femme-machos (successful ones, anyway) are watched with amusement and at times revered if they are willing to pay the price of their adaptation.

8. Madonna, too, has mainstreamed bisexuality and plays visually with "deviant" sexual behavior. In the U.S., however, sexual repression is so strong that there is no public space for handling this visual play with humor. And, unlike Chicano/Mexicano culture, in which the virgin/whore/femme-macho tripartite allows for *playing* with the edge of "propriety," no such playfulness exists in the U.S. without going over the edge.

9. María Félix, with her wicked sense of humor, considered playing the part on film of the principal character in *Zona Sagrada,* with her son, also an actor, playing opposite.

10. This is a play on the word *chingar,* which means "to go fuck yourself."

11. Emma Pérez indicates that Hernán Córtez did not feel Malintzín (or Malinche) was worthy of marriage because she was the "*other,* the inferior, disdained female," and when he was finished with her he passed her on to his soldier (1993, 61).

12. The mixture of European and Indian races.

13. The word *piedra* literally means "stone" in Spanish. The character Piedra in this skit was actually the Aztec calendar made of stone placed in front of a bright red cloth screen. La Piedra served as the main narrator in the play.

14. See Alarcón 1981, for an in-depth analysis of this reinterpretation of la Malinche's role in the conquest of Mexico.

15. *Chingada* literally means in Spanish "the one who has been fucked."

16. *El chingón* literally means in Spanish "the fucker," or "the one who has the ability to fuck," implying the possession of a penis, which is the instrument used to fuck.

17. Although sexual attitudes and sexual behaviors are one of the most underresearched areas for Chicanos (Almaguer 1991), the emergent literature

indicates that there are strong attitudes that support what Patricia Zavella (1994) calls "the cult of virginity." For example, Padilla and Baird (1991, 100–101) find that, among a sample of Mexican American adolescents between the ages of fourteen and nineteen years, a full 80 percent of all participants in the study agreed that women should be virgins when they marry, but only 37 percent of the respondents thought that men should be the same. Men felt more strongly about this than women but not significantly so.

18. Padilla and Baird (1991, 102) find that most of the Mexican American adolescents they studied did not approve of sex without love; young men were more likely to believe this was acceptable (45 percent) than young women (22 percent).

19. Chicana lesbians, like the Malinche, are also characterized as "*vendidas* [sell-outs] to the race" because they have caught white women's sexual disease (Trujillo 1991, ix).

20. Emma Pérez also denounces Octavio Paz's analysis of Chicanas as traitors because of their sexuality's potential for betrayal: "We dispute a historically specific moment that denigrates us, immortalizes us as 'the betrayer' for all time, eternally stuck in an image, *la puta* (the whore). Long before the arrival of the *Virgen de Guadalupe,* we were *La Chingada*. The metaphor cuts to the core of each Chicana; each *mestiza* is flouted as *la india* / whore. Worse yet is that *la india* is our mother, and Paz slashes away at her beauty. He subordinates our first love object by violently raping her in historical text, in male language" (1993, 61).

21. Padilla and Baird note that "it is more important for the males (94%) to have boy children than it was for the females (68%). The male adolescents also want a median of 2 boys, whereas the females want a median of 1 boy" (1991, 101). For a historical view of some of these norms in Mexican American communities, see Ruiz 1993, 118–19.

22. Other white communities, for example some working-class white communities, may judge women's worth according to their virginity, but that is not relevant to my argument here. It would be interesting to start mapping the "convergences and differences" between different groups of women as advocated by Lamphere et al. 1993.

23. Hortensia Amaro indicates that 91 percent of Mexican American women in her study report that the role of mother is either extremely important or has an important place in their lives, whereas only 8.8 percent report that motherhood is somewhat important (1988, 11).

24. *La jefita* is a term of endearment for mothers used among working-class Chicanos and Mexicans. It literally means "little boss."

25. Jose Montoya's poem is reprinted in Mirandé and Enriquez 1979, 165–66.

26. In *La Bamba* the mother's dedication is reciprocated in different ways by each of her children. In fact, when Ritchie Valens is asked by his promoter to leave the rest of his band behind to record his first record, the only reason he agrees is because, as he says, "his family." Ritchie also uses the royalties of his albums to buy his mother "the home of her dreams" (see Fregoso 1993, 141).

27. In *La Bamba* Rosalinda Fregoso notes that, "since the film's dominant tendency is to refuse the mother a subject role within the narrative at the same time that it disallows her any other interests or desires apart from Ritchie, the Ritchie Valens story advances an image of a sacrificial mother whose only object of desire is the 'good son'" (1993, 143).

28. In some extreme cases, if the *expectation* of submissiveness is violated, it can result in violence against women, which further encourages compliance for fear of the consequences (Amaro 1994, 443–44). Another effective threat used by some Chicanos to force Chicanas into compliance is to create competition among women and to threaten to leave them for another partner.

29. *Soldaderas* literally means "female soldier." Soldaderas actually participated in battle during the armed struggle in 1910 to help democratize Mexico from a feudal country to one in which land was distributed among peasants.

30. This particular play is of great significance to the women in El Teatro because La Virgen del Tepeyac is the Catholic version of the Aztec goddess Tonanztin. La Virgen del Tepeyac is the only Indian woman to be beautified by the Catholic Church. To women in El Teatro the role of the Virgen represented a tribute to female potentiality (see Broyles 1986, 171). La Virgen de Guadalupe also has significance outside of El Teatro Campesino. Manuel de Jesús Vega not only agrees with this assessment but also quotes Paz to reinforce his point: "No se puede hablarse de la religiosidad del mexicano sin hacer mención de la importancia que tiene en su vida la Virgen de Guadalupe. Recordemos que César Chávez y el sindicato que dirige siempre marchan trás de un estandarte con la imagen de la Virgen. . . . "La Virgen es el consuelo de los pobres, el escudo de los débiles, el amparo de los oprimidos. En suma es la Madre de los huérfanos'" (It is not possible to speak of Mexicans' religiosity without the mention of the importance to their lives of the Virgen of Guadalupe. Let us remember that César Chavez and the union he directs always walk behind a banner with the image of the Virgen. . . . "The Virgen is solace for the poor, the shield of the weak, the protector of the oppressed. In summary, she is the Mother of all orphans") (1983, 378–80).

31. *Indigena* means "Indian" in Spanish.

32. Ironically, El Teatro members' internalized racism helped to rewrite history by casting La Virgen as a white Madonna when the significance of the character is precisely that she is *Indian*! bell hooks makes a similar point about the beauty standards in society at large as well as in Black communities, in which "the images of black female bitchiness, evil temper, and treachery continue to be marked by darker skin. . . . We see these images continually in the mass media whether they be presented to us in television sitcoms (such as the popular show 'Martin'), on cop shows, (the criminal black woman is usually dark), and in movies made by black and white directors alike" (1994, 179).

33. Dances, baptisms, Mexican bingo, barbecues, birthday parties, mass, Christmas celebrations, fifteen-year-old birthdays for young women, funerals.

34. Baptisms, afternoon gatherings, dances, wakes.

35. The interconnectedness of El Teatro Campesino's position on family, community, and the ownership of land is summarized in its statement that:

"We are family . . . who live communally. We are all brothers and sisters because we have a Common Father. . . . He created us, He who uplifted us, Our Father of the Astros, GOD THE FATHER" (quoted in Morton 1974).

36. The importance of *la tierra* (earth) is also manifested in the Teatro Campesino's artistic production. See, for example, *Bernabé* and the analysis of this play by Donald H. Frischmann (1982, 264–69).

37. *Carnalismo* is derived from the word *carne*, which literally means "one's flesh," as in the biological ties that are the result of being from the same flesh.

38. *Raza* refers to José Vasconcelos's notion of a unified "cosmic race" in North America and Latin America that would result in a new social order combining the best elements of all cultures. Chicanos adopted this term, *raza*, to refer to the ties Chicanos feel as a group (see Vasconcelos 1979).

39. *El Fin del Mundo* (The End of the World) was the last play produced by El Teatro Campesino. Like most of the productions by the Teatro Campesino, *El Fin del Mundo* went through various stages in its four-year evolution, which began in 1974. The fourth, and last, version was created under Valdez's guidance and was directed by his sister, Socorro Valdez, in 1978 (Huerta 1982, 209). *El Fin del Mundo* showed the evolution of the Teatro Campesino by this mixed-gendered collaboration and the sympathetic portrayal of a Chicana lesbian.

40. Zavella (1994, 201, 207) rightly indicates that the crossing of borders by Chicanas is not an easy journey that is accomplished by all and that, in fact, material conditions as well as cultural restrictions work more often than not against women crossing borders.

41. Lugones (1990) takes the concept of limen from Turner 1974.

42. *Gabacha:* a Chicano term for a white woman.

43. *Mestiza:* of mixed race.

44. *Mulata:* of African American and white race heritage.

45. *Rajetas:* literally "split," that is, having betrayed your word.

46. When you live in the borderlands.

47. *Burra:* donkey; *buey:* oxen.

48. *Chile:* hot sauce.

49. Tex-Mex is a speech style particular to Texas, where Chicanos (and some Anglos) mix English and Spanish to create a dialect. It is creative language because new combinations can constantly be made, and it has been used by Chicano poets as emphasizing Chicano cultural expression. Some expressions include *troca* (truck), *parkearse* (to park), *watcha* (to watch).

50. *Migra:* slang word used by Chicanos for the Immigration and Naturalization Service (INS).

51. *Sin fronteras:* without borders.

52. Emma Pérez advocates Chicanas' reacquisition of that part of them that is *india* and that has been "plundered through conquest and colonization." She proclaims that "we reclaim the core for our women-tempered *sitios y lenguas* (spaces and languages)" (Pérez 1993, 62).

53. Lugones (1990, 10) makes explicit that she is referring to white women in another part of her manuscript, although it is not explicit in this quote.

Chapter 3

1. Connell describes the historical developments and the cross-cultural variations in the definition of masculinity. For example, he notes that the industrial revolution, which displaced peasants and converted them into members of the working class, led to working-class hegemonic masculinities. He describes the process: "The separation of household from workplace in the factory system, the dominance of the wage form, and the development of industrial struggle, were conditions for the emergence of norms of masculinity organized around wage-earning capacity, skill and endurance in labor, domestic patriarchy, and combative solidarity among wage earners" (1993, 611).

2. Alice Echols provides an excellent overview of the literature produced on the 1960s and analyzes the different perspectives of these analyses (1992, 12). See also Elizabeth Martínez 1989.

3. Cheryl Harris (1993a) argues persuasively that whiteness has been legally constructed to be valuable property and that, in order to maintain its value, non-white members have to be kept out of the group.

4. In fact, the *liberal subject* remained basically male even in the progressive political movements of the 1960s. As Echols (1992, 10) points out, many of its intellectuals and former activities have produced a host of memoirs, histories, and films in which "citizenship, principled protest, and rock 'n' roll genius are assumed to be the unique preserve of men"—the only true civil subjects (1992, 10).

5. Cheryl Harris (1993a) answers Brown's challenge and goes beyond "speculation" to demonstrate *systematically* how the state is racist in favoring whiteness as valuable property.

6. In the United States lack of money often means lack of privacy or space (Frankenberg 1993, 200).

7. Connell points out that there are a range of masculinities varying across cultures and through historical times and even within a particular culture at a given time (1992, 736). Such is the case with heterosexual and homosexual masculinities and the masculinities of different ethnic and age groups. I would also add class.

8. As Ruth Frankenberg points out: "Integral to this set of linked discursive, economic, and political histories [against intermarriage] were constructions of masculinities and femininities along racially differentiated lines. Foremost was the construction in racist discourses of the sexuality of men and women of color as excessive, animalistic, or exotic in contrast to the ostensibly restrained or 'civilized' sexuality of white women and men" (1993, 75).

9. Wealthy white women also appear competent, aggressive leaders in comparison to men of Color—especially poor ones. For example, there are documented cases of wealthy plantation owners who could run complex operations in the absence of white men by "directing," "leading," and "managing" large cadres of black slaves—both men and women. The same is true of pioneer women in the West where in the absence of white men they were portrayed as able people by using Native Americans—both men and women—as cheap

labor. Currently, white women in corporate America manage both men and women of Color and their main source of sexism is other CEOs who are almost exclusively white men.

10. Ann Phoenix (1990) also echoes Davis in stating that Black men of African-Caribbean origin are stereotyped as feckless, violent, criminal, and oversexed and dangerous.

11. A recent article in *Newsweek* reports that Black children are three times more likely than whites to live in a single-parent household, that 43.2 percent of all African American children live in poverty, and that African Americans now account for 28.8 percent of U.S. AIDS cases. Furthermore, African Americans constitute 52 percent of women with AIDS, and African American children represent 53 percent of all pediatric AIDS cases (Morganthau 1992).

12. In the same *Newsweek* article they report that homicide is now the leading cause of death for African American males between the ages of fifteen and thirty-four; nearly half of all U.S. murder victims are African American; in 1989, 23 percent of all African American men aged twenty to twenty-nine were either in prison or on probation or parole; one study finds that one-fifth of all African American males between fifteen and thirty-four now have a criminal record (Morganthau 1992).

13. The signing of the Treaty of Guadalupe Hidalgo in 1848 gave birth to Chicanos *as a people.* The treaty ended the Mexican-American War, in which Mexico was defeated and lost over 50 percent of its territory. Overnight the people residing in what has become the southwestern United States had a new government that used a different language, a different culture, and had the victor's power over them (Almaguer 1971; García 1973). Although the Mexican government tried to provide safeguards for its former citizenry by insuring their language and U.S. citizenship, the conquerors ignored their contractual agreements and proceeded to dispossess the vanquished people of their land, language, culture, and history and place them not much above a slave status. As Rodolfo Alvarez summarizes: "*as a people,* Mexican Americans are a creation of the imperial conquest of one nation by another through military force . . . with the signing of the Treaty of Guadalupe Hidalgo, the Mexican American people were *created as a people:* Mexican by birth, language, and culture; U.S. citizens by the might of arms" (1973, 924).

14. Part of the gender socialization for men in general is to defame them by calling them pussies and bitches. This socialization is especially intensified in organized sports and military training (Fine, Weis, and Addelston 1994).

15. In the United States the legal definition of who is Black follows the "one-drop rule," in which any African ancestry makes the person Black. This is also called the hypodescent rule; the children of one subordinate and one superordinate parent is assigned the race of the subordinate parent. A Black and white couple who have children would automatically be classified as Black (M. Harris 1964, 37, 56; Davis 1991, 5; C. I. Harris 1993a, 1738–41).

16. bell hooks points out that "the black male slave was primarily exploited as a laborer in the fields; the black female was exploited as a laborer

in the fields, a worker in the domestic household, a breeder, and as an object of white male sexual assault" (1981, 22).

17. hooks observes that "white women and men justified the sexual exploitation of enslaved black women by arguing that they were the initiators of sexual relationships with men. From such thinking emerged the stereotype of black women as sexual savages, and in sexist terms a sexual savage, a non-human, an animal cannot be raped" (1981, 52).

18. The notion of "race" being constituted purely by blood through biological inheritance is at the core of white privilege. Furthermore, this Black blood is so tainted and apart from the white race that a person with "one drop" of Black blood is considered Black. It would take many generations before Blacks could join the white privileged group. Cheryl Harris analyzes how legally the hypodescent rule overrode other types of considerations in determining who is white; for example, "if an individual's blood was tainted, she could not claim to be 'white' as the law understood, regardless of the fact that phenotypically she may have been completely indistinguishable from a white person, may have lived as a white person, and have descended from a family that lives as whites. Although socially accepted as white, she could not *legally* be white" (1993b, 1739). The interracial coupling taboo is very much related to viewing Blacks as not human because of their "blood." Similarly for Chicanos, their mestizo (hybrid) background is also considered as tainted, especially because of their Indian background.

19. An example of the blurring of gender boundaries between Black women and men was the fact that, during the period when Jim Crow laws were instituted in the United States, there were single toilet facilities for both black men and women (Lerner 1973).

20. Of course, since the 1960s there have been troubling questions raised about John Kennedy's sincerity of commitment to the ideals of justice (see Reeves 1991).

21. See Ruiz 1991 for the difficulties involved for women in the Chicano movement to bring their concerns about gender to the forefront.

22. Because of the urgency of the struggle for economic and cultural survival, only recently have there been concerted efforts to address issues of sexuality within Chicano communities. This important work has been done primarily, although not exclusively, by Chicana lesbians (Anzaldúa 1990; Almaguer 1991; Trujillo 1991; Zavella 1994).

23. A political slogan of the Chicano movement, which roughly translates as "Up with Our People!"

24. Dough used to make tamales, a Mexican food that looks like a small pie made out of corn dough and wrapped in corn husk leaves.

25. *Mija* is a term of endearment between lovers that is a contraction of the Spanish *mi hija* and literally means "my little daughter"; it is equivalent to calling a lover "babe."

26. See chapter 2 for the cultural significance of la Malinche.

27. This was the first major political party created in the 1970s on the basis of Chicano concerns.

28. Alice Echols points out that, while the Black Civil Rights Movement was searching for the black inside the Negro, white women feminists were "daring to be bad" by violating sanctions against assertiveness, while New Left (white) men were trying to find the "rebel underneath the gray flannel suit" (1992, 23–24). Oddly enough, Echols fails to see how this search for the new person as a product of progressive politics is racialized in such a way that it literally leaves out women of Color—what did their progressive person look like?—and, of course, other men of Color besides Blacks who did not have access to the gray flannel suit to begin with and whose progressive person is more culturally specific. All of these points I address in this chapter.

29. As Juan Gómez-Quiñones indicates: "Cultural resistance, the rejection of cultural domination, is the negation of assimilation. This may take two routes: 'tradition' for its own sake, or a synthesis of tradition and creation" (1977, 8). Activists within the Chicano movement explicitly took the latter route, synthesis, because Chicanos have never been accepted by Mexico or the United States. They felt that the Chicanos' strength came from being between cultures and that out of that position they could create a superior culture that combined all the influences their conquest had exposed them to.

30. La Raza Cósmica refers to José Vasconcelos's (1979) notion of a unified "cosmic race" in North America and Latin America that would result in a new social order combining the best elements of all cultures. Chicanos adopted this term, *raza*, to refer to the ties Chicanos feel as a group.

31. See Richard Rodriguez 1982 and Laura Rendón 1992 for two different ways of coping with the psychic costs of being educationally successful as a Chicano/a. In the case of Rodriguez, the success comes at the cost of deep ambivalence about his Mexican background to the point that he tries to "shave" his brown skin with a razor and finally concludes that complete assimilation is the only way to escape the pain. For Rendón the pain is no less, as she becomes one of the few Chicanas to hold a doctorate degree and pursue an academic career. She concludes, however, that the pain will stop only when institutions change to accommodate culturally diverse students. In the meantime she commits herself to political mobilization on behalf of her group.

32. Although some white feminists have pursued religion as a political goal, most of the mobilization has been around spirituality rather than organized religion. The quest for spirituality has been sparked especially by radical feminists who see women's capacity to procreate as the basis for women's "special ways of knowing and conceiving the world" (Jaggar 1983, 95). In contrast, the Black and Chicano movements used the existing commitment among their groups to organized religion for political mobilization: for Martin Luther King it was Blacks' commitment to the Protestant religions, for César Chavez it was Chicanos' commitment to Catholicism, and for Malcolm X it was Blacks' conversion to Islam.

33. The Catholic Church has been central to the political mobilization of Chicanos. For example, Communities Organized for Public Service (COPS) in San Antonio, Texas, and its counterpart in Los Angeles, United Neighborhoods Association (UNO), started by being partially financed by the Catholic

Church's hierarchy (Barrera 1990, 59). The strong commitment of most Chicano activists to the Catholic Church has put them at odds with both Chicano and non-Chicano participants within their movement who see the Catholic Church as reactionary. For example, Dolores Huerta, one of the main leaders in the United Farmworkers Union, recalls how César Chávez and Saul Alinsky had a strong disagreement over Chávez's religious commitment to Catholicism as the basis for his political organizing. Huerta recalls Alinsky's discomfort at having to explain to his organization, Industrial Areas Foundation, Chávez's political strategy of fasting and prayer. Ultimately, Chávez's actions were extremely successful at uniting the farmworkers, and

> Saul was at a loss for words. . . . But that was the reaction of many liberals and radicals. . . . Guys can be liberal about homosexuality, about dope, about capital punishment, about everything but the Catholic church. There the liberalism ends. So he [Chávez] doesn't want to feed the bigotry that the average person has against the church. He tries to overcome that bigotry by his example. (Levy 1975, 277–78)

34. There is a popular joke in Mexico in which an Anglo Marxist walking by the Basilica de Nuestra Señora de Guadalupe (the church of Mexico's patron saint) sees a fellow Mexican Marxist involved in the Catholic ritual of walking on his knees from the entrance of the shrine to the Virgin of Guadalupe's altar. The Anglo Marxist is astonished and says to the Mexican Marxist, "I thought you were a Marxist!" His comrade replies, "Yes, I am, but I'm Mexican first."

35. Toni Morrison (1989) questions what appears to be the universal wisdom in the United States that adolescents not have children until later in life. She asserts that perhaps the reason young people are having children is because that's when human beings are best suited to be parents. The question, according to Morrison, is how do we construct a society that helps young people fulfill their potential *at the same time* that they are raising children?

36. Susan Ostrander's ethnography confirms Beth Vanfossen's work that indicates that upper-class women have larger number of children to increase their lineage: "Children are valued as carriers of the family's elite status, and, accordingly, the number of children per family is considerably higher than in the middle class" (Vanfossen 1979, 296; Ostrander 1984, 71). In the 1980s, during the Reagan era, there was a call for educated white women to reproduce before there was "race suicide"—the result of their low fertility rates (Kimmel 1993, 33).

37. Except when their children are needed to be laborers.

38. *Rasquache* means "low down"; a glorification of "low class" as desirable because of its members' potential authenticity.

39. Labor camps where farmworkers live during the picking season.

40. Metaphorically *puro pedo* means "hot air," and literally it means "a pure form of flatulence."

41. *Gringo seco* means "dried-up Anglo" in informal Spanish.

42. *Que suenen la campanita!* is an announcement usually made at the

beginning of the play so that the audiences quiet down; it means, "Let the little bell ring!" (Valdez 1973, 190).

43. Gómez-Quiñones characterizes the participants in the Chicano student movement as coming predominantly from the working class, being few in number, and organizing such student organizations as the United Mexican American Students, the Mexican American Student Confederation, the Mexican American Student Organization, and the Mexican American Youth Organization, among others (1990, 118). Contrast the class origins of the white student movement from the preamble to *The Port Huron Statement* written by Tom Hayden: "We are the people of this generation, bred in at least modest comfort, housed now in universities, looking uncomfortably at the world we inherit" (1989, 92). There are several key differences to highlight between these two student movements. The participants in the white student movement acknowledge the comfort with which they were raised and the explicit expectation that they would be inheriting the existing power structure. Both of these elements are missing in the Black and Chicano movements.

44. Muñoz indicates that the class differences between the white student movement and the Chicano student movement are also reflected in their goals: whereas the white youth radicalism

> contributed to the making of a counterculture stressing humanistic values, Chicano youth radicalism represented a return to the humanistic cultural values of the Mexican working class. This in turn led to the shaping of a nationalist ideology, which although antiracist in nature, stressed the non-white indigenous aspects of Mexican working-class culture. This nationalism defined Mexican Americans as *mestizos,* a mixed race people, and rejected identification with the white European/Hispanic roots of Mexican culture. It further called for the rejection of assimilation into the dominant, white Anglo-Saxon Protestant culture of the United States. (1989, 15).

45. Interestingly enough, thirty years after this speech Derrick Bell takes a similar position in indicating that individual protest highlights the illegitimacy of authority even when the concrete material results may seem insignificant (1994, 8).

46. Elizabeth Martínez reviews the proliferation of books on the political movements of the 1960s and the fact that almost all had been written by white males. The result is that ethnic/racial movements that took place during that time are completely ignored. For example, Todd Gitlin's book does not mention any ethnic/racial movements besides the Black Civil Rights movement until the last third of his 513-page book. Even then Martínez notes that "he speaks of 'an amalgam of reform efforts, especially for civil rights (ultimately for Hispanics, Native Americans, and other minorities as well as blacks). . . .' Six words, and in parentheses at that, for the thousands of Asian, Latino, and Native American people who worked for liberation and social justice in those years." Besides a racial/ethnic bias in the books of the 1960s, there is also a class bias in favor of student and middle-class elites (Martínez 1989, 49).

47. Evans 1980, 151; quoted in Echols 1992, 18.

48. Tom Hayden explicitly uses the rhetoric of conquest and sports by stating that he, like others in the movement, were not only interested in rebellion for its own sake but what he wanted was to win (1989, 77).

49. Trimberger and Dennis (1979) make the point that *The Port Huron Statement* authored by Tom Hayden opened the possibility of making the personal political by indicating that "re-assertion of the personal" was essential to change society. Echols uses Trimberger's work to reinforce this point in her book on the 1960s (1989, 28–29).

50. For example, Chicana academics created their own professional organization, Mujeres Activas in Letras y Cambio Social (MALCS) (Women Active in Letters and Social Change), in response to men's domination of the National Association for Chicano Studies (NACS). Most of the MALCS members, however, participate in NACS. Chicana feminists have not officially proposed to boycott or otherwise disengage from NACS. Instead, there have been a series of confrontations over the exclusion of women and the absence of gender issues in the annual meetings of NACS. (I also make this point in chap. 2.)

51. *The New York Times* reported that there were dozens of pickets at the opening of the film "The Color Purple" protesting the portrayal of Black men as extremely violent. The same article reports that nearly a thousand blacks crammed into the Progressive Community Church for a heated discussion of the film (Shipp 1986). There were also numerous editorials lamenting the one-sided portrayal of black men as wife beaters and sexual abusers (Rasperry 1986).

52. Kimmel points out that hegemonic white masculinity is used to give men, as a group, the power to determine the distribution of rewards in society. Yet not all men have equal power; rather it is mediated by men's differential access to class, race, or ethnic privileges or privileges based on sexual orientation (1993, 30).

53. This analysis of Connell is provided by Caroline Ramazanoglu (1992, 343).

54. Although Echols mentions that there were other ethnic/racial groups that were not incorporated into the analyses of the 1960s, she simply refers to a book review that notes the exclusion of women in the male accounts of the Chicano movement without remedying the situation in her own excellent analysis of the exclusion of white women in white men's accounts of the 1960s (1992, 13, 30). Elizabeth Martínez (1989) documents in depth how most books on the 1960s do not address the contributions made by the political mobilization of ethnic/racial groups.

55. See the following as examples of this tendency: Abernathy 1989; Muñoz 1989; Gómez-Quiñones 1990.

56. For a review of this issue, see Echols 1992, 13, 30.

Chapter 4

1. The goal of a masculinist positivist Western tradition is to measure as precisely as possible the hierarchical relationship between the different variables that constitute a particular phenomemon.

2. Also see Mirandé 1988, for an analysis for the positive aspects of machismo (another word for manhood), including responsibility for one's family and honest relationships with others. Stoltenberg (1993, 9) also calls this "being a man of conscience"—"loving justice more than loving manhood."

3. There are a few budding exceptions but as yet not a well-developed scholarship or theoretical framework. For examples, see Sturgis 1988; McIntosh 1992; and Frankenberg 1993.

4. Morrison sees this appropriation as one way that whites gain identity. She puts it this way in explaining the writer Willa Cather's use of a "slave girl" in one of her novels: "the reckless, unabated power of a white woman gathering identity unto herself from the wholly available and serviceable lives of Africanist others. This seems to me to provide the coordinates of an immensely important moral debate" (1992, 25). I would add a silent debate.

5. Among critical race theorists are such scholars as Kimberlé Crenshaw, Richard Delgado, Angela Harris, Cheryl Harris, Mari Matsuda, and Patricia Williams.

6. These observations are from the bottom up. It would still be immensely helpful to have the socialization practices of the privilege *from birth* to break their silence. Those of us who have gained some measure of privilege as adults are still handicapped in fully understanding how privilege is constructed through a lifetime of practice.

7. There are many examples of these moral arguments in the United States, such as by César Chávez, Dolores Huerta, Audrey Lorde, and Malcolm X, among others.

8. In Spanish there is a saying *no te hagas pendejo,* meaning "don't play dumb." This is a rhetorical device used in conversation in which individuals claim not to understand so as not to be overpowered by the other speaker in the conversation. It is an expression used mostly by working-class Mexicans in order to subvert the power of those who claim not to know, especially when the factual evidence is overwhelming. Even though this device is usually not used when there is a power disparity—that is, between a subordinate speaker and a dominant speaker—it is used by working-class Mexicans to refer to the mechanism when they are out of the presence of those who use it. Thus, a worker may say about her boss, *se hace pendejo* (he plays dumb), when her boss refuses her request to have her salary increased because of the extra duties he has assigned to her by claiming that he does not know what extra duties she is speaking about.

9. Deborah Tannen's book *You Just Don't Understand* (1990) and John Gray's book *Men Are from Mars, Women Are from Venus* (1992) are examples of addressing "speech style" differences without addressing the underlying power differentials. See West 1995, for the fallacies in these type of analyses.

10. An example that comes to mind is special admissions to top universities for children of alumni. Former president George Bush falls into this category.

11. A *pastorela* is a Catholic passion play brought to the Americas by colonizing Spaniards in the sixteenth century. The play, performed throughout the

U.S. southwest and Latin America, consists of stock characters whose dialogue and specific plot twists get reinvented by those who perform it. The adaptability of the play includes substituting the dialogue with local slang to make it more accessible and enjoyable to working-class communities. Several scholars attribute the endurance of this play to its flexibility, which insures it from becoming "set" and therefore obsolete (Broyles 1994, 60–62).

12. Much of the analysis presented here on the research of whiteness has appeared previously in Hurtado and Stewart 1995.

13. A most recent example is California governor Pete Wilson's assertion that he does not remember the Mexican immigrant who served him for a number of years. He actually did not "see" her.

14. Gutiérrez points out that the Kingdom of New Mexico's settled population in the eighteenth century consisted of four major groups: the nobility (the dominant class), landed peasants, the indians (the middle group), and at the bottom were the *genízaros*. The *genízaros* were ". . . slaves, detribalized Indians, primarily of Apache and Navajo origin, who had been captured by the Spanish and pressed into domestic service" (1991, 148).

15. Angela Harris makes a similar point in her analysis of the essentialist nature of Catherine MacKinnon and Robin West's feminist jurisprudence. She clearly states that her "aim is not to establish a new essentialism in its place based on the essential experience of black women. . . . Accordingly, I invite the critique and subversion of my own generalizations" (1990, 238).

16. Take, for example, Derrick Bell's statement in the introduction to his book that chronicles his protest against Harvard University because it would not hire a woman of Color: "The protester, while seeking always to carry the banner of truth and justice, must remember that the fires of commitment do not bestow the gift of infallibility" (1994, xxi). Interestingly, Bell's principled protest was questioned by African American feminists, who saw his action, made without consulting Regina Austin, the professor whom Bell sought to have hired at Harvard, as usurping their right to participate in the decision of whether Bell should undertake his protest on her behalf.

Bibliography

Abernathy, Ralph David. 1989. *And the Walls Came Tumbling Down: An Autobiography*. New York: Harper and Row.

Alarcón, Norma. 1990. "The Theoretical Subject(s) of This Bridge Called My Back and Anglo-American Feminism." In *Making Face, Making Soul: Haciendo Caras*, ed. Gloria Anzaldúa, 356–69. San Francisco: Aunt Lute Foundation Books.

———. 1981. "Chicana's Feminist Literature: A Re-vision through Malintzin/or Malintzin: Putting Flesh Back on the Object." In *This Bridge Called My Back: Writings by Radical Women of Color*, ed. Cherríe Moraga and Gloria Anzaldúa, 182–90. Watertown, Mass.: Persephone Press.

Almaguer, Tomás. 1994. *Racial Fault Lines: The Historical Origins of White Supremacy in California*. Berkeley: University of California Press.

———. 1991. "Chicano Men: A Cartography of Homosexual Identity and Behavior." *differences: A Journal of Feminist Cultural Studies* 3(2): 75–100.

———. 1971. "Toward the Study of Chicano Colonialism." *Aztlán: Chicano Journal of the Social Sciences and Arts* 2(2): 7–21.

Alvarez, Rodolfo. 1973. "The Psycho-Historical and Socioeconomic Development of the Chicano Community in the United States." *Social Science Quarterly* 53(4): 920–42.

Amaro, Hortensia. 1988. "Women in the Mexican-American Community: Religion, Culture, and Reproductive Attitudes and Experiences." *Journal of Community Psychology* 16 (January): 6–20.

Anzaldúa, Gloria. 1990. "La Conciencia de la Mestiza: Towards a New Consciousness." In *Making Face, Making Soul—Haciendo Caras: Creative and Critical Perspectives by Women of Color*, ed. Gloria Anzaldúa, 377–89. San Francisco: Spinsters / Aunt Lute.

———, ed. 1990. *Making Face, Making Soul—Haciendo Caras: Creative and Critical Perspectives by Women of Color*. San Francisco: Spinsters / Aunt Lute.

———. 1987. *Borderlands—La Frontera: The New Mestiza*. San Francisco: Spinsters / Aunt Lute.

———. 1981. "La Prieta." In *This Bridge Called My Back: Writings by Radical Women of Color*, ed. Cherríe Moraga and Gloria Anzaldúa, 198–209. Watertown, Mass.: Persephone Press.

Apfelbaum, Erika. 1979. "Relations of Domination and Movements for Liberation: An Analysis of Power between Groups." In *The Social Psychology of Intergroup Relations*, ed. William G. Austin and Stephen Worchel, 188–204. Monterey, Calif.: Brooks/Cole Publishing.

Aptheker, Bettina. 1982. *Woman's Legacy: Essays on Race, Sex, and Class.* Amherst: University of Massachusetts Press.

Ardener, Shirley. 1975. *Perceiving Women.* New York: Wiley.

Bailey, Richard. 1993. Review of *A Question of Character: A Life of John F. Kennedy* by Thomas C. Reeves. *Southwestern Historical Quarterly* 96 (April): 620–21.

Barrera, Mario. 1990. *Beyond Aztlán Ethnic Autonomy in Comparative Perspective.* Notre Dame, Ind.: University of Notre Dame Press.

Barrera, Marta. 1991. "Café con Leche." In *Chicana Lesbians: The Girls Our Mothers Warned Us About,* ed. Carla Trujillo, 80–83. Berkeley, Calif.: Third Woman Press.

Beard, Henry, and Christopher Cerf. 1992. *The Official Politically Correct Dictionary and Handbook.* New York: Villard Books.

Beckwith, Francis J., and Bauman, Michael E., eds. 1993. *Are You Politically Correct? Debating America's Cultural Standards.* Buffalo, N.Y.: Prometheus Books.

Behar, Ruth. 1993. *Translated Woman: Crossing the Border with Esperanza's Story.* Boston: Beacon Press.

Belenky, Mary Field, Blythe McVicker Clinchy, Nancy Rule Goldberger, and Jill Mattuck Tarule. 1986. *Women's Ways of Knowing.* New York: Basic Books.

Bell, Derrick. 1994. *Confronting Authority: Reflections of an Ardent Protester.* New York: Basic Books.

———. 1992. *Faces at the Bottom of the Well: The Permanence of Racism.* New York: Basic Books.

Bennett, Claudette E. 1995. *The Black Population in the United States: March 1994 and 1993.* U.S. Bureau of the Census, Current Population Reports, P20–480. Washington, D.C.: U.S. Government Printing Office.

Biennial Higher Education Staff Information (EEO-6) Reports. 1993. University of California, Office of the President.

Blumstein, Alfred. 1983. "On the Racial Disproportionality of United States Prison Populations." *Journal of Criminal Law and Criminology* 73: 1259–81.

Bly, Robert. 1990. *Iron John: A Book about Men.* Reading, Mass.: Addison-Wesley.

Boynton, Robert. 1995. "The New Intellectuals." *Atlantic Monthly,* March, 53–70.

Brant, Beth, ed. 1984. *A Gathering of Spirit: Writing and Art of North American Indian Women.* Montpelier, Vt.: Sinister Wisdom Books.

Brod, Harry, ed. 1987. *The Making of Masculinities: The New Men's Studies.* Boston: Allen and Unwin.

Brown, Edward G. 1980. "The Teatro Campesino's Vietnam Trilogy." *Minority Voices* 4(1): 29–38.

Brown, Elaine. 1992. *A Taste of Power: A Black Woman's Story.* New York: Doubleday.

Brown, Wendy. 1992. "Finding the Man in the State." *Feminist Studies* 18(1): 7–34.

Broyles, Yolanda Julia. 1994. *El Teatro Campesino: Theater in the Chicano Movement*. Austin: University of Texas Press.

———. 1986. "Women in El Teatro Campesino: ¿Apoco Estaba Molacha La Virgen de Guadalupe?" In *Chicana Voices: Intersections of Class, Race and Gender*, ed. Ricardo Romo, 162–87. Austin: Center for Mexican-American Studies, University of Texas at Austin.

———. 1985. "Toward a Re-Vision of Chicano Theatre History: The Women of El Teatro Campesino." In *Making a Spectacle: Feminist Essays on Contemporary Women's Theatre*, ed. Linda Hart, 209–38. Ann Arbor: University of Michigan Press.

Bruce-Novoa, Juan. 1988. "De Los Actos a La Bamba: La Evolución de Valdez." Paper presented at the Third International Conference on the Hispanic Cultures of the United States, Barcelona, 7–10 June.

———. 1978. "*El Teatro Campesino* de Luis Valdez." *Texto Crítico* 4(10): 65–75.

Cabezas, Amado, and Gary Kawaguchi. 1987. "Empirical Evidence for Continuing Asian American Income Inequality: The Human Capital Model and Labor Market Segmentation." Paper presented at the Fourth Asian American Studies Conference of the Association of Asian American Studies, San Francisco State University, 19–21 March.

Cade, Toni. 1970a. "On The Issue of Roles." In *The Black Woman: An Anthology*, ed. Toni Cade, 101–10. New York: New American Library.

———. 1970b. "The Pill: Genocide or Liberation?" In *The Black Woman: An Anthology*, ed. Toni Cade, 162–69. New York: New American Library.

Cameron, Barbara. 1981. " 'Gee, You Don't Seem like an Indian from the Reservation.' " In *This Bridge Called My Back: Writings by Radical Women of Color*, ed. Cherríe Moraga and Gloria Anzaldúa, 46–52. Watertown, Mass.: Persephone Press.

Canaan, Joyce, and Christine Griffin. 1990. "The New Men's Studies: Part of the Problem or Part of the Solution?" In *Men, Masculinities and Social Theory*, ed. Jeff Hearn and David Morgan, 206–14. London: Unwin Hyman.

Caraway, Nancie. 1991. *Segregated Sisterhood: Racism and the Politics of American Feminism*. Knoxville: University of Tennessee Press.

Carter, Deborah J., and Reginald Wilson. 1993. *Twelfth Annual Status Report: Minorities in Higher Education*. Washington, D.C.: American Council on Education.

Castillo, Ana. 1995. *Massacre of the Dreamers*. New York: Plume Book.

———. 1991. "La Macha: Toward a Beautiful Whole Self." In *Chicana Lesbians: The Girls Our Mothers Warned Us About*, ed. Carla Trujillo, 24–48. Berkeley, Calif.: Third Woman Press.

Cervantes, Lorna Dee. 1977. "You Cramp My Style Baby." *El Fuego de Aztlán* 4(Summer): 39.

Chavez, Linda. 1991. *Out of the Barrio: Toward a New Politics of Hispanic Assimilation*. New York: Basic Books.

Childs, John Brown. 1994. "The Value of Transcommunal Identity Politics." *Z Magazine* 7(7–8): 48–51.

Chodorow, Nancy. 1978. *The Reproduction of Mothering: Psychoanalysis and the Sociology of Gender.* Berkeley and Los Angeles: University of California Press.

Cisneros, Sandra. 1994. *Loose Woman.* New York: Alfred A. Knopf.

Cleaver, Eldridge. 1968. *Soul on Ice.* New York: McGraw-Hill.

Cliff, Michelle. 1990. "Women Warriors: Black Writers Load the Cannon." *Village Voice Supplement,* May, 20–22.

Collins, Patricia Hill. 1991. *Black Feminist Thought.* New York: Routledge.

————. 1989. "The Social Construction of Black Feminist Thought." *Signs: Journal of Women in Culture and Society* 14(4): 745–73.

————. 1986. "Learning from the Outsider Within: The Sociological Significance of Black Feminist Thought." *Social Problems* 33(6): 14–32.

Connell, R. W. 1995. *Masculinities.* Berkeley: University of California Press.

————. 1993. "The Big Picture: Masculinities in Recent World History." *Theory and Society* 22: 597–623.

————. 1992. "A Very Straight Gay: Masculinity, Homosexual Experience, and the Dynamics of Gender." *American Sociological Review* 57 (December): 735–51.

————. 1987. *Gender and Power: Society, the Person, and Sexual Politics.* Stanford, Calif.: Stanford University Press.

————. 1985. "Theorizing Gender." *Sociology* 19(2): 260–72.

Cotera, Marta. 1977. *Chicana Feminism.* Austin, Tex.: Information System Development.

Crenshaw, Kimberlé. 1993. "Demarginalizing the Intersection of Race and Sex: A Black Feminist Critique of Antidiscrimination Doctrine, Feminist Theory and Anti-Racist Politics." In *Feminist Legal Theory: Foundations,* ed. D. Kelly Weisberg, 383–95. Philadelphia: Temple University Press.

Cuadraz, Gloria Holguín. 1996. "Experiences of Multiple Marginality: A Case Study of Chicana 'Scholarship Women.'" In *Racial and Ethnic Diversity in Higher Education. ASHE Reader Series,* ed. Caroline Turner, Mildred García, Amaury Nora, and Laura Rendón, 210–222. New York: Simon & Schuster Custom Publishing.

Cuadraz, Gloria Holguín, and Jennifer Pierce. 1994. "From Scholarship Girls to Scholarship Women: Surviving the Contradictions of Class and Race in Academe." *Explorations in Ethnic Studies* 17(1): 1–23.

Davis, Angela Y. 1981. *Women, Race and Class.* New York: Random House.

————. 1974. *With My Mind on Freedom: An Autobiography.* New York: Bantam Books.

————. 1971. "Reflections on the Black Woman's Role in the Community of Slaves." *Black Scholar* 3(4): 3–15.

Davis, F. James. 1991. *Who Is Black? One Nation's Definition.* University Park: Pennsylvania State University Press.

de Beauvoir, Simone. 1952. *The Second Sex.* New York: Random House.

de la Torre, Adela, and Beatríz M. Pesquera, eds. 1993. *Building with Our Hands: New Directions in Chicana Studies.* Berkeley: University of California Press.

Del Castillo, Adelaida. 1974. "Malintzin Tenépal: A Preliminary Look into a New Perspective." *Encuentro Femenil* 1(2): 58–77.

Delgado, Abelardo. 1978. "An Open Letter to Carolina . . . or Relations between Men and Women." *Revista Chicano-Riqueña* 6(2): 33–41.

Diamond, Betty Ann. 1977. "Brown Eyed Children of the Sun: The Cultural Politics of El Teatro Campesino." Ph.D. diss., Modern Literature, University of Wisconsin.

Domhoff, G. William. (1983). *Who Rules American Now?* Englewood Cliffs, N.J.: Prentice-Hall.

Du Bois, W. E. B. 1973. *The Souls of Black Folk.* Millwood, N.Y.: Kraus-Thomson Organization.

duCille, Ann. 1994. "The Occult of True Black Womanhood: Critical Demeanor and Black Feminist Studies." *Signs: Journal of Women in Culture and Society* 19(3): 591–629.

Dworkin, Andrea. 1987. *Intercourse.* New York: Free Press.

Eagleton, Terry. 1984. "Uses of Criticism." *New York Times Book Review* 9 December, section 1, 45.

Echols, Alice. 1992. " 'We Gotta Get out of This Place': Notes toward a Remapping of the Sixties." *Socialist Review* 22(2): 9–33.

———. 1989. *Daring to Be Bad: Radical Feminism in America, 1967–1975.* Minneapolis: University of Minnesota Press.

Ehrenreich, Barbara, and Deirdre English, eds. 1978. *For Her Own Good: 150 Years of the Experts' Advice to Women.* Garden City, N.Y.: Anchor.

Elgin, Susette Haden. 1984. *Native Tongue.* New York: Dawn Books.

Ellison, Ralph. 1952. *Invisible Man.* New York: Random House.

Espín, Oliva M. 1995. " 'Race,' Racism, and Sexuality in the Life Narratives of Immigrant Women." *Feminism and Psychology* 5(2): 223–38.

———. 1984. "Cultural and Historical Influences on Sexuality in Hispanic/Latin Women." In *Pleasure and Danger: Exploring Female Sexuality,* ed. Carol S. Vance, 149–63. London: Routledge and Kegan Paul.

Evans, Sara. 1980. *Personal Politics: The Roots of Women's Liberation in the Civil Rights Movement and the New Left.* New York: Vintage.

Fernández, Roberta. 1994. "Abriendo-Caminos in the Brotherland: Chicana Writers Respond to the Ideology of Literary Nationalism." *Frontiers—A Journal of Women Studies* 14(2): 23–50.

Fine, Michelle, Lois Weis, and Judi Addelston. 1994. "(In)Secure Times: Constructing White Hetero-Masculinity in the 1980s and 90s." MS, City University of New York, Graduate Center.

Flores, Arturo Conrado. 1986. "El Teatro Campesino de Luis Valdez, 1965–1980." Ph.D. diss., Department of Spanish and Portuguese, University of Arizona.

Fonow, Mary Margaret, and Judith A. Cook. 1991. *Beyond Methodology.* Bloomington: Indiana University Press.

Frankenberg, Ruth. 1993. *White Women, Race Matters: The Social Construction of Whiteness.* Minneapolis: University of Minnesota Press.

Fregoso, Rosa Linda. 1993. "The Mother Motif in *La Bamba* and *Boulevard Nights.*" In *Building with Our Hands—New Directions in Chicana Studies,* ed.

Adela de la Torre and Beatríz M. Pesquera, 130–45. Berkeley: University of California Press.

Friday, Nancy. 1982. *My Mother / Myself: The Daughter's Search for Identity*. New York: Delacorte.

Friedan, Betty. 1963. *The Feminine Mystique*. New York: Penguin.

Frischmann, Donald H. 1982. "El Teatro Campesino y su Mito Bernabe: Un Regreso a la Madre Tierra." *Aztlán* 12(2): 259–70.

Frye, Marilyn. 1992. *Willful Virgin*. Freedom, Calif.: The Crossing Press.

———. 1983. *The Politics of Reality: Essays in Femnist Theory*. Trumansburg, N.Y.: The Crossing Press.

Fuentes, Carlos. 1967. *Zona Sagrada*. Mexico: Siglo Veintiuno Editores.

Gallagher, C. A. 1995. "White Reconstruction in the University." *Socialist Review* 24(1–2): 165–85.

García, Chris F. 1973. *Political Socialization of Chicano Children: A Comparative Study with Anglos in California Schools*. New York: Praeger Press.

Garza, Mario. 1976. *Un Paso Más, One More Step: Collected Poems*. Lansing, Mich.: El Renacimiento Publications.

Gilman, Charlotte Perkins. 1973. *The Yellow Wallpaper*. New York: The Feminist Press.

Goffman, Erving. 1959. *The Presentation of Self in Everyday Life*. Garden City, N.Y.: Doubleday-Anchor.

Gomez-Quiñones, Juan. 1990. *Chicano Politics Reality and Promise, 1940–1990*. Albuquerque: University of New Mexico Press.

———. 1977. "On Culture." *Revista Chicano-Riqueña* 5(2): 29–47.

"The Good News: It's No Longer 59 Cents; Bad News: Income Gap between Women and Men Continues to Loom Large." 1992. *Los Angeles Times*, 30 December, B6.

Graham, Lawrence O. 1995. *Member of the Club: Reflections on Life in a Racially Polarized World*. New York: Harper Collins Publishers.

Gray, John. 1992. *Men Are from Mars, Women Are from Venus : A Practical Guide for Improving Communication and Getting What You Want in Your Relationships*. New York: Harper Collins.

Gutiérrez, Ramón A. 1993. Community, Patriarchy and Individualism: The Politics of Chicano History and the Dream of Equality. *American Quarterly* 45(1): 44–72.

———. 1991. When Jesus Came, the Corn Mothers Went Away: Marriage, Sexuality, and Power in New Mexico, 1500–1846. Stanford, Calif.: Stanford University Press.

Haney, Craig. 1985. "The State of Prisons: What Happened to Justice in the '80s?" Paper presented at the American Psychological Association Meetings, Los Angeles, August.

Haney, Craig, and Aída Hurtado. 1994. "The Jurisprudence of Race and Meritocracy Standardized Testing and 'Race-Neutral' Racism in the Workplace." *Law and Human Behavior* 18(3): 223–47.

Haraway, Donna. 1988. "Situated Knowledges: The Science Question in Feminism and the Privilege of Partial Perspective." *Feminist Studies* 14(3): 575–99.

Harding, Sandra. 1991. *Whose Science? Whose Knowledge? Thinking from Women's Lives.* Ithaca, N.Y.: Cornell University Press.

———. 1986. *The Science Question in Feminism.* Ithaca, NY: Cornell University Press.

Harris, Angela P. 1990. "Race and Essentialism in Feminist Legal Theory." *Stanford Law Review* 42: 581–616.

Harris, Cheryl I. 1993a. "Bell's Blues." *University of Chicago Law Review* 60(568): 783–93.

———. 1993b. "Whiteness as Property." *Harvard Law Review* 106(8): 1709–91.

Harris, Marvin. 1964. *Patterns of Race in the Americas.* New York: Walker.

Hart, Janet. 1996. *New Voices in the Nation: Women and the Greek Resistance, 1941–1964.* Ithaca, London: Cornell University Press.

———. 1992. "Cracking the Code: Narrative and Political Mobilization in the Greek Resistance." *Social Science History* 16(4): 631–68.

Hartmann, Heidi. 1981. "The Unhappy Marriage of Marxism and Feminism: Towards a More Progressive Union." In *Women and Revolution*, ed. Lydia Sargent. Boston: South End Press.

Hayden, Tom. 1989. *Reunion: A Memoir.* New York: Macmillan.

Henley, Nancy. 1986. *Body Politics: Power, Sex, and Nonverbal Communication.* New York: Simon and Schuster.

———. 1979. "Assertiveness Training: Making the Political Personal." Paper presented at the Society for the Study of Social Problems, Boston, August.

Hernández, E. D. 1991. "Discussion, Discourse and Direction: The Dilemmas of a Chicana Lesbian." In *Chicana Lesbians: The Girls Our Mothers Warned Us About*, ed. Carla Trujillo, 138–40. Berkeley, Calif.: Third Woman Press.

Herrera, Hayden. 1983. *Frida: A Biography of Frida Kahlo.* New York: Harper and Row.

Higginbotham, Elizabeth. 1985. "Race and Class Barriers to Black Women's College Attendance." *Journal of Ethnic Studies* 13: 89–107.

"Homicide Rates Highest in South—U.S. Record Worst in Developed World." 1995. *San Francisco Chronicle*, 2 February, A3, col. 5.

hooks, bell. 1994. *Outlaw Culture: Resisting Representations.* New York: Routledge.

———. 1993. *Sisters of the Yam: Black Women and Self-Recovery.* Boston: South End Press.

———. 1990. *Yearning: Race, Gender, and Cultural Politics.* Boston: South End Press.

———. 1989. *Talking Back: Thinking Feminist, Thinking Black.* Boston: South End Press.

———. 1988. "Straightening Our Hair." *Z Magazine* (September): 33, 35.

———. 1984. *Feminist Theory from Margin to Center.* Boston: South End Press.

———. 1981. *Ain't I a Woman? Black Women and Feminism.* Boston: South End Press.

hooks, bell, and Cornel West. 1991. *Breaking Bread: Insurgent Black Intellectual Life.* Boston: South End Press.

Huerta, Jorge A. 1982. *Chicano Theater Themes and Forms.* Ypsilanti, Mich.: Bilingual Press / Editorial Binlingue.

Hurtado, Aída. 1996. "Strategic Suspensions: Feminists of Color Theorize the Production of Knowledge." In Knowledge, Difference, and Power: Essays Inspired by Women's Ways of Knowing, ed. Nancy Goldberger, with Mary Belenky, Blythe Clinchy, and Jill Tarule. New York: Basic Books.

———. 1995. "Variations, Combinations, and Evolutions: Latino Families in the United States." In *Understanding Latino Families: Scholarship, Policy, and Practice,* ed. Ruth E. Zambrana, 40–61. Thousand Oaks, Calif.: Sage Publications.

———. 1993. "Media Representations and the Beating of Rodney King." *Revista Mujeres* 10 (June, special issue): 47–57.

———. 1989. "Reflections on White Feminism: A Perspective from a Woman of Color." In *Social and Gender Boundaries in the United States,* ed. Sucheng Chan, 155–86. Lewiston: Edwin Mellen Press.

———. 1988. "Chicana Feminism: A Theoretical Perspective." Paper presented at the Third International Conference on the Hispanic Cultures of the United States, Barcelona, 7–10 June.

———. 1987–88. "A View from Within: Midwife Practices in South Texas." *International Quarterly of Community Health Education* 8(4): 317–39.

Hurtado, Aída, and Abigail Stewart. 1996. "Through the Looking Glass: Implications of Studying Whiteness for Feminists Methods." In *Off White: Readings on Society, Race and Culture,* ed. Michelle Fine, Linda Powell, Lois Weis, and Mun Wong. New York: Routledge.

Hutchinson, Louise Daniel. 1982. *Anna Cooper: A Voice from the South.* Washington, D.C.: Smithsonian Institution Press.

Jaggar, Alison. 1983. *Feminist Politics and Human Nature.* Totowa, N.J.: Rowman and Allanheld.

James, Aley. 1994. "The Pay Gap Narrows, but . . . (the Gap between Men and Women's Salaries Has Narrowed, but Much of That Is Due to Lower Wages for Men)." *Fortune,* September, 32.

Joseph, Gloria I. 1981. "White Promotion, Black Survival." In *Common Differences: Conflicts in Black and White Feminists' Perspectives,* ed. Gloria I. Joseph and Jill Lewis, 19–42. New York: Anchor.

Joseph, Gloria I., and Jill Lewis, eds. 1981. *Common Differences: Conflicts in Black and White Feminists' Perspectives.* New York: Anchor.

Keller, Evelyn Fox. 1984. *Reflections on Gender and Science.* New Haven: Yale University Press.

Kelley, Dennis. 1994. "Ph.D.s Go to More Women." *USA Today,* 17 January, 1D.

Kimmel, Michael S. 1993. "Invisible Masculinity." *Society* 30(6): 28–35.

Klahn, Norma. 1994. "Writing the Border: The Languages and Limits of Representation." *Journal of Latin American Cultural Studies* 3(1–2): 29–55.

Lamphere, Louise, Patricia Zavella, Felipe Gonzalez, with Peter B. Evan. 1993. *Sunbelt Working Mothers: Reconciling Family and Factory.* Ithaca and London: Cornell University Press.

Leal, Luis. 1981. "In Search of Aztlán." *Denver Quarterly* 16(16): 18.

Lerner, Gerda. 1973. *Black Women in White America: A Documentary History*. New York: Random House, Vintage Books.

Levy, Jacques. 1975. *César Chavez: Autobiography of La Causa*. New York: W. W. Norton.

Lewin, Kurt. 1948. *Resolving Social Conflicts: Selected Papers on Group Dynamics (1935–1946)*. New York: Harper.

Littleton, Christine. 1989. "Feminist Jurisprudence: The Difference Method Makes" (book review). *Stanford Law Review* 41: 751–64.

Lorde, Audre. 1984. *Sister Outsider*. Trumansburg, N.Y.: Crossing Press.

Lugones, Maria C. 1992. Structure/Antistructure and Agency under Oppression. MS, Carleton College.

MacKinnon, Catherine A. 1993. *Only Words*. Cambridge, Mass.: Harvard University Press.

MacKinnon, Catherine A. 1983. "Feminism, Marxism, Method, and the State: Toward Feminist Jurisprudence." *Signs: Journal of Women in Culture and Society* 8(4): 635–58.

———. 1982. "Feminism, Marxism, Method, and the State: An Agenda for Theory." *Signs: Journal of Women in Culture and Society* 7(31): 515–44.

Malcolm X, with the assistance of Alex Haley. 1973. *The Autobiography of Malcolm X*. New York: Ballantine.

Malcolm X. 1970. *By Any Means Necessary: Speeches, Interviews, and a Letter by Malcolm X*. New York: Pathfinder.

Marks, Elaine, and Isabelle de Courtivron, eds. 1981. *New French Feminisms: An Anthology*. New York: Schocken Books.

Martínez, Elizabeth. 1989. "That Old (White) Male Magic." *Z Magazine* 27(8): 48–52.

Matsuda, Mari J., Charles R. Lawrence III, Richard Delgado, and Kimberlè Williams Crenshaw. 1993. *Words That Wound. Critical Race Theory, Assaultive Speech, and the First Amendment*. San Francisco: Westview Press.

McIntosh, Peggy. 1992. "White Privilege and Male Privilege: A Personal Account of Coming to See Correspondences through Work in Women's Studies." In *Race, Class, and Gender*, ed. M. L. Andersen and P. Hill Collins, 70–81. Belmont, Calif.: Wadsworth.

Memmi, Albert. 1965. *The Colonizer and the Colonized*. New York: Orient Press.

Mirandé, Alfredo. 1988. "Qué Gacho es ser Macho: It's a Drag to Be a Macho Man." *Aztlán* 17(2): 63–89.

Mirandé, Alfredo, and Evangelina Enriquez. 1979. *La Chicana: The Mexican-American Woman*. Chicago: University of Chicago Press.

Mitchell, Juliet. 1971. *Woman's Estate*. Harmondsworth: Penguin.

Montoya, Jose. 1979. "La Jefita." In *La Chicana: The Mexican-American Woman*, ed. Alfredo Mirandé and Evangelina Enriquez, 165–66. Chicago: University of Chicago Press.

Moraga, Cherríe, and Gloria Anzaldúa, eds. 1981. *This Bridge Called My Back: Writings by Radical Women of Color*. Watertown, Mass.: Persephone Press.

Morganthau, Tom. 1992. "Losing Ground: New Fears and Suspicions as Black America's Outlook Looks Bleaker." *Newsweek* 119(14): 20–22.

Morrison, Toni. 1992. *Playing in the Dark: Whiteness and the Literary Imagination.* Cambridge, Mass.: Harvard University Press.

———. 1989. "The Pain of Being Black." *Time* 133(21): 120–22.

Morton, Carlos. 1974. "*La Serpiente* Sheds Its Skin—The *Teatro Campesino.*" *Drama Review* 18(4): 71–76.

Muñoz, Carlos. 1989. *Youth Identity, Power: The Chicano Movement.* New York: Verso.

Muñoz, Carlos, and Barrera, Mario. 1988. "La Raza Unida Party and the Chicano Student Movement in California." In *Latinos in the Political System,* ed. F. Chris García, 213–35. Notre Dame, Ind.: University of Notre Dame Press.

Navarro, Marta A. 1991. "Interview with Ana Castillo." In *Chicana Lesbians: The Girls Our Mothers Warned Us About,* ed. Carla Trujillo, 113–32. Berkeley, Calif.: Third Woman Press.

Neidert, Lisa J., and Reynolds Farley. 1985. "Assimilation in the United States: An Analysis of Ethnic and Generation Differences in Status and Achievement." *American Sociological Review* 50: 840–50.

Orbach, Susie. 1978. *Fat Is a Feminist Issue.* New York: Paddington.

Orozco, Cynthia. 1986. "Sexism in Chicano Studies and the Community." In *Chicana Voices: Intersections of Class, Race, and Gender,* ed. Ricardo Romo, 11–18. Austin: Center for Mexican American Studies, University of Texas at Austin.

Ortíz, Vilma. 1995. "The Diversity of Latino Families." In *Understanding Latino Families: Scholarship, Policy, and Practice,* ed. Ruth E. Zambrana, 18–39. Thousand Oaks, Calif.: Sage Publications.

Ostrander, Susan. 1984. *Women of the Upper Class.* Philadelphia: Temple University Press.

Padilla, Amado M., and Traci L. Baird. 1991. "Mexican-American Adolescent Sexuality and Sexual Knowledge: An Exploratory Study." *Hispanic Journal of Behavioral Sciences* 13(1): 95–104.

Palmer, Phyllis Marynick. 1983. "White Women / Black Women: The Dualism of Female Identity and Experience in the United States." *Feminist Studies* 9(1): 151–70.

Parker, Bettye J. 1979. "Complexity: Toni Morrison's Women—An Interview Essay." In *Sturdy Black Bridges: Visions of Black Women in Literature,* ed. Roseanne Bell, Bettye Parker, and Beverly Guy-Sheftall, 251–57. New York: Anchor/Doubleday.

Paz, Octavio. 1985. *The Labyrinth of Solitude.* Trans. from the Spanish by Lysander Kemp, Yara Milos, and Rachel Phillips Belash. New York: Grove Press.

Pena, Devón. 1987. "'Tortuosidad': Shop Floor Struggles of Female Maquiladora Workers." In *Women on the U.S.-Mexico Border: Responses to Change,* ed. Vicki L. Ruiz and Susan Tiano, 129–54. Boston: Allen and Unwin.

Pérez, Emma. 1996. *Gulf Dreams.* Berkeley, Calif.: Third Woman Press.

———. 1993. "Speaking from the Margin: Uninvited Discourse on Sexuality and Power." In *Building with Our Hands: New Directions in Chicana Studies,* ed. Adela de la Torre and Beatríz M. Pesquera, 51–71. Berkeley: University of California Press.

Perry, Bruce, ed. 1989. *Malcolm X: The Last Speeches.* New York: Pathfinder.

Pesquera, Beatríz. 1994. "We're Still Tied to an Image: Chicana Workers and Motherhood." Paper presented at the Sixth European Conference on Latino Cultures in the United States, Bordeaux, 7–10 July.

———. 1985. "Work and Family: A Comparative Analysis of Professional, Clerical, and Blue-Collar Chicana Workers." Ph.D. diss. Sociology Department, University of California, Berkeley.

Pettigrew, Thomas F., and Joanne Martin. 1987. "Shaping the Organizational Context for Black American Inclusion." *Journal of Social Issues* 43: 41–78.

Phoenix, Ann. 1990. "Theories of Gender and Black Families." In *British Feminist Thought,* ed. Terry Lovell, 119–33. Oxford: Blackwell.

"Pregnancy Deaths More Common for Blacks." 1995. *San Francisco Chronicle,* 13 January, A3.

Quintana, Alvina E. 1989. "Challenge and Counter-Challenge: Chicana Literary Motifs." In *Social and Gender Boundaries in the United States,* ed. Sucheng Chan, 187–203. Lewiston, N.Y.: Edwin Mellen Press.

Rabine, Leslie Wahl. 1988. "A Feminist Politics of Non-Identity." *Feminist Studies* 14(1): 11–31.

Ramazanoglu, Caroline. 1992. "What Can You Do with a Man? Feminism and the Critical Appraisal of Masculinity." *Women's Studies International Forum* 15(3): 28–35.

Ramirez, Elizabeth Cantú. 1974. "The Annals of Chicano Theater: 1965–1973." Master's thesis, University of California, Los Angeles.

Rasperry, William. 1986. "An Absence of Context." *Washington Post,* 5 March.

Rausing, Sigrid. 1991. "Men of Tin." *Trouble and Strife* 22: 40–44.

Reese, Nigel. 1993. *The Politically Correct Phrasebook: What They Say You Can and Cannot Say in the 1990s.* London: Bloomsbury.

Reeves, Thomas C. 1991. *A Question of Character: A Life of John F. Kennedy.* New York: Free Press.

Rendón, Laura I. 1992. "From the Barrio to the Academy: Revelations of a Mexican American 'Scholarship Girl.'" *New Directions in Community Colleges* 90 (Winter): 55–64.

Rich, Adrienne. 1986. *Blood, Bread, and Poetry: Selected Prose 1979–1985.* New York: W. W. Norton.

———. 1979. *On Lies, Secrets, and Silence: Selected Prose, 1966–1973.* New York: W. W. Norton.

Rodriguez, Richard. 1982. *Hunger of Memory: The Education of Richard Rodriguez.* New York: Bantam Books.

Roediger, David R. 1991. *The Wages of Whiteness: Race and the Making of the American Working Class.* New York: Verso.

Rollins, Judith. 1985. *Between Women: Domestics and Their Employers.* Philadelphia: Temple University Press.

Romero, Mary. 1992. *Maid in the U.S.A.* New York: Routledge.

Root, Maria, ed. 1992. *Racially Mixed People in America.* Newbury Park, Calif.: Sage Publications.

Rosch, E. H. 1973. "Natural Categories." *Cognitive Psychology* 4(3): 328–50.

Ruiz, Vicki L. 1993. " 'Star Struck' Acculturation, Adolescence, and the Mexican American Woman, 1920–1950." *In Building with Our Hands: New Directions in Chicana Studies,* ed. Adela de la Torre and Beatríz M. Pesquera, 109–29. Berkeley: University of California Press.

———. 1991. "Review of *Youth Identity, Power: The Chicano Movement,* by Carlos Muñoz." *American Historical Review* (December): 1638.

Ryan, Jake, and Charles Sackrey. 1984. *Strangers in Paradise: Academics from the Working Class.* Boston: South End Press.

Ryan, William. 1971. *Blaming the Victim.* New York: Pantheon.

Salvo, Joseph J., and John M. McNeil. 1984. *Lifetime Work Experience and Its Effect on Earnings: Retrospective Data from the 1979 Income Survey Development Program.* U.S. Department of Commerce, Bureau of the Census, Current Population Reports, Series P-23, no. 136. Washington, D.C.: U.S. Government Printing Office.

Sánchez, Elba. 1992. *Tallos de Luna / Moon Shoots.* Santa Cruz, Calif.: Moving Arts Press.

Sánchez, Marta E. 1985. *Contemporary Chicana Poetry: A Critical Approach to an Emerging Literature.* Berkeley: University of California Press.

Sandoval, Chela. 1991. "U.S. Third World Feminism: The Theory and Method of Oppositional Consciousness in the Postmodern World." *Genders* 10 (spring): 1–24.

Scott, Joan W. 1991. "The Evidence of Experience." *Social Inquiry* 17(4): 773–97.

———. 1988. "Deconstructing Equality-versus-Difference: or, The Uses of Post-structuralist Theory for Feminism." *Feminist Studies* 14(1): 33–51.

———. 1986. "Gender: A Useful Category of Historical Analysis." *American Historical Review* 91(5): 1053–75.

Segura, Denise. 1994. "Beyond Machismo: Chicanas, Work, and Family." Paper presented at the Sixth European Conference on Latino Cultures in the United States, Bordeaux, 7–10 July.

———. 1986. "Chicanas and Mexican Immigrant Women in the Labor Market: A Study of Occupational Mobility and Stratification." Ph.D. diss., Sociology Department, University of California, Berkeley.

Segura, Denise A., and Jennifer L. Pierce. 1993. "Chicana/o Family Structure and Gender Personality: Chodorow, Familism, and Psychoanalytic Sociology Revisited." *Signs: Journal of Women in Culture and Society* 19(1): 62–91.

Shipp, E. R. 1986. "Blacks in Heated Debate over 'The Color Purple.' " *New York Times,* 27 January, A13(L).

Smith, Dorothy E. 1978. "A Peculiar Eclipsing: Women's Exclusion from Man's Culture." *Women's Studies International Quarterly* 1: 281–95.

Sosa-Ridell, Adeljiza, ed. 1983. "Mujeres Activas en Letras y Cambio Social." *Noticiera de M.A.L.C.S.* Davis: University of California, Davis, Chicano Studies Program.

Spelman, Elizabeth. 1988. *Inessential Woman: Problems of Exclusion in Feminist Thought.* Boston: Beacon Press.

Spender, Dale. 1980. *Man Made Language.* London: Routledge, Chapman and Hall.

Stanton, Elizabeth Cady, Susan B. Anthony, and Matilda Joslyn Gage, eds. 1889. *History of Woman Suffrage,* 2d ed. Rochester, N.Y.: Susan B. Anthony.

———. 1887. *History of Woman Suffrage.* Rochester, N.Y.: Charles Mann.

Staples, Robert. 1973. *The Black Woman in America.* Chicago: Nelson Hill.

Steele, Shelby. 1990. *The Content of Our Character: A New Vision of Race in America.* New York: St. Martin's Press.

Sterling, Dorothy. 1979. *Black Foremothers: Three Lives.* New York: McGraw-Hill.

Sternback, Nancy Saporta. 1989. "A Deep Memory of Love: The Chicana Feminism of Cherríe Moraga." In *Breaking Boundaries: Latina Writing and Critical Readings,* ed. Asuncion Horno-Delgado, Eliana Ortega, Nina M. Scott, and Nancy Saporta Sternback, 48–61. Amherst: University of Massachusetts Press.

Stimpson, Catharine. 1971. "'Thy Neighbor's Wife, Thy Neighbor's Servants': Women's Liberation and Black Civil Rights." In *Woman in Sexist Society: Studies in Power and Powerlessness,* ed. Vivian Gornick and Barbara K. Morgan, 452–79. New York: Basic Books.

Stoltenberg, John. 1993. *The End of Manhood: A Book for Men of Conscience.* New York: Dutton Books.

Sturgis, Susanna J. 1988. "Class/Act: Beginning a Translation from Privilege." In *Out the Other Side: Contemporary Lesbian Writing,* ed. C. McEwan and S. O'Sullivan, 7–13. London: Virago.

Susuki, Bob H. 1977. "Education and the Socialization of Asian Americans: A Revisionist Analysis of the 'Model Minority' Thesis." *Amerasia Journal* 4(2): 23–51.

Taeuber, Cynthia M. 1991. *Statistical Handbook on Women in America.* Phoenix, Ariz.: Oryx Press.

Taeuber, Cynthia M., and Victor Baldisera, 1986. *Women in the American Economy.* U.S. Bureau of the Census, Current Population Reports, Series P-23, no. 146. Washington, D.C.: U.S. Government Printing Office.

Taibo, Paco Ignacio. 1985. *Maria Félix: 47 Pasos por el Cine.* Mexico: J. Mortiz / Planeta.

Tajfel, Henri. 1974. "Social Identity and Intergroup Behavior." *Social Science Information* 13: 65–93.

Tannen, Deborah. 1990. *You Just Don't Understand: Women and Men in Conversation.* New York: Ballantine Books.

Tatum, Beverly D. 1992. "Talking about Race, Learning about Racism: The Application of Racial Identity Development Theory in the Classroom. *Harvard Educational Review* 62(1): 1–24.

Tavris, Carol. 1982. *Anger: The Misunderstood Emotion.* New York: Simon and Schuster.

Terrell, Mary Church. 1940. *A Colored Woman in a White World.* Washington, D.C.: Ransdell.

Trebilcot, Joyce. 1979. "Conceiving Women: Notes on the Logic of Feminism." *Sinister Wisdom* (11): 43–50.

Trimberger, Ellen Kay, and Peggy Dennis. 1979. "Women in the Old and New Left: The Evolution of a Politics of Personal Life." *Feminists Studies* 5(3): 432–50.

Trotter, Robert T., III, and Juan Antonio Chavira. 1981. *Curanderismo: Mexican/American Folk Healing.* Athens: University of Georgia Press.

Trujillo, Carla, ed. 1991. *Chicana Lesbians: The Girls Our Mothers Warned Us About.* Berkeley, Calif.: Third Woman Press.

Turner, Victor. 1974. *Dramas, Fields, and Metaphors.* Ithaca and London: Cornell University Press.

U.S. Bureau of the Census. 1993. *Poverty in the United States: 1991.* U.S. Department of Commerce, Series P-60, no. 181. Washington, D.C.: U.S. Government Printing Office.

———. 1992. *Money Income of Households, Families, and Persons in the United States: 1991,* U.S. Department of Commerce, Current Population Reports, Series P-60, no. 180. Washington, D.C.: U.S. Government Printing Office.

Valdez, Luis. 1978. *Actos.* San Juan Bautista, Calif.: Menyah Productions.

———. 1973. "El Teatro Campesino: Notes on Chicano Theater." In *Guerrilla Street Theater,* ed. Henry Lesnick, 190–94. New York: Avon Books.

———. 1972. "Life in the Barrios." In *Aztlán: An Anthology of Mexican American Literature,* ed. Luis Valdez and Stan Steiner. New York: Vintage Books.

———. 1971. "El Teatro Campesino—Its Beginnings." In *The Chicanos: Mexican American Voices,* ed. Ed Ludwig and James Santibañez, 115–19. Baltimore: Penguin Books.

Vanfossen, Beth. 1979. *The Structure of Social Inequality.* Boston: Little, Brown.

Vasconcelos, José. 1979. *The Cosmic Race = La Raza Cósmica.* Los Angeles: Centro de Publicaciones, Department of Chicano Studies, California State University at Los Angeles.

Vega, Manuel de Jesús. 1983. "El Teatro Campesino Chicano y La Vanguardia Teatral: 1965–1975." Ph.D. diss., Literature and Latin American Studies, Middlebury College.

Vigil, Evangelina. 1982. *Thirty an' Seen a Lot.* Houston: Arte Público Press.

Walker, Alice. 1967. *Meridian.* New York: Harcourt, Brace, Jovanovich.

Wellman, David T. 1993. *Portraits of White Racism,* 2d ed. New York: Cambridge University Press.

Wells, Ida B. 1970. *Crusade for Justice: The Autobiography of Ida B. Wells,* ed. Alfreda M. Duster. Chicago: University of Chicago Press.

West, Candace. 1997. "Public Speaking." In *The Reader's Companion to U.S. Women's History,* ed. Wilma Mankiller, Gwendolyn Mink, Marysa Navarro, Barbara Smith, and Gloria Steinem. Boston: Houghton Mifflin.

———. 1995. Women's Competence in Conversation." *Discourse and Society* 6(1): 107–31.

———. 1992. "Rethinking 'Sex Differences' in Conversational Topics: It's Not What They Say but How They Say It." *Advances in Group Processes* 9: 131–62.

West, Candace, and Sarah Fenstermaker. 1993. "Power, Inequality and the

Accomplishment of Gender: An Ethnomethodological View." In *Theory on Gender / Feminism on Theory*, ed. Paula England, 151–74. New York: Aldine.

West, Candace, and Don H. Zimmerman. 1987. "Doing Gender." *Gender and Society* 1(2): 125–51.

West, Cornel. 1993. *Race Matters.* Boston: Beacon Press.

White, Deborah Gray. 1985. *"Ar'n't I a Woman?" Female Slaves in the Plantation South.* New York: W. W. Norton.

Williams, Gregory Howard. 1995. *Life on the Color Line: The True Story of a White Boy Who Discovered He Was Black.* New York: E. P. Dutton.

Williams, Patricia J. 1995. *The Rooster's Egg: On the Persistence of Prejudice.* Cambridge: Harvard University Press.

"Women Reached 70% of Pay Parity with Men in '87." 1988. *San Jose Mercury News,* 2 February, C1.

Woo, Deborah. 1992. "The Gap between Striving and Achieving: The Case for Asian American Women." In *Race, Class, and Gender in the United States: An Integrated Study,* ed. Paula S. Rothenberg, 174–82. New York: St. Martin's Press.

———. 1985. "The Socioeconomic Status of Asian American Women in the Labor Force: An Alternative View." *Sociological Perspectives* 28(3): 307–38.

Wyche, Karen Fraser, and Graves, Sherryl B. 1992. "Minority Women in Academia—Access and Barriers to Professional Participation." *Psychology of Women Quarterly* 16(4): 429–37.

Xavier, Roy Eric. 1983. *Politics and Chicano Culture: A Perspective on El Teatro Campesino.* Berkeley: Chicano Studies Library Publications, University of California.

Yarbro-Bejarano, Yvonne. 1986. "The Female Subject in Chicano Theater: Sexuality, 'Race,' and Class." *Theater Journal* 38(1): 389–407.

———. 1985. "Chicanas' Experience in Collective Theater: Ideology and Form." *Women and Performance* 2(2): 45–58.

Ybarra-Fraustro, Tomás. 1986. "When Cultures Meet: Integration or Disintegration?" MS, Department of Spanish, Stanford University.

Young, Iris M. 1990. "The Ideal Community and the Politics of Difference." In *Feminism/Postmodernism,* ed. Linda J. Nicholson, 300–23. New York: Routledge.

Zavella, Patricia. 1994a. "Playing with Fire: The Gendered Construction of Chicano/Mexican Sexuality." Paper presented at the Sixth European Conference on Latino Cultures in the United States, Bordeaux, 7–10 July.

———. 1994b. "Reflections on Diversity among Chicanas." In *Race,* ed. Steven Gregory and Roger Sanjek, 199–212. New Brunswick, N.J.: Rutgers University Press.

———. 1993. "Feminist Insider Dilemmas: Constructing Ethnic Identity with 'Chicana' Informants." *Frontiers* 18(3): 53–76.

———. 1991a. "Mujeres in Factories: Race and Class Perspectives on Women, Work, and Family." In *Gender at the Crossroads of Knowledge: Feminist Anthropology in the Post-Modern Era,* ed. Micaela de Leonardo, 312–36. Berkeley: University of California Press.

————. 1991b. "Reflections on Diversity among Chicanas." *Frontiers* 12(2): 763–85.

————. 1988. "The Problematic Relationship of Feminism and Chicana Studies." *Women's Studies* 17: 123–34.

————. 1987. *Women's Work and Chicano Families: Cannery Workers of the Santa Clara Valley.* Ithaca, N.Y.: Cornell University Press.

Zinn, Maxine Baca. 1975a. "Chicanas: Power and Control in the Domestic Sphere." *De Colores* 2(2): 19–31.

————. 1975b. "Political Familism: Towards Sex Role Equality in Chicano Families." *Aztlán: Chicano Journal of the Social Sciences and the Arts* 6(1): 13–26.

Zinn, Maxine Baca, Lynn Weber Cannon, Elizabeth Higginbotham, and Bonnie Thornton Dill. 1986. "The Costs of Exclusionary Practices in Women's Studies." *Signs: Journal of Women in Culture and Society* 11(21): 290–303.

Index

5403